ACL Joint Workshop on Statistical Parsing and Semantic Processing of Morphologically Rich Languages

(SP-Sem-MRL 2012)

Held at the 50th Annual Meeting of the Association for Computational Linguistics 2012 (ACL 2012)

Jeju Island, Korea
12 July 2012

ISBN: 978-1-62276-595-9

Printed from e-media with permission by:

Curran Associates, Inc.
57 Morehouse Lane
Red Hook, NY 12571

Some format issues inherent in the e-media version may also appear in this print version.

Printed by Curran Associates, Inc. (2012)

For permission requests, please contact the Association for Computational Linguistics at the address below.

Association for Computational Linguistics
209 N. Eighth Street
Stroudsburg, Pennsylvania 18360

Phone: 1-570-476-8006
Fax: 1-570-476-0860

acl@aclweb.org

Additional copies of this publication are available from:

Curran Associates, Inc.
57 Morehouse Lane
Red Hook, NY 12571 USA
Phone: 845-758-0400
Fax: 845-758-2634
Email: curran@proceedings.com
Web: www.proceedings.com

Preface to SP-SEM-MRL 2012

Morphologically Rich Languages (MRLs) are languages in which grammatical relations such as Subject, Predicate, and Object, are largely indicated morphologically (e.g., through inflection) instead of positionally. This poses serious challenges for current (English-centric) syntactic and semantic processing. Furthermore, since grammatical relations provide the interface to compositional semantics, morpho-syntactic phenomena may significantly complicate processing the syntax–semantics interface. In statistical parsing, English parsing performance has reached a high plateau in certain genres. Semantic processing of English has similarly seen much progress in recent years. MRL processing presents new challenges, such as optimal morphological representation, non position-centric algorithms, or different semantic distance measures.

These challenges lurk in areas where parses may be used as input, such as semantic role labeling, distributional semantics, paraphrasing and textual entailment; inadequate representation or pre-processing of morphological variation is likely to hurt parsing and semantic tasks alike.

This joint workshop aims to build upon the first and second SPMRL workshops (at NAACL-HLT 2010 and IWPT 2011, respectively) while extending the overall scope to include semantic processing. We aim to encourage cross-fertilization among researchers working on different languages and among those working on different levels of processing.

The syntax track received 11 papers of which 7 were accepted for publication. This year's collection of papers describe work on Korean, Basque, French, Spanish, Portuguese and Tamil (the latter three are a first for SPMRL), and encompass several different parsing approaches and combinations thereof, including dependency parsing, PCFG-LA parsing, rule-based parsing and precision-grammar-based parsing.

A trend of this year's papers is the problem of data sparsity in statistical parsing of MRLs: Candito et al. present a technique that involves the use of word clusters, lemmas and Wordnet synsets to alleviate the problem of OOV words in statistical parsing with the French Treebank; Silva and Branca investigate whether dependency information can be used to assign lexical types to OOV words in a HPSG precision grammar approach to Portuguese parsing; Le Roux et al. investigate the problem of data sparsity in the context of Spanish constituency parsing and show that optimising the processes of lemmatisation and part-of-speech tagging can lead to improved parsing performance; Green et al. tackle the problem of small training sets by applying ensemble parsing models trained on subsets of the entire training set. (They test their approach on the Tamil language but suggest that it is applicable to any language with minimal treebank resources).

We are also happy to present parsing papers that describe general parsing techniques that are applicable to any language, but which have been tested on MRLs: Goenaga et al. explore an approach which involves the combination of rule-based and data-driven parsing, and test this combined approach on the Basque language; Le Roux et al. present a reranking technique in which the n-best trees produced by a constituency parser are then converted to dependency trees and reranked using dependency information. (The approach is tested on a language with scant morphology, English, and a language with a richer inflectional system, French); Finally, Choi et al. present work which aims to reduce ambiguity in statistical parsing of Korean by transforming eojeol-based trees into entity-based trees. Their work is relevant to all languages where the word is not the natural unit of syntactic analysis.

Five papers, of seven submissions, were accepted for the Semantic Track of SP-SEM-MRL 2012. The

selected papers reflect a healthy diversity of semantic models and the fertile breadth of applications for semantics in morphologically rich languages: Versley applies supervised learning to the task of classifying German noun-verb semantic relations. The experiments evaluate a wide range of corpus- and lexicon-based features for representing the noun-verb pairs; Lorenzo and Cerisara present a Bayesian model for unsupervised Semantic Role Labeling for English and French, with promising results; Hawwari, Bar, and Diab propose a method for creating a resource of Arabic multi-word expressions. The method handles MWEs with gaps, which can be problematic for Arabic; Versley and Henrich describe an approach to word sense discrimination based on the hypothesis that an ambiguous word is unambiguous when embedded in the context of a compound word. Their findings support the utility of the hypothesis.
In research which combines both syntactic and semantic processing, Acedański, Slaski, and Przepiórkowski introduce a procedure for extracting dependency information from chunked data. Given the output of a chunker without prepositional phrase attachment information, their procedure is able to make attachment decisions using lexical, morphosyntactic, lexico-semantic, and association features.

It is our hope that the rich programme of SP-Sem-MRL 2012 will foster interactions and collaborations between the syntax and the semantics community on the topic of Morphologically Rich Languages processing. Our aim is to help to bring ideas (and solutions) to the fore and promote a more rapid advance of the state-of-the-art in the field.

We thank our authors and the Program Committee for making SP-Sem-MRL 2012 a success.

Marianna Apidianaki, Ido Daga, Katryn Erk, Jennifer Foster, Yuval Marton, Ines Rehbein, Djamé Seddah, Reut Tsarfaty and Peter Turney

General Chairs:

Marianna Apidianaki (LIMSI-CNRS, France)
Ido Dagan (Bar-Ilan University, Israel)
Jennifer Foster (Dublin City University, Ireland)
Yuval Marton (IBM Watson Research Center, USA)
Djamé Seddah (University of Paris Sorbonne, France)
Reut Tsarfaty (Uppsala University, Sweden)

Shared Session Chairs:

Katrin Erk (University of Texas at Austin, USA)
Ines Rehbein (University of Potsdam, Germany)
Peter Turney (National Research Council, Canada)
Yannick Versley (University of Tuebingen, Germany)

Invited Speakers:

Mark Steedman (University of Edinburgh, UK)
Ivan Titov (Saarland University, Germant)

Program Committee:

Ion Androutsopoulos (Athens Univ. of Economics and Business, Greece)
Mohammed Attia (Dublin City University, Ireland)
Adriane Boyd (Ohio State University, US)
Bernd Bohnet (University of Stuttgart, Germany)
Marie Candito (University of Paris 7, France)
Aoife Cahill (Educational Testing Service, US)
Gülşen Cebiroğlu Eryiğit (Istambul Technical University, Turkey)
Ozlem Cetinoglu (University of Stuttgart, Germany)
Jinho Choi (University of Colorado at Boulder, US)
Grzegorz Chrupala (Saarland University, Germany)
Benoit Crabbé (University of Paris 7, France)
Josef van Genabith (Dublin City University, Ireland)
Yoav Goldberg (Google Research NY, US)
Spence Green (Stanford University, US)

Veronique Hoste (University College Ghent, Belgium)
Samar Husain (Potsdam University, Germany)
Sandra Kübler (Indiana University, US)
Jonas Kuhn (University of Stuttgart, Germany)
Mirella Lapata (University of Edinburgh, UK)
Alberto Lavelli (FBK-irst, Italy)
Alessandro Lenci (University of Pisa, Italy)
Joseph Le Roux (Université Paris-Nord, France)
Wolfgang Maier (University of Düsseldorf, Germany)
Nitin Madnani (Educational Testing Service, NJ)
Takuya Matsuzaki (University of Tokyo, Japan)
Aurélien Max (LIMSI-CNRS, France)
Yusuke Miyao (University of Tokyo, Japan)
Preslav Nakov (Qatar Computing Research Institute, Qatar)
Roberto Navigli (Sapienza University of Rome, Italy)
Kemal Oflazer (Carnegie Mellon University, Qatar)
Sebastian Pado (University of Heidelberg, Germany)
Patrick Pantel (Microsoft Research, US)
Sameer Pradhan (BBN Technologies, US)
Benoit Sagot (INRIA Rocquencourt, France)
Kenji Sagae (University of Southern California, US)
Idan Szpektor (Bar-Ilan University, Israel)
Lamia Tounsi (Dublin City University, Ireland)
Tim Van de Cruys (University of Cambridge, UK)
Stephen Wan (CSIRO ICT Centre, Australia)
Deniz Yuret (Koc University Istanbul, Turkey)
Zdenek Zabokrtsky (Charles University, Czech Republic)
Wajdi Zaghouani (Université de Montréal, Canada)
Shiqi Zhao (Baidu Inc., China)

Table of Contents

Conference Program

Thursday, July 12, 2012

Session 1: (08:50-10:05) Opening Session

08:50-09:05 Statistical Parsing and Semantic Processing of MRLs: Overview of the workshop by Reut Tsarfaty

09:05-10:05 Invited Talk (I) by Ivan Titov

Session 2: (10:05-10:30) Syntactic Parsing of MRLs (I)

10:05–10:30 *Probabilistic Lexical Generalization for French Dependency Parsing*
Enrique Henestroza Anguiano and Marie Candito

10:30-11:00 Coffee Break

Session 3: (11:00-12:25) Semantic Processing of MRLs

11:00–11:25 *Supervised Learning of German Qualia Relations*
Yannick Versley

11:25–11:40 *Building an Arabic Multiword Expressions Repository*
Abdelati Hawwari, Kfir Bar and Mona Diab

11:40–11:55 *Unsupervised frame based Semantic Role Induction: application to French and English*
Alejandra Lorenzo and Christophe Cerisara

11:55–12:10 *Using Synthetic Compounds for Word Sense Discrimination*
Yannick Versley and Verena Henrich

12:10–12:25 *Machine Learning of Syntactic Attachment from Morphosyntactic and Semantic Co-occurrence Statistics*
Szymon Acedański, Adam Slaski and Adam Przepiórkowski

12:30-14:00 Lunch Break

Thursday, July 12, 2012 (continued)

Session 4: (14:00-15:30) Syntactic Parsing of MRLs (II)

14:00-15:00 Invited Talk (II) by Mark Steedman

15:00–15:15 *Combining Rule-Based and Statistical Syntactic Analyzers*
Iakes Goenaga, Koldobika Gojenola, María Jesús Aranzabe, Arantza Díaz de Ilarraza and Kepa Bengoetxea

15:15–15:30 *Statistical Parsing of Spanish and Data Driven Lemmatization*
Joseph Le Roux, Benoit Sagot and Djamé Seddah

15:30-16:00 Coffee Break

Session 5: (16:00-17:30) Syntactic Parsing of MRLs (III)

16:00–16:25 *Assigning Deep Lexical Types Using Structured Classifier Features for Grammatical Dependencies*
João Silva and António Branco

16:25–16:40 *Using an SVM Ensemble System for Improved Tamil Dependency Parsing*
Nathan Green, Loganathan Ramasamy and Zdeněk Žabokrtský

16:40–17:05 *Korean Treebank Transformation for Parser Training*
DongHyun Choi, Jungyeul Park and Key-Sun Choi

17:05–17:30 *Generative Constituent Parsing and Discriminative Dependency Reranking: Experiments on English and French*
Joseph Le Roux, Benoit Favre, Alexis Nasr and Seyed Abolghasem Mirroshandel

17:30-17:40 Short Break

Thursday, July 12, 2012 (continued)

Session 6: (17:40-18:20) Closing Session

17:40-18:10 Panel: Disclosing the SPMRL 2013 Shared Task

18:10-18:20 Concluding Remarks by Reut Tsarfaty

Probabilistic Lexical Generalization for French Dependency Parsing

Enrique Henestroza Anguiano and Marie Candito
Alpage (Université Paris Diderot / INRIA)
Paris, France
enrique.henestroza_anguiano@inria.fr, marie.candito@linguist.jussieu.fr

Abstract

This paper investigates the impact on French dependency parsing of lexical generalization methods beyond lemmatization and morphological analysis. A distributional thesaurus is created from a large text corpus and used for distributional clustering and WordNet automatic sense ranking. The standard approach for lexical generalization in parsing is to map a word to a single generalized class, either replacing the word with the class or adding a new feature for the class. We use a richer framework that allows for probabilistic generalization, with a word represented as a probability distribution over a space of generalized classes: lemmas, clusters, or synsets. Probabilistic lexical information is introduced into parser feature vectors by modifying the weights of lexical features. We obtain improvements in parsing accuracy with some lexical generalization configurations in experiments run on the French Treebank and two out-of-domain treebanks, with slightly better performance for the probabilistic lexical generalization approach compared to the standard single-mapping approach.

1 Introduction

In statistical, data-driven approaches to natural language syntactic parsing, a central problem is that of accurately modeling lexical relationships from potentially sparse counts within a training corpus. Our particular interests are centered on reducing lexical data sparseness for linear classification approaches for dependency parsing. In these approaches, linear models operate over feature vectors that generally represent syntactic structure within a sentence, and feature templates are defined in part over the word forms of one or more tokens in a sentence. Because treebanks used for training are often small, lexical features may appear relatively infrequently during training, especially for languages with richer morphology than English. This may, in turn, impede the parsing model's ability to generalize well outside of its training set with respect to lexical features.

Past approaches for achieving lexical generalization in dependency parsing have used WordNet semantic senses in parsing experiments for English (Agirre et al., 2011), and word clustering over large corpora in parsing experiments for English (Koo et al., 2008) as well as for French (Candito et al., 2010b). These approaches map each word to a single corresponding generalized class (synset or cluster), and integrate generalized classes into parsing models in one of two ways: (i) the *replacement strategy*, where each word form is simply replaced with a corresponding generalized class; (ii) a strategy where an additional feature is created for the corresponding generalized class.

Our contribution in this paper is applying *probabilistic lexical generalization*, a richer framework for lexical generalization, to dependency parsing. Each word form is represented as a categorical distribution over a *lexical target space* of generalized classes, for which we consider the spaces of lemmas, synsets, and clusters. The standard single-mapping approach from previous work can be seen as a subcase: each categorical distribution assigns a probability of 1 to a single generalized class. The method we use for introducing probabilistic information into a feature vector is based on that used by Bunescu (2008), who tested the use of probabilistic part-of-speech (POS) tags through an NLP pipeline.

In this paper, we perform experiments for French that use the replacement strategy for integrating generalized classes into parsing models, comparing the single-mapping approach for lexical generalization with our probabilistic lexical generalization approach. In doing so, we provide first results on the application to French parsing of WordNet automatic sense ranking (ASR), using the method of McCarthy et al. (2004). For clustering we deviate from most previous work, which has integrated Brown clusters (Brown et al., 1992) into parsing models, and instead use distributional lexical semantics to create both a distributional thesaurus - for probabilistic generalization in the lemma space and ASR calculation - and to perform hierarchical agglomerative clustering (HAC). Though unlexicalized syntactic HAC clustering has been used to improve English dependency parsing (Sagae and Gordon, 2009), we provide first results on using distributional lexical semantics for French parsing. We also include an out-of-domain evaluation on medical and parliamentary text in addition to an in-domain evaluation.

In Section 2 we describe the lexical target spaces used in this paper, as well as the method of integrating probabilistic lexical information into a feature vector for classification. In Section 3 we discuss dependency structure and transition-based parsing. In Section 4 we present the experimental setup, which includes our parser implementation, the construction of our probabilistic lexical resources, and evaluation settings. We report parsing results both in-domain and out-of-domain in Section 5, we provide a summary of related work in Section 6, and we conclude in Section 7.

2 Probabilistic Lexical Target Spaces

Using terms from probability theory, we define a *lexical target space* as a sample space Ω over which a categorical distribution is defined for each lexical item in a given *source vocabulary*. Because we are working with French, a language with relatively rich morphology, we use lemmas as the base lexical items in our source vocabulary. The outcomes contained in a sample space represent generalized classes in a *target vocabulary*. In this paper we consider three possible target vocabularies, with corresponding sample spaces: Ω_l for lemmas, Ω_s for synsets, and Ω_c for clusters.

2.1 Ω_l Lemma Space

In the case of the lemma space, the source and target vocabularies are the same. To define an appropriate categorical distribution for each lemma, one where the possible outcomes also correspond to lemmas, we use a *distributional thesaurus* that provides similarity scores for pairs of lemmas. Such a thesaurus can be viewed as a similarity function $D(x, y)$, where $x, y \in V$ and V is the vocabulary for both the source and target spaces.

The simplest way to define a categorical distribution over Ω_l, for a lemma $x \in V$, would be to use the following probability mass function p_x:

$$p_x(y) = \frac{D(x,y)}{\sum_{y' \in V} D(x,y')} \tag{1}$$

One complication is the identity similarity $D(x, x)$: although it can be set equal to 1 (or the similarity given by the thesaurus, if one is provided), we choose to assign a pre-specified probability mass m to the identity lemma, with the remaining mass used for generalization across other lemmas. Additionally, in order to account for noise in the thesaurus, we restrict each categorical distribution to a lemma's k-nearest neighbors. The probability mass function p_x over the space Ω_l that we use in this paper is finally as follows:

$$p_x(y) = \begin{cases} m, & \text{if } y = x \\ \dfrac{(1-m)D(x,y)}{\sum_{y' \in N_x(k)} D(x,y')}, & \text{if } y \in N_x(k) \\ 0, & \text{otherwise} \end{cases} \tag{2}$$

2.2 Ω_s Synset Space

In the case of the synset space, the target vacabulary contains synsets from the Princeton WordNet sense hierarchy (Fellbaum, 1998). To define an appropriate categorical distribution over synsets for each lemma x in our source vocabulary, we first use the WordNet resource to identify the set S_x of different senses of x. We then use a distributional thesaurus to perform ASR, which determines the prevalence with respect to x of each sense $s \in S_x$, following the approach of McCarthy et al. (2004). Representing the thesaurus as a similarity function $D(x, y)$, letting $N_x(k)$ be the set of k-nearest neighbors for x, and letting $W(s_1, s_2)$ be a similarity function over synsets in WordNet, we define a prevalence function $R_x(s)$ as follows:

$$R_x(s) = \sum_{y \in N_x(k)} D(x, y) \frac{\max_{s' \in S_y} W(s, s')}{\sum_{t \in S_x} \max_{s' \in S_y} W(t, s')} \tag{3}$$

This function essentially weights the semantic contribution that each distributionally-similar neighbor adds to a given sense for x. With the prevalence scores of each sense for x having been calculated, we use the following probability mass function p_x over the space Ω_s, where $S_x(k)$ is the set of k-most prevalent senses for x:

$$p_x(s) = \begin{cases} \dfrac{R_x(s)}{\sum_{s' \in S_x(k)} R_x(s')}, & \text{if } s \in S_x(k) \\ 0, & \text{otherwise} \end{cases} \tag{4}$$

Note that the first-sense ASR approach to using WordNet synsets for parsing, which has been previously explored in the literature (Agirre et al., 2011), corresponds to setting k=1 in Equation 4.

2.3 Ω_c Cluster Space

In the case of the cluster space, any approach for word clustering may be used to create a reduced target vocabulary of clusters. Defining a categorical distribution over clusters would be interesting in the case of *soft clustering* of lemmas, in which a lemma can participate in more than one cluster, but we have not yet explored this clustering approach.

In this paper we limit ourselves to the simpler *hard clustering* HAC method, which uses a distributional thesaurus and iteratively joins two clusters together based on the similarities between lemmas in each cluster. We end up with a simple probability mass function p_x over the space Ω_c for a lemma x with corresponding cluster c_x:

$$p_x(c) = \begin{cases} 1, & \text{if } c = c_x \\ 0, & \text{otherwise} \end{cases} \tag{5}$$

2.4 Probabilistic Feature Generalization

In a typical classifier-based machine learning setting in NLP, feature vectors are constructed using indicator functions that encode categorical information, such as POS tags, word forms or lemmas.

In this section we will use a running example where a and b are token positions of interest to a classifier, and for which feature vectors are created. If we let t stand for POS tag and l stand for lemma, a *feature template* for this pair of tokens might then be $[t_a l_b]$. Feature templates are instantiated as actual features in a vector space depending on the categorical values they can take on. One possible instantiation of the template $[t_a l_b]$ would then be the feature $[t_a{=}verb \wedge l_b{=}avocat]$, which indicates that a is a verb and b is the lemma *avocat* ("avocado" or "lawyer"), with the following indicator function:

$$f = \begin{cases} 1, & \text{if } t_a{=}verb \wedge l_b{=}avocat \\ 0, & \text{otherwise} \end{cases} \tag{6}$$

To perform probabilistic feature generalization, we replace the indicator function, which represents a single original feature, with a collection of weighted functions representing a set of derived features. Suppose the French lemma *avocat* is in our source vocabulary and has multiple senses in Ω_s (s_1 for the "avocado" sense, s_2 for the "lawyer" sense, etc.), as well as a probability mass function p_{av}. We discard the old feature $[t_a{=}verb \wedge l_b{=}avocat]$ and add, for each s_i, a derived feature of the form $[t_a{=}verb \wedge x_b{=}s_i]$, where x represents a target space generalized class, with the following weighted indicator function:

$$f(i) = \begin{cases} p_{av}(s_i), & \text{if } t_a{=}verb \wedge l_b{=}avocat \\ 0, & \text{otherwise} \end{cases} \tag{7}$$

This process extends easily to generalizing multiple categorical variables. Consider the bilexical feature $[l_a{=}manger \wedge l_b{=}avocat]$, which indicates that a is the lemma *manger* ("eat") and b is the lemma *avocat*. If both lemmas *manger* and *avocat* appear

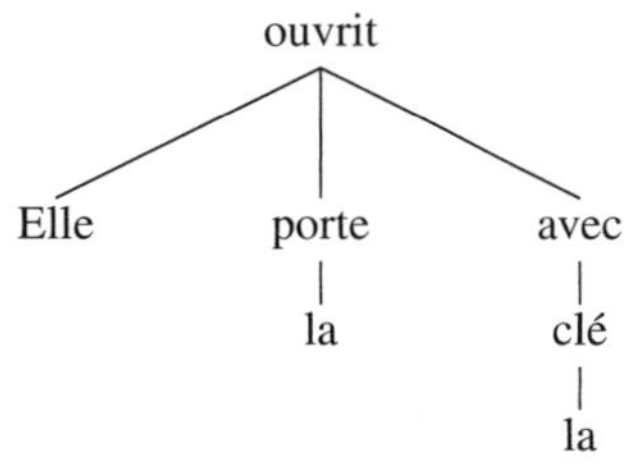

Figure 1: An unlabeled dependency tree for "Elle ouvrit la porte avec la clé" ("She opened the door with the key").

in our source vocabulary and have multiple senses in Ω_s, with probability mass functions p_{ma} and p_{av}, then for each pair i, j we derive a feature of the form $[x_a{=}s_i \wedge x_b{=}s_j]$, with the following weighted indicator function:

$$f(i,j) = \begin{cases} p_{ma}(s_i)p_{av}(s_j), & \text{if } l_a{=}manger \wedge l_b{=}avocat \\ 0, & \text{otherwise} \end{cases} \quad (8)$$

3 Dependency Parsing

Dependency syntax involves the representation of syntactic information for a sentence in the form of a directed graph, whose edges encode word-to-word relationships. An edge from a *governor* to a *dependent* indicates, roughly, that the presence of the dependent is syntactically legitimated by the governor. An important property of dependency syntax is that each word, except for the root of the sentence, has exactly one governor; dependency syntax is thus represented by trees. Figure 1 shows an example of an unlabeled dependency tree.[1] For languages like English or French, most sentences can be represented with a *projective* dependency tree: for any edge from word g to word d, g dominates any intervening word between g and d.

Dependency trees are appealing syntactic representations, closer than constituency trees to the semantic representations useful for NLP applications. This is true even with the projectivity requirement, which occasionally creates syntax-semantics mismatches. Dependency trees have recently seen a surge of interest, particularly with the introduction of supervised models for dependency parsing using linear classifiers.

[1]Our experiments involve labeled parsing, with edges additionally labeled with the surface grammatical function that the dependent bears with respect to its governor.

3.1 Transition-Based Parsing

In this paper we focus on transition-based parsing, whose seminal works are that of Yamada and Matsumoto (2003) and Nivre (2003). The parsing process applies a sequence of incremental actions, which typically manipulate a buffer position in the sentence and a stack for built sub-structures. In the *arc-eager* approach introduced by Nivre et al. (2006) the possible actions are as follows, with s_0 being the token on top of the stack and n_0 being the next token in the buffer:

- SHIFT: Push n_0 onto the stack.
- REDUCE: Pop s_0 from the stack.
- RIGHT-ARC(r): Add an arc labeled r from s_0 to n_0; push n_0 onto the stack.
- LEFT-ARC(r): Add an arc labeled r from n_0 to s_0; pop s_0 from the stack.

The parser uses a greedy approach, where the action selected at each step is the best-scoring action according to a classifier, which is trained on a dependency treebank converted into sequences of actions. The major strength of this framework is its $O(n)$ time complexity, which allows for very fast parsing when compared to more complex global optimization approaches.

4 Experimental Setup

We now discuss the treebanks used for training and evaluation, the parser implementation and baseline settings, the construction of the probabilistic lexical resources, and the parameter tuning and evaluation settings.

4.1 Treebanks

The treebank we use for training and in-domain evaluation is the French Treebank (FTB) (Abeillé and Barrier, 2004), consisting of 12,351 sentences from the *Le Monde* newspaper, converted to projective[2] dependency trees (Candito et al., 2010a). For our experiments we use the usual split of 9,881 training, 1,235 development, and 1,235 test sentences.

[2]The projectivity constraint is linguistically valid for most French parses: the authors report $< 2\%$ non-projective edges in a hand-corrected subset of the converted FTB.

Moving beyond the journalistic domain, we use two additional treebank resources for out-of-domain parsing evaluations. These treebanks are part of the Sequoia corpus (Candito and Seddah, 2012), and consist of text from two non-journalistic domains annotated using the FTB annotation scheme: a medical domain treebank containing 574 development and 544 test sentences of public assessment reports of medicine from the European Medicines Agency (EMEA) originally collected in the OPUS project (Tiedemann, 2009), and a parliamentary domain treebank containing 561 test sentences from the Europarl[3] corpus.

4.2 Parser and Baseline Settings

We use our own Python implementation of the arc-eager algorithm for transition-based parsing, based on the arc-eager setting of MaltParser (Nivre et al., 2007), and we train using the standard FTB training set. Our baseline feature templates and general settings correspond to those obtained in a benchmarking of parsers for French (Candito et al., 2010b), under the setting which combined lemmas and morphological features.[4] Automatic POS-tagging is performed using MElt (Denis and Sagot, 2009), and lemmatization and morphological analysis are performed using the L*efff* lexicon (Sagot, 2010). Table 1 lists our baseline parser's feature templates.

4.3 Lexical Resource Construction

We now describe the construction of our probabilistic lexical target space resources, whose prerequisites include the automatic parsing of a large corpus, the construction of a distributional thesaurus, the use of ASR on WordNet synsets, and the use of HAC clustering.

4.3.1 Automatically-Parsed Corpus

The text corpus we use consists of 125 million words from the *L'Est Republicain* newspaper[5], 125 million words of dispatches from the *Agence France-Presse*, and 225 million words from a French Wikipedia backup dump[6]. The corpus is preprocessed using the Bonsai tool[7], and parsed using our baseline parser.

	Feature Templates
Unigram	t_{n_0}; l_{n_0}; c_{n_0}; w_{n_0}; t_{s_0}; l_{s_0}; c_{s_0}; w_{s_0}; d_{s_0}; t_{n_1}; l_{n_1}; t_{n_2}; t_{n_3}; t_{s_1}; t_{s_2}; $t_{n_{0l}}$; $l_{n_{0l}}$; $d_{n_{0l}}$; $d_{s_{0l}}$; $d_{s_{0r}}$; $l_{s_{0h}}$; $\{m^i_{n_0} : i \in \|M\|\}$; $\{m^i_{s_0} : i \in \|M\|\}$
Bigram	$t_{s_0}t_{n_0}$; $t_{s_0}l_{n_0}$; $l_{s_0}l_{n_0}$; $l_{n_0}t_{n_1}$; $t_{n_0}t_{n_{0l}}$; $t_{n_0}d_{n_{0l}}$; $\{m^i_{s_0}m^j_{n_0} : i; j \in \|M\|\}$; $\{t_{n_0}m^i_{n_0} : i \in \|M\|\}$; $\{t_{s_0}m^i_{s_0} : i \in \|M\|\}$
Trigram	$t_{s_2}t_{s_1}t_{s_0}$; $t_{s_1}t_{s_0}t_{n_0}$; $t_{s_0}t_{n_0}t_{n_1}$; $t_{n_0}t_{n_1}t_{n_2}$; $t_{n_1}t_{n_2}t_{n_3}$; $t_{s_0}d_{s_{0l}}d_{s_{0r}}$

Table 1: Arc-eager parser feature templates. c = coarse POS tag, t = fine POS tag, w = inflected word form, l = lemma, d = dependency label, m^i = morphological feature from set M. For tokens, n_i = i^{th} token in the buffer, s_i = i^{th} token on the stack. The token subscripts l, r, and h denote partially-constructed syntactic left-most dependent, right-most dependent, and head, respectively.

4.3.2 Distributional Thesaurus

We build separate distributional thesauri for nouns and for verbs,[8] using straightforward methods in distributional lexical semantics based primarily on work by Lin (1998) and Curran (2004). We use the FreDist tool (Henestroza Anguiano and Denis, 2011) for thesaurus creation.

First, *syntactic contexts* for each lemma are extracted from the corpus. We use all syntactic dependencies in which the secondary token has an open-class POS tag, with labels included in the contexts and two-edge dependencies used in the case of prepositional-phrase attachment and coordination. Example contexts are shown in Figure 2. For verb lemmas we limit contexts to dependencies in which the verb is governor, and we add unlexicalized versions of contexts to account for subcategorization. For noun lemmas, we use all dependencies in which the noun participates, and all contexts are lexicalized. The vocabulary is limited to lemmas with at least 1,000 context occurrences, resulting in 8,171 nouns and 2,865 verbs.

Each pair of lemma x and context c is subsequently weighted by mutual informativeness using the point-wise mutual information metric, with

[3]http://www.statmt.org/europarl/

[4]That work tested the use of Brown clusters, but obtained no improvement compared to a setting without clusters. Thus, we do not evaluate Brown clustering in this paper.

[5]http://www.cnrtl.fr/corpus/estrepublicain/

[6]http://dumps.wikimedia.org/

[7]http://alpage.inria.fr/statgram/frdep/fr_stat_dep_parsing.html

[8]We additionally considered adjectives and adverbs, but our initial tests yielded no parsing improvements.

· One-Edge Context:	$-obj\rightarrow N\|avocat$
· One-Edge Context: (unlexicalized)	$-obj\rightarrow N$
· Two-Edge Context:	$-mod\rightarrow P\|avec\ -obj\rightarrow N\|avocat$
· Two-Edge Context: (unlexicalized)	$-mod\rightarrow P\|avec\ -obj\rightarrow N$

Figure 2: Example dependency contexts for the verb lemma *manger*. The one-edge contexts corresponds to the phrase "manger un avocat" ("eat an avocado"), and the two-edge contexts corresponds to the phrase "manger avec un avocat" ("eat with a lawyer").

probabilities estimated using frequency counts:

$$I(x,c) = log\left(\frac{p(x,c)}{p(x)p(c)}\right) \quad (9)$$

Finally, we use the cosine metric to calculate the distributional similarity between pairs of lemmas x, y:

$$D(x,y) = \frac{\sum_c I(x,c)I(y,c)}{\sqrt{\left(\sum_c I(x,c)^2\right) \times \left(\sum_c I(y,c)^2\right)}} \quad (10)$$

4.3.3 WordNet ASR

For WordNet synset experiments we use the French EuroWordNet[9] (FREWN). A WordNet synset mapping[10] allows us to convert synsets in the FREWN to Princeton WordNet version 3.0, and after discarding a small number of synsets that are not covered by the mapping we retain entries for 9,833 nouns and 2,220 verbs. We use NLTK, the Natural Language Toolkit (Bird et al., 2009), to calculate similarity between synsets. As explained in Section 2.2, ASR is performed using the method of McCarthy et al. (2004). We use k=8 for the distributional nearest-neighbors to consider when ranking the senses for a lemma, and we use the synset similarity function of Jiang and Conrath (1997), with default information content counts from NLTK calculated over the British National Corpus[11].

[9] http://www.illc.uva.nl/EuroWordNet/

[10] http://nlp.lsi.upc.edu/tools/download-map.php

[11] http://www.natcorp.ox.ac.uk/

	Source Vocabulary	Evaluation Set		
		FTB Eval	EMEA Eval	Europarl
Nouns	FTB train	95.35	62.87	94.69
	Thesaurus	96.25	79.00	97.83
	FREWN	80.51	73.09	87.06
Verbs	FTB train	96.54	94.56	97.76
	Thesaurus	98.33	97.82	99.54
	FREWN	88.32	91.48	91.98

Table 2: Lexical occurrence coverage (%) of source vocabularies over evaluation sets. FTB Eval contains both the FTB development and test sets, while EMEA Eval contains both the EMEA development and test sets. Proper nouns are excluded from the analysis.

4.3.4 HAC Clustering

For the HAC clustering experiments in this paper, we use the CLUTO package[12]. The distributional thesauri described above are taken as input, and the UPGMA setting is used for cluster agglomeration. We test varying levels of clustering, with a parameter z which determines the proportion of cluster vocabulary size with respect to the original vocabulary size (8,171 for nouns and 2,865 for verbs).

4.3.5 Resource Coverage

The coverage of our lexical resources over the FTB and two out-of-domain evaluation sets, at the level of token occurrences of verbs and common nouns, is described in Table 2. We can see that the FTB training set vocabulary provides better coverage than the FREWN for both nouns and verbs, while the coverage of the thesauri (and derived clusters) is the highest overall.

4.4 Tuning and Evaluation

We evaluate four lexical target space configurations against the baseline of lemmatization, tuning parameters using ten-fold cross-validation on the FTB training set. The feature templates are the same as those in Table 1, with the difference that features involving lemmas are modified by the probabilistic feature generalization technique described in Section 2.4, using the appropriate categorical distributions. In all configurations, we exclude the French auxiliary verbs *être* and *avoir* from participation in lexical generalization, and we replace proper nouns

[12] http://glaros.dtc.umn.edu/gkhome/cluto/cluto/download

with a special lemma[13]. Below we describe the tuned parameters for each configuration.

– **RC: Replacement with cluster in Ω_c**
For clusters and the parameter z (cf. Section 4.3.4), we settled on relative cluster vocabulary size z=0.6 for nouns and z=0.7 for verbs. We also generalized lemmas not appearing in the distributional thesaurus into a single unknown class.

– **PKNL: Probabilistic k-nearest lemmas in Ω_l**
For the parameters k and m (cf. Section 2.1), we settled on k=4 and m=0.5 for both nouns and verbs. We also use the unknown class for low-frequency lemmas, as in the RC configuration.

– **RS: Replacement with first-sense (k=1) in Ω_s**
Since the FREWN has a lower-coverage vocabulary, we did not use an unknown class for out-of-vocabulary lemmas; instead, we mapped them to unique senses. In addition, we did not perform lexical generalization for verbs, due to low cross-validation performance.

– **PKPS: Probabilistic k-prevalent senses in Ω_s**
For this setting we decided to not place any limit on k, due to the large variation in the number of senses for different lemmas. As in the RS configuration, we mapped out-of-vocabulary lemmas to unique senses and did not perform lexical generalization for verbs.

5 Results

Table 3 shows labeled attachment score (LAS) results for our baseline parser (Lemmas) and four lexical generalization configurations. For comparison, we also include results for a setting that only uses word forms (Forms), which was the baseline for previous work on French dependency parsing (Candito et al., 2010b). Punctuation tokens are not scored, and significance is calculated using Dan Bikel's randomized parsing evaluation comparator[14], at significance level p=0.05.

Parse Configuration	Evaluation Set LAS			
	FTB Test	EMEA Dev	EMEA Test	Europarl
Forms	86.85	84.08	85.41	86.01
Lemmas	87.30	84.34	85.41	86.26
RC	87.32	84.28	85.71*	86.28
PKNL	87.46	84.63*	85.82*	86.26
RS	87.34	84.48	85.54	86.34
PKPS	87.41	84.63*	85.68*	86.22

Table 3: Labeled attachment score (LAS) on in-domain (FTB) and out-of-domain (EMEA, Europarl) evaluation sets for the baseline (Lemmas) and four lexical generalization configurations (RC, PKNL, RS, PKPS). Significant improvements over the baseline are starred. For comparison, we also include a simpler setting (Forms), which does not use lemmas or morphological features.

5.1 In-Domain Results

Our in-domain evaluation yields slight improvements in LAS for some lexical generalization configurations, with PKNL performing the best. However, the improvements are not statistically significant. A potential explanation for this disappointing result is that the FTB training set vocabulary covers the FTB test set at high rates for both nouns (95.25%) and verbs (96.54%), meaning that lexical data sparseness is perhaps not a big problem for in-domain dependency parsing. While WordNet synsets could be expected to provide the added benefit of taking word sense into account, sense ambiguity is not really treated due to ASR not providing word sense disambiguation in context.

5.2 Out-Of-Domain Results

Our evaluation on the medical domain yields statistically significant improvements in LAS, particularly for the two probabilistic target space approaches. PKNL and PKPS improve parsing for both the EMEA dev and test sets, while RC improves parsing for only the EMEA test set and RS does not significantly improve parsing for either set. As in our in-domain evaluation, PKNL performs the best overall, though not significantly better than other lexical generalization settings. One explanation for the improvement in the medical domain is the substantial increase in coverage of nouns in EMEA afforded

[13] Proper nouns tend to have sparse counts, but for computational reasons we did not include them in our distributional thesaurus construction. We thus chose to simply generalize them into a single class.

[14] http://www.cis.upenn.edu/~dbikel/software.html

by the distributional thesaurus (+26%) and FREWN (+16%) over the base coverage afforded by the FTB training set.

Our evaluation on the parliamentary domain yields no improvement in LAS across the different lexical generalization configurations. Interestingly, Candito and Seddah (2012) note that while Europarl is rather different from FTB in its syntax, its vocabulary is surprisingly similar. From Table 2 we can see that the FTB training set vocabulary has about the same high level of coverage over Europarl (94.69% for nouns and 97.76% for verbs) as it does over the FTB evaluation sets (95.35% for nouns and 96.54% for verbs). Thus, we can use the same reasoning as in our in-domain evaluation to explain the lack of improvement for lexical generalization methods in the parliamentary domain.

5.3 Lexical Feature Use During Parsing

Since lexical generalization modifies the lexical feature space in different ways, we also provide an analysis of the extent to which each parsing model's lexical features are used during in-domain and out-of-domain parsing. Table 4 describes, for each configuration, the number of lexical features stored in the parsing model along with the *average lexical feature use* (ALFU) of classification instances (each instance represents a parse transition) during training and parsing.[15]

Lexical feature use naturally decreases when moving from the training set to the evaluation sets, due to holes in lexical coverage outside of a parsing model's training set. The single-mapping configurations (RC, RS) do not increase the number of lexical features in a classification instance, which explains the fact that their ALFU on the FTB training set (6.0) is the same as that of the baseline. However, the decrease in ALFU when parsing the evaluation sets is less severe for these configurations than for the baseline: when parsing EMEA Dev with the RC configuration, where we obtain a significant LAS improvement over the baseline, the reduction in ALFU is only 13% compared to 22% for the baseline parser. For the probabilistic generalization configurations, we also see decreases in ALFU when parsing the evaluation sets, though their higher absolute ALFU may help explain the strong medical domain parsing performance for these configurations.

[15]We define the lexical feature use of a classification instance to be the number of lexical features in the parsing model that receive non-zero values in the instance's feature vector.

Parse Configuration	Lexical Feats In Model	Average Lexical Feature Use		
		FTB Train	FTB Dev	EMEA Dev
Lemmas	294k	6.0	5.5	4.7
RC	150k	6.0	5.8	5.2
PKNL	853k	15.7	14.8	12.0
RS	253k	6.0	5.6	4.9
PKPS	500k	9.2	8.6	7.0

Table 4: Parsing model lexical features (rounded to nearest thousand) and average lexical feature use in classification instances across different training and evaluation sets, for the baseline (Lemmas) and four lexical generalization configurations (PKNL, RC, PKPS, and RS).

5.4 Impact on Running Time

Another factor to note when evaluating lexical generalization is the effect that it has on running time. Compared to the baseline, the single-mapping configurations (RC, RS) speed up feature extraction and prediction time, due to reduced dimensionality of the feature space. On the other hand, the probabilistic generalization configurations (PKNL, PKPS) slow down feature extraction and prediction time, due to an increased dimensionality of the feature space and a higher ALFU. Running time is therefore a factor that favors the single-mapping approach over our proposed probabilistic approach.

Taking a larger view on our findings, we hypothesize that in order for lexical generalization to improve parsing, an approach needs to achieve two objectives: (i) generalize sufficiently to ensure that lemmas not appearing in the training set are nonetheless associated with lexical features in the learned parsing model; (ii) substantially increase lexical coverage over what the training set can provide. The first of these objectives seems to be fulfilled through our lexical generalization methods, as indicated in Table 4. The second objective, however, seems difficult to attain when parsing text in-domain, or even out-of-domain if the domains have a high lexical overlap (as is the case for Europarl). Only for our parsing experiments in the medical domain do both objectives appear to be fulfilled, as evidenced by our LAS improvements when parsing EMEA with lexical generalization.

6 Related Work

We now discuss previous work concerning the use of lexical generalization for parsing, both in the classic in-domain setting and in the more recently popular out-of-domain setting.

6.1 Results in Constituency-Based Parsing

The use of word classes for parsing dates back to the first works on generative constituency-based parsing, whether using semantic classes obtained from hand-built resources or less-informed classes created automatically. Bikel (2000) tried incorporating WordNet-based word sense disambiguation into a parser, but failed to obtain an improvement. Xiong et al. (2005) generalized bilexical dependencies in a generative parsing model using Chinese semantic resources (CiLin and HowNet), obtaining improvements for Chinese parsing. More recently, Agirre et al. (2008) show that replacing words with WordNet semantic classes improves English generative parsing. Lin et al. (2009) use the HowNet resource within the split-merge PCFG framework (Petrov et al., 2006) for Chinese parsing: they use the first-sense heuristic to append the most general hypernym to the POS of a token, obtaining a semantically-informed symbol refinement, and then guide further symbol splits using the HowNet hierarchy. Other work has used less-informed classes, notably unsupervised word clusters. Candito and Crabbé (2009) use Brown clusters to replace words in a generative PCFG-LA framework, obtaining substantial parsing improvements for French.

6.2 Results in Dependency Parsing

In dependency parsing, word classes are integrated as features in underlying linear models. In a seminal work, Koo et al. (2008) use Brown clusters as features in a graph-based parser, improving parsing for both English and Czech. However, attempts to use this technique for French have lead to no improvement when compared to the use of lemmatization and morphological analysis (Candito et al., 2010b). Sagae and Gordon (2009) augment a transition-based English parser with clusters using unlexicalized syntactic distributional similarity: each word is represented as a vector of counts of emanating unlexicalized syntactic paths, with counts taken from a corpus of auto-parsed phrase-structure trees, and HAC clustering is performed using cosine similarity. For semantic word classes, (Agirre et al., 2011) integrate WordNet senses into a transition-based parser for English, reporting small but significant improvements in LAS (+0.26% with synsets and +0.36% with semantic files) on the full Penn Treebank with first-sense information from Semcor.

We build on previous work by attempting to reproduce, for French, past improvements for in-domain English dependency parsing with generalized lexical classes. Unfortunately, our results for French do not replicate the improvements for English using semantic sense information (Agirre et al., 2011) or word clustering (Sagae and Gordon, 2009). The primary difference between our paper and previous work, though, is our evaluation of a novel probabilistic approach for lexical generalization.

6.3 Out-Of-Domain Parsing

Concerning techniques for improving out-of-domain parsing, a related approach has been to use self-training with auto-parsed out-of-domain data, as McClosky and Charniak (2008) do for English constituency parsing, though in that approach lexical generalization is not explicitly performed. Candito et al. (2011) use word clustering for domain adaptation of a PCFG-LA parser for French, deriving clusters from a corpus containing text from both the *source* and *target* domains, and they obtain parsing improvements in both domains. We are not aware of previous work on the use of lexical generalization for improving out-of-domain dependency parsing.

7 Conclusion

We have investigated the use of probabilistic lexical target spaces for reducing lexical data sparseness in a transition-based dependency parser for French. We built a distributional thesaurus from an automatically-parsed large text corpus, using it to generate word clusters and perform WordNet ASR. We tested a standard approach to lexical generalization for parsing that has been previously explored, where a word is mapped to a single cluster or synset. We also introduced a novel probabilistic lexical generalization approach, where a lemma is represented by a categorical distribution over the space of lemmas, clusters, or synsets. Probabilities for the lemma space were calculated using the distributional thesaurus, and probabilities for the WordNet synset space were calculated using ASR sense prevalence scores, with probabilistic clusters left for future work.

Our experiments with an arc-eager transition-based dependency parser resulted in modest but significant improvements in LAS over the baseline when parsing out-of-domain medical text. However, we did not see statistically significant improvements over the baseline when parsing in-domain text or out-of-domain parliamentary text. An explanation for this result is that the French Treebank training set vocabulary has a very high lexical coverage over the evaluation sets in these domains, suggesting that lexical generalization does not provide much additional benefit. Comparing the standard single-mapping approach to the probabilistic generalization approach, we found a slightly (though not significantly) better performance for probabilistic generalization across different parsing configurations and evaluation sets. However, the probabilistic approach also has the downside of a slower running time.

Based on the findings in this paper, our focus for future work on lexical generalization for dependency parsing is to continue improving parsing performance on out-of-domain text, specifically for those domains where lexical variation is high with respect to the training set. One possibility is to experiment with building a distributional thesaurus that uses text from both the source and target domains, similar to what Candito et al. (2011) did with Brown clustering, which may lead to a stronger *bridging* effect across domains for probabilistic lexical generalization methods.

Acknowledgments

This work was funded in part by the ANR project Sequoia ANR-08-EMER-013.

References

A. Abeillé and N. Barrier. 2004. Enriching a French treebank. In *Proceedings of the 4th International Conference on Language Resources and Evaluation*, Lisbon, Portugal, May.

E. Agirre, T. Baldwin, and D. Martinez. 2008. Improving parsing and PP attachment performance with sense information. In *Proceedings of the 46th Annual Meeting of the Association for Computational Linguistics*, pages 317–325, Columbus, Ohio, June.

E. Agirre, K. Bengoetxea, K. Gojenola, and J. Nivre. 2011. Improving dependency parsing with semantic classes. In *Proceedings of the 49th Annual Meeting of the Association for Computational Linguistics*, pages 699–703, Portland, Oregon, June.

D.M. Bikel. 2000. A statistical model for parsing and word-sense disambiguation. In *Proceedings of the EMNLP/VLC-2000*, pages 155–163, Hong Kong, October.

S. Bird, E. Loper, and E. Klein. 2009. *Natural Language Processing with Python*. O'Reilly Media Inc.

P.F. Brown, P.V. Desouza, R.L. Mercer, V.J.D. Pietra, and J.C. Lai. 1992. Class-based n-gram models of natural language. *Computational Linguistics*, 18(4):467–479.

R.C. Bunescu. 2008. Learning with probabilistic features for improved pipeline models. In *Proceedings of the Conference on Empirical Methods in Natural Language Processing*, pages 670–679, Honolulu, Hawaii, October.

M. Candito and B. Crabbé. 2009. Improving generative statistical parsing with semi-supervised word clustering. In *Proceedings of the 11th International Conference on Parsing Technologies*, pages 138–141, Paris, France, October.

M. Candito and D. Seddah. 2012. Le corpus Sequoia : annotation syntaxique et exploitation pour l'adaptation d'analyseur par pont lexical. In *Actes de la 19ème conférence sur le traitement automatique des langues naturelles*, Grenoble, France, June. To Appear.

M. Candito, B. Crabbé, and P. Denis. 2010a. Statistical French dependency parsing: Treebank conversion and first results. In *Proceedings of the 7th International Conference on Language Resources and Evaluation*, Valetta, Malta, May.

M. Candito, J. Nivre, P. Denis, and E. Henestroza Anguiano. 2010b. Benchmarking of statistical dependency parsers for French. In *Proceedings of the 23rd International Conference on Computational Linguistics*, pages 108–116, Beijing, China, August.

M. Candito, E. Henestroza Anguiano, D. Seddah, et al. 2011. A Word Clustering Approach to Domain Adaptation: Effective Parsing of Biomedical Texts. In *Proceedings of the 12th International Conference on Parsing Technologies*, Dublin, Ireland, October.

J.R. Curran. 2004. *From distributional to semantic similarity*. Ph.D. thesis, University of Edinburgh.

P. Denis and B. Sagot. 2009. Coupling an annotated corpus and a morphosyntactic lexicon for state-of-the-art

POS tagging with less human effort. In *Proceedings of the 23rd Pacific Asia Conference on Language, Information and Computation*, Hong Kong, China, December.

C. Fellbaum, editor. 1998. *WordNet: An Electronic Lexical Database*. MIT Press, Cambridge, MA.

E. Henestroza Anguiano and P. Denis. 2011. FreDist: Automatic construction of distributional thesauri for French. In *Actes de la 18ème conférence sur le traitement automatique des langues naturelles*, pages 119–124, Montpellier, France, June.

J.J. Jiang and D.W. Conrath. 1997. Semantic similarity based on corpus statistics and lexical taxonomy. In *International Conference on Research in Computational Linguistics*, Taiwan.

T. Koo, X. Carreras, and M. Collins. 2008. Simple semi-supervised dependency parsing. In *Proceedings of the 46th Annual Meeting of the Association for Computational Linguistics*, pages 595–603, Columbus, Ohio, June.

X. Lin, Y. Fan, M. Zhang, X. Wu, and H. Chi. 2009. Refining grammars for parsing with hierarchical semantic knowledge. In *Proceedings of the 2009 Conference on Empirical Methods in Natural Language Processing*, pages 1298–1307, Singapore, August.

D. Lin. 1998. Automatic retrieval and clustering of similar words. In *Proceedings of the 36th Annual Meeting of the Association for Computational Linguistics and 17th International Conference on Computational Linguistics, Volume 2*, pages 768–774, Montreal, Quebec, August.

D. McCarthy, R. Koeling, J. Weeds, and J. Carroll. 2004. Finding predominant word senses in untagged text. In *Proceedings of the 42nd Meeting of the Association for Computational Linguistics*, pages 279–286, Barcelona, Spain, July.

D. McClosky and E. Charniak. 2008. Self-training for biomedical parsing. In *Proceedings of the 46th Annual Meeting of the Association for Computational Linguistics*, pages 101–104, Columbus, Ohio, June.

J. Nivre, J. Hall, J. Nilsson, G. Eryi it, and S. Marinov. 2006. Labeled pseudo-projective dependency parsing with support vector machines. In *Proceedings of the Tenth Conference on Computational Natural Language Learning*, pages 221–225, New York City, NY, June.

J. Nivre, J. Hall, J. Nilsson, A. Chanev, G. Eryigit, S. Kübler, S. Marinov, and E. Marsi. 2007. MaltParser: A language-independent system for data-driven dependency parsing. *Natural Language Engineering*, 13(02):95–135.

J. Nivre. 2003. An efficient algorithm for projective dependency parsing. In *Proceedings of the 8th International Workshop on Parsing Technologies*, pages 149–160, Nancy, France, April.

S. Petrov, L. Barrett, R. Thibaux, and D. Klein. 2006. Learning accurate, compact, and interpretable tree annotation. In *Proceedings of the 21st International Conference on Computational Linguistics and the 44th annual meeting of the Association for Computational Linguistics*, pages 433–440, Sydney, Australia, July.

K. Sagae and A. Gordon. 2009. Clustering words by syntactic similarity improves dependency parsing of predicate-argument structures. In *Proceedings of the 11th International Conference on Parsing Technologies*, pages 192–201, Paris, France, October.

B. Sagot. 2010. The Lefff, a freely available, accurate and large-coverage lexicon for French. In *Proceedings of the 7th International Conference on Language Resources and Evaluation*, Valetta, Malta, May.

J. Tiedemann. 2009. News from OPUS - A collection of multilingual parallel corpora with tools and interfaces. In *Recent Advances in Natural Language Processing*, volume 5, pages 237–248. John Benjamins, Amsterdam.

D. Xiong, S. Li, Q. Liu, S. Lin, and Y. Qian. 2005. Parsing the penn chinese treebank with semantic knowledge. In *Proceedings of the International Joint Conference on Natural Language Processing*, pages 70–81, Jeju Island, Korea, October.

H. Yamada and Y. Matsumoto. 2003. Statistical dependency analysis with support vector machines. In *Proceedings of the 8th International Workshop on Parsing Technologies*, pages 195–206, Nancy, France, April.

Supervised Learning of German Qualia Relations

Yannick Versley
SFB 833
Universität Tübingen
versley@sfs.uni-tuebingen.de

Abstract

In the last decade, substantial progress has been made in the induction of semantic relations from raw text, especially of hypernymy and meronymy in the English language and in the classification of noun-noun relations in compounds or other contexts. We investigate the question of learning qualia-like semantic relations that cross part-of-speech boundaries for German, by first introducing a hand-tagged dataset of associated noun-verb pairs for this task, and then provide classification results using a general framework for supervised classification of lexical relations.

1 Introduction

Ever since the introduction of wordnets (Miller and Fellbaum, 1991) or more generally machine-readable dictionaries containing semantic relations, researchers have investigated ways to learn such examples automatically from large text corpora, or generalize them from existing instances. Substantial research exists on the learning of hyperonymy relations (Hearst, 1992; Snow et al., 2005; Tjong Kim Sang and Hofmann, 2009), meronymy relations (Hearst, 1998; Berland and Charniak, 1999; Girju et al., 2003) and selectional preferences (Erk et al., 2010; Bergsma et al., 2008; Ó Séaghdha, 2010).

Both lexicographic research (Chaffin and Herrmann, 1987; Morris and Hirst, 2004) and research in cognitive psychology (Vigliocco et al., 2004; McRae et al., 2005), argue that it is important to consider relations beyond the classical inventory of hyperonymy and meronymy relations; furthermore psychological research on priming (Hare et al., 2009) suggests different processing for different relations, which would entail that cognitively plausible modeling of human language should model these relations explicitly rather than simply recording untyped associations between concepts (as in the 'evocation' relation proposed for WordNet by Boyd-Graber et al., 2006).

One set of suggestions for an extended inventory of relations can be found in the telic and agentive qualia relations of Pustejovsky (1991) which have been shown to be useful in recognizing discourse relations (Wellner et al., 2006), or metonymy/coercion phenomena (Verspoor, 1997; Rüd and Zarcone, 2011), and have the property of linking different parts-of-speech groups, unlike meronymy and hyperonymy/troponymy.

The work we present in this paper consists of a dataset of noun-verb associations for German concrete nouns, which we present in more detail in section 3, and a state-of-the-art approach to the supervised classification of such cross-part-of-speech relations using informative features from large collections of unannotated text, which we present in section 4. Experimental results are discussed in section 6.

2 Related Work

Most of earlier work on discovering novel instances of semantic relations was based on surface pattern matching, as presented by Hearst (1998). In the domain of finding qualia relations, Cimiano and Wenderoth (2005) propose patterns such as "*...purpose* *of X is ...*" or "*... X is used to ...*", whereas they argue that agentive qualia are best chosen from a small, fixed inventory of verbs (e.g., *make*, *bake*, *create ...*). Katrenko and Adriaans (2008a) additionally propose "*to Y a (new|complete) X*" and "*a (new|complete) X has been Y'd*" as patterns for agentive qualia.

Some of the more recent work starts out from matches extracted by means of such a pattern, but use supervised training data to learn semantic constraints that improve the precision by filtering the extracted examples. Berland and Charniak (1999) use some handcrafted rules to exclude abstract objects from the part-of relations they extract from a corpus, and additionally rank pattern extractions by collocation strength. Girju et al. (2003) propose an iterative refinement scheme based on taxonomic information from WordNet: In this learning approach, general constraints using top-level semantic classes (entity, abstraction, causal-agent) are passed to a decision tree learner and iteratively refined until the semantic constraints induced from the classes are no longer ambiguous.

Katrenko and Adriaans (2008b, 2010) present approaches to learn semantic constraints for the use in recognizing semantic relations between word tokens (SemEval 2007 shared task, see Girju et al., 2009), either in a graph-based generalization of Girju's iterative refinement approach that is able to handle sense ambiguities more gracefully, or by clustering pairs of words by the joint similarity of both relation arguments.

A complementary aspect is to improving recall beyond the possibilities of a few hand-selected patterns. Following Hearst (1998), Girju et al. (2003) show that it is possible to find usable patterns by exploiting known positive examples and looking for co-occurrences of these relation arguments in a corpus. However, these patterns usually have low precision and/or very limited recall, meaning that a more elaborate approach (such as Girju et al.'s induction of semantic constraints) is needed to make the best use of them.

Yamada and Baldwin (2004) propose to use a combination of templates typical of telic and agentive qualia relations (X is worth Ying, X deserves Ying, a well-Yed X) and a statistical ranking combining association and a classifier learned on positive and negative examples for that role. They find that the combination of association statistic and classification worked somewhat better than the templates alone.

One approach targeted at exploiting a greater number of patterns for hyperonymy relations can be found in the work of Snow et al. (2005): they extract patterns consisting of the shortest path in the dependency graph plus an optional satellite and use the set of all found paths as features in a linear classifier. The resulting classifier for hyperonymy relations outperforms single patterns both in terms of precision and in terms of recall; a further improvement can be achieved if the frequency of pattern instances is binned instead of just occurrence or non-occurrence being recorded.

Tjong Kim Sang and Hofmann (2009) investigate the question whether it is necessary to use syntactic (rather than surface) patterns for the hyperonym classification approach of Snow et al. They compare a method of extracting features based on syntax as in Snow et al.'s approach with a surface-based alternative where the string between two words, plus optionally one word to the left or right side of the word, is extracted. Tjong Kim Sang and Hofmann argue that the benefit of the parser (additional recall due to the better generalization capability of the syntactic patterns) is mostly negated by parsing errors: In some informative contexts that the system based on POS patterns is able to find without problems, parsing errors lead to a parse tree that does not exhibit the intended (dependency path) pattern.

Several researchers have applied such pattern classification approaches to a larger set of relations, and have demonstrated that extracting a pattern distribution between occurrences and performing supervised classification based on this distribution is a promising solution for semantic relations that go beyond hyperonymy.

Ó Séaghdha and Copestake (2007) use a supervised classification approach for noun-noun compounds combining context features for each of the single words with features characterizing the joint occurrences of the two nouns that are part of the target compound. In their experiments, they found that linear classification using informative (bag-of-words and bag-of-triples) features in conjunction with features aimed at the similarity of each word of the target pair yields good results. In particular, the results of using a linear classifier with informative corpus-based features that are quite close to those that can be achieved using a (more accurate, but computationally quite expensive) string kernel or those that Ó Séaghdha (2007) achieves using taxonomic information from WordNet.

Turney (2008) presents a general approach for classifying word pairs into semantic relations by extracting the strings occurring between the two words of a pair (up to three words in-between, up to one word on either side) and using a frequency-based selection process to select sub-patterns where words from the extracted context pattern may have been replaced by a wildcard. Using standard machine learning tools (a support vector machine with radial base function kernel), he is able to reach results that are close to those possible with previous more specialized approaches.

Similarly, Herdağdelen and Baroni (2009) tackle a variety of problems in semantic relation classification using a unified approach where frequent unigrams and bigrams are extracted from co-occurrence contexts of the target word pair (in addition to features extracted from general occurrence contexts of each word). Herdağdelen and Baroni's approach uses a linear SVM (which is faster and better-suited to large data sets in general than either kernelized support vector machines or nearest-neighbour approaches) yet is able to reach competitive accuracy.

In contrast to approaches using generic machine learning, Ó Séaghdha and Copestake (2009) and Nakov and Kozareva (2011) model the similarities between related word pairs more explicitly in terms of distributional kernels (Ó Séaghdha and Copestake), or as a similarity metric between word pairs (Nakov and Kozareva). Such approaches allow more flexibility in the modeling of similarity and the combination of lexical and relational similarity measures, but are less well-suited for scaling up to more training data.[1]

Because of the need for sufficient training data, purely supervised approaches to learning relations in morphologically-rich languages are often limited to the classical relations found in wordnets. Tjong Kim Sang and Hofmann (2009) use a Dutch corpus and hyperonymy relations from the Dutch Cornetto wordnet and mention relatively few differences to approaches on English such as Snow et al. (2005). Kurc and Piasecki (2008) apply the semi-supervised approach of Pantel and Pennachiotti (2006) for learning hyperonymy relations, but modify the patterns used to enforce morphosyntactic agreement and accommodate a more flexible word order. Versley (2007) uses Web pattern queries for finding hyperonymy relations and mentions the fact that greater morphological richness and the smaller size of the German Web make the use of Web queries more complex than for English.

Outside the realm of hyperonymy, Regneri (2006) uses Web-based pattern search to classify verb-verb associations into the semantic classes proposed for English by Chklovski and Pantel (2004). Rüd and Zarcone (2011) perform a corpus study of patterns indicative of telic and agentive qualia relations in a German Web corpus, but perform no automatic classification.

In summary, the research of Tjong Kim Sang and Hofmann (2009) seems to indicate that at least hyperonymy relations can be found using a shallow pattern approach despite greater word order flexibility of languages such as Dutch and German. For cross-part-of-speech relations, such as telic and agentive qualia, such a question has been unaddressed as of yet, which prompted us to create a dataset that is suitable for such an investigation.

3 Material

In order to investigate general-domain Noun-Verb relations in German, we first had to create an appropriate dataset that captures a realistic notion of the relationships that humans infer in a text. Existing datasets that explore this space (most of them for English) use a variety of approaches: One approach starts from examples (such as the popular analogy dataset for English introduced by Turney and Littman, 2003); other approaches such as the data collection for the SemEval task on identifying relations between nominals (Girju et al., 2009; Hendrickx et al., 2010) start from common semantic re-

[1] Ó Séaghdha and Copestake (2009) reports training times of slightly more than one day for their most efficient method whereas a ten-fold crossvalidation run using SVM_{perf} – see the presentation on p. 6 – takes under an hour, i.e., using linear classification is more efficient by a factor of about 100.

lations and use patterns to gather positive and negative examples by Web queries.

In our case, we started from noun-verb associations found in a sample of human-produced associations to concrete noun stimuli (Melinger et al., 2006); starting from the original association data, we excluded items that were produced by less than three subjects and used the part-of-speech information attached to the data to retrieve only the verb associates.

The classification scheme was motivated by existing generative lexicon research (Pustejovsky, 1991; Lenci et al., 2003), but was modeled to achieve a good fit to the associations present in the data rather than to force a good fit to any particular theory.

- *agentive* relations exist between an artifact and an event that creates or procures it (e.g. *bread-bake*)
- the *telic* relations exist between an entity and an event that is related to its purpose or (actual or intended) role:
  - *telic-artifact* holds between an artifact and its intended usage (e.g. *plane-fly*)
  - *telic-role* holds between a role (i.e., a profession, organizational position etc.) and activities related to that role (e.g. *cowboy-ride*)
  - *telic-bodypart* holds between a body part and its intended uses (e.g. *eye-see*)
- the *behaviour* group of relations hold between an entity and events that are caused by it, but are not necessarily intentional or related to a role that it fulfills:
  - *behaviour-animate* are typical activities performed by animate entities that are unrelated to the role that they fulfill for humans (e.g., *dog-bark*)
  - *behaviour-artifact* relates artifacts to (usually) unintended behaviour associated with them (e.g., *moped-rattle*)
  - *behaviour-environment* relates elements of the environment to events that go on around them (e.g., *sun-shine*)
- *location* relations hold between elements of the environment and activities typically performed in or at them (e.g., *mountain-climb*)
- *grooming* relations hold between artifacts and activities that contribute to the readiness of an artifact (or body part) for its intended use but are not directly related to it (e.g., *plant-water*, *hair-dye*)

In comparison to standard schemes such as SIMPLE (Lenci et al., 2003), we have extended the set of *telic* and *agentive* qualia from the original generative lexicon approach by supplementing it with relations that describe the affordances of objects or guides the interpretative linking of objects and events, namely *location* for affordances of elements of the environment and *grooming* for object-related actions that may not be necessary for a differently-built object with that same function, and finally *behaviour* describes events that co-occur with objects but are usually not part of a human agent's action plan.

As a refinement, we subdivided the *telic* qualia and *behaviour* relations, in particular specifying any *telic* relation with the reason a concrete object may be relevant for goal-directed processing – either by teleological interpretation of body parts, by the creation of artifacts with a specific purpose, or the establishment of roles with social conventions supporting certain types of actions.

Among the responses collected by Melinger et al. (2006), we found relatively few instances that were genuinely ambiguous (*Drachen - fliegen*, which may either be interpreted as 'kite/fly', in which case it would be a *telic-artifact* relation, or as 'dragon/fly', in which case it would be a *behaviour-animate* relation), but found that domestic animals (cows, horses, dogs) have affordances such as *horse-ride* or *dog-bark* that indicate they are conceptualized as instruments serving a particular goal (which means that the relation should be labeled as *telic-artifact* rather than as *behaviour-animate*).

In the associated word pairs, we also found relations such as *Zwiebel-schneiden* ('onion-cut') or *Handtuch-duschen* ('towel-shower') where the action is related to a thing's purpose but not identical to it (towels are used to dry yourself *after* showering, and people acquire onions to eat them *after* having cut them). Our initial annotation included a combination between the qualia-like relations presented here and an additional event-semantic relation linking the elicited event and the intended affordance of the object. However, the event relation was left out of the dataset used in the experiments to avoid data sparsity.

In our dataset with 641 items, the most frequent relations are *telic-artifact* (425 instances), *behaviour-animate* (94 instances), *telic-role* (35 instances), *telic-bodypart* (24 instances). The other relations have between 2 and 17 instances each (see table 3). The relationship data is therefore heavily skewed.

4 Classification Approach

Our classification approach is aimed at a practical toolkit for supervised classification of lexical-semantic relations, similar in spirit to the BagPack approach of Herdağdelen and Baroni (2009) but adapted for the use in morphologically-rich languages, in particular German.

In addition to the surface-based unigram and bigram features, we use features based on dependency syntax, which is more robust against variation in word order, and allows to reattach separable verb prefixes.

4.1 Preprocessing

To see why a very shallow approach may be less useful for German, let us consider a simple direct (accusative) object relation such as between *aufessen* (eat up) and *Kuchen* (cake): this relation could be realized in a variety of ways depending on clause type and constituent order, as illustrated in example (1).

(1) a. Peter isst den Kuchen auf.
Peter eats the cake up.
"Peter eats up the cake".
b. Den Kuchen hat Peter aufgegessen.
The cake$_{acc}$ has Peter eaten-up.
"Peter has eaten up the cake".
c. ... dass Peter den Kuchen aufisst.
... that Peter the cake up-eat.
"... that Peter eats up the cake".

In German, clause type decides whether the verb is in verb-second position (1a) or at the end of the clause (1b,1c); additionally, as in (1a), prefixes of verbs may be stranded at the end of a clause with the verb in verb-second position.

In addition to morphological analysis, hence, reattachment is necessary in such cases as (1a), and parsing is necessary to reattach prefix and verb. In cases such as (1b), word order variation also needs to be taken into account in order to recover the direct object relation, unlike in languages with less-flexible word order.

As a text collection that furnishes contexts for the words or word pairs that interest us, we use the *webnews* corpus, a collection of online news articles collected by Versley and Panchenko (2012). For the processing of this 1.7 billion word corpus, we use a pipeline that relies on deterministic dependency parsing to provide complete dependency parses at a speed that is suitable for the processing of Web-scale corpora.

The parsing model is based on MALTParser, a transition-based parser, and uses part-of-speech and morphological information as input. Morphological information is annotated using RFTagger (Schmid and Laws, 2008), a state-of-the-art morphological tagger based on decision trees and a large context window (which allows it to model morphological agreement more accurately than a normal trigram-based sequence tagger). While transition-based parsers are quite fast in general, an SVM classifier (which is used in MALTParser by default) becomes slower with increasing training set. In contrast, using the MALTParser interface to LibLinear by Cassel (2009), we were able to reach a much larger speed of 55 sentences per second (against 0.4 sentences per second for a more feature-rich SVM-based model that reaches state of the art performance).

For lemmatization, we use the syntax-based TüBa-D/Z lemmatizer (Versley et al., 2010), which uses a separate morphological analyzer and some fallback heuristics. The SMOR morphology (Schmid et al., 2004) serves to provide morphological analyses for novel words, covering inflection, derivation and composition processes. For unanalyzed novel words that are not covered by SMOR, the lemmatizer falls back to surface-based guessing heuristics. It uses morphological and syntactic information to provide more accurate lemmas; In addition to dependency structures, the morphological tags from RFTagger as well as global frequency information are used.

4.2 Classification

For classification, we use the following learning methods:

- For the **SVMperf** classifier, the set of possible labels is decomposed into binary problems using the one-vs-all scheme (for each possible label, a classifier is trained that receives the instances of this label as positive instances and the others as negative instances). SVMperf allows the training of models that either optimize (an upper bound for) the accuracy (SVM_{acc}) or the f-measure (SVM_F) of positive instances (Joachims, 2005).

- The **Maximum Entropy** (MaxEnt) classifier directly learns the multiclass decision. Here, we used the AMIS package by Miyao and Tsujii (2002).

All experiments are run in a ten-fold crossvalidation setup where the data is split ten portions and each portion (fold) is tagged using a classifier trained on the remaining nine folds. This setup leads to decreased variation

As noted in section 6, SVM_{perf} using optimization for accuracy (i.e., a standard linear kernel SVM with hinge loss and a one-versus-all reduction to handle the multiclass problem) performs best on the two aggregate measures that we used (accuracy and macro-averaged F). Hence, most results we report in the later part only use the standard SVM learner.

4.3 Features

The first group of **surface-based** features uses a similar technique to Herdağdelen and Baroni (2009): given the co-occurrences of two words X and Y with at most 4 words in-between, we extract frequent unigrams and bigrams. Because we can maintain the sparsity of the resulting feature vector (see section 5), we can use a larger list of 10 000 each of the most frequent unigrams and bigrams (`w12`) alternatively to a list with only 2 000 entries each (`w12:2k`). The `lem12` feature uses the same approach, but uses lemmas instead.

A second group of features uses a **path-based** representation based on a modified version of the dependency parse (where the main verb, and not the auxiliary verb is the head of a clause and is connected to both the subject and its other arguments).

In the path-based representation, we can extract the (shortest) path between the two target words in the dependency graph. The `rel` feature records the complete path (labeled dependency edges as well as lemmas of intervening nodes) between the target words. In contrast, the `sat` feature records labeled dependency edges as well as lemmas of the dependents of one of the target words.

Because the `rel` feature yields relatively large (and therefore sparse) strings, we also decompose the dependency path in triples consisting of labeled dependency edge in the path and the two nodes adjacent to it (with the endpoints replaced by "w_1" and "w_2", respectively) for the `triples` feature.

In order to emulate the feature extraction of Snow et al. (2005), we introduce a `relsat` feature, which pairs the path (as in the `rel` feature) with one dependent of either target word. The `relsat` feature would be able to model patterns such as "w_1 and other w_2", where a modifier ("other") is not part of the shortest dependency path between w_1 and w_2.

In addition, a feature based on GermaNet (Henrich and Hinrichs, 2010) uses **taxonomic** information: possible hypernyms of the noun and verb in the pair are extracted, and are used by themselves (e.g. "noun is a hyponym of 'thing' ", or "verb is a hyponym of 'communicate' ") and in combinations of up to two of these possible hypernym labels.

In addition to taxonomic information from GermaNet, we use **distributional similarity** features for single words. For the nouns, we use distributional features based on the co-occurrence of premodifying adjectives, which Versley and Panchenko (2012) found to work better than other grammatical-relation-based collocates (`attr1`), while we use Padó and Lapata's (2007) method of gathering and weighting collocates based on distance in the dependency graph for the verbs (`p12`). Herdağdelen and Baroni (2009) simply use a window-based approach for gathering collocates, which we reimplemented as a simpler way of capturing distributional similarity. The resulting features are named `w1` and `w2`.

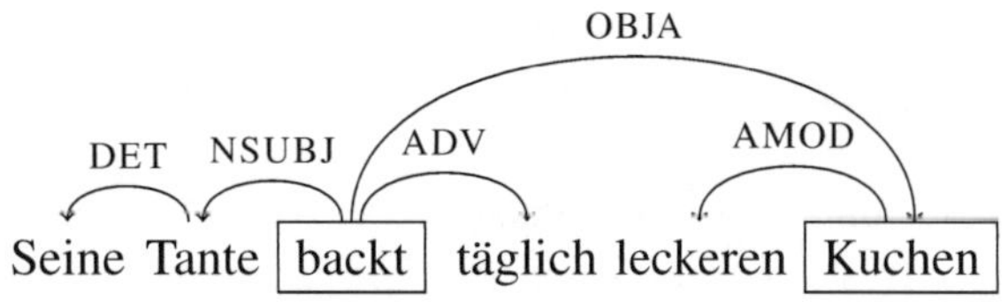

His aunt bakes daily luscious cake
"his aunt bakes luscious cake every day"

`w12`	Seine_{w_2,w_1} Tante_{w_2,w_1} $_{w_2}\text{täglich}_{w_1}$
`lem12`	sein_{w_2,w_1} Tante_{w_2,w_1} $_{w_2}\text{täglich}_{w_1}$
`rel`	↑OBJA
`sat`	w_2ADV:täglich w_1AMOD:lecker w_1NSUBJ:Tante
`triples`	w_1 ↑OBJA w_2
`relsat`	↑OBJA/w_2ADV:täglich ↑OBJA/w_1AMOD:lecker ↑OBJA/w_1NSUBJ:Tante

Due to the short path between w_1 and w_2, the `triples` and `rel` features are not very different in the example. In case of more complicated constructions, the `triples` approach would yield multiple simpler features whereas `rel` would yield one single complex string.

Figure 1: Kinds of features

5 Count Transformations

It is a well-known fact in distributional semantics that raw observation counts for context items (be they elements surrounding single word occurrences or elements extracted from the occurences of two words together) are incomparable for different target words/target pairs (since their frequency can differ) as well as for different context items. As a result, researchers have proposed different approaches to produce transformed vectors using more sophisticated association statistics (see Dumais, 1991, Weeds et al., 2004, Turney and Pantel, 2010, *inter alia*).

In our case, we implemented L_1 normalization (which normalizes for target word frequency), a conservative estimate for pointwise mutual information (which normalizes for the frequencies of both target word and feature), and the G^2 log-likelihood measure of Dunning (1993), which gives significance scores (i.e., numbers that invariably grow both with target and feature frequency, even if the association strength – the relation between actual occurrences and those that would be expected when assuming no association – is constant). In both cases, very frequent features would be emphasized in comparison to medium- and low-frequency features.

In the realm of supervised learning, an additional choice has to be made among learning methods that can classify words or word pairs using large feature vectors – most commonly using nearest-neighbour classification (Nakov and Kozareva, 2011), using custom kernels in support vector classification (Ó Séaghdha and Copestake, 2009; Turney, 2008), or by using appropriate techniques to represent the feature vectors in linear classification.

In comparison to the former methods, linear classification scales better with the number of examples (where nearest-neigbour and kernel-based techniques both show strongly superlinear behaviour) and would be the method of choice for large-scale classification.

Herdağdelen and Baroni (2009) propose to map the values computed by association statistics by computing mean and standard deviation of each feature and mapping the range $[\mu - 2\sigma, \mu + 2\sigma]$ of association scores for that feature (seen over the values of that feature for all target pairs) to the range $[0, 1]$ in the input for the classifier, clamping values outside that range to 0 or 1, respectively.

Unfortunately, the approach proposed by Herdağdelen and Baroni has the property that an association score of 0 is mapped to a non-zero feature value for the classifier, which means that feature vectors are no longer sparse (i.e., instead of only storing non-zero values for context items that are informative, values for all context items have to be processed).

To keep the sparsity of the transformed counts, we always use 0 as the lower bound of the mapping (such that zero values stay zero values). In addition to the Herdagdelen and Baroni's mean/variance-based threshold, we investigated the following possibilities for fixing the upper bound:

- **MI scale**: use a constant upper bound of 1 on (a conservative estimate of) the pointwise mutual information.[2]

[2]To yield a conservative MI estimate, we use the discounting factor introduced by Pantel and Lin (2002). The pointwise mutual information value normalizes the frequency of both words of a pair, hence all mutual information values are on a common scale. A threshold of 1 in this case corresponds to two items oc-

baselines/single features	Acc	MacroF
random	0.463	0.090
telic-artifact	0.663	0.080
w12/L_1-norm/AMIS	0.677	0.181
w12/L_1-norm/SVM$_{acc}$	0.715	0.212
w12/L_1-norm/SVM$_F$	0.674	0.120
w12/L_1-norm	0.715	0.212
lem12/G^2-quant	0.703	0.204
rel/L_1-quant	0.722	0.154
sat/L_1-norm	0.700	0.185
triples/L_1-quant	**0.741**	0.192
triples/G^2-norm	0.739	**0.212**
relsat/L_1-quant	0.698	0.154
attr1+pl2/MI-thr	0.800	0.460
w1+w2/MI-thr	0.807	0.468
GermaNet, no combination	0.846	0.450
GermaNet, degree=2	**0.851**	**0.516**

Table 1: Trivial and single-feature baselines (using SVM-acc unless noted otherwise)

combinations	Acc	MacroF
triples/G^2-norm	**0.739**	**0.212**
triples+w12/G^2-norm	0.733	0.206
triples+rel/G^2-norm	0.725	0.190
triples+sat/G^2-norm	0.738	0.200
triples+relsat/G^2-norm	0.729	0.184
triples+w1+w2/MI-thr	0.816	0.469
triples+attr1+pl2/MI-thr	0.807	0.431
GermaNet	0.851	**0.516**
GermaNet+triples/G^2-norm	0.853	0.482
GermaNet+triples/MI-thr	0.855	0.484
GermaNet+w12/G^2-norm	0.855	0.496
GermaNet+w12/MI-thr	**0.858**	0.510
GWN+w12+triples/G^2-norm	0.852	0.462
GWN+w12+triples/MI-thr	0.849	0.478
GermaNet+w1+w2/MI-thr	0.828	0.496

Table 2: Combination results (using SVMacc)

- **norm**: use a value based on mean and standard deviation of the occurring values for one given feature ($\mu + 2\sigma$).
- **quant**: use a fixed quantile (99%) of all values for a feature for the upper bound of the mapping interval.

In addition, to mapping feature values onto the unit interval $[0, 1]$, we investigated the usefulness of making the features binary-valued by mapping all values lower than the threshold to zero. While intuitively a continuous-valued feature should be more informative, the high dimensionality of the feature space may mean that noisy feature extraction ultimately leads to a worse model in the continuous-feature case.

6 Results and Discussion

Because of the skewed distribution, it is useful to look not only at the overall accuracy (Acc) but also at the macro-average of the F-measure of all relations (MacroF). The macro-averaged F-measure reflects the ability of the system to recognize all relations since it weighs all relation types equally, instead of (implicitly) weighting by token count where under-predicting rare relation types normally yields a higher accuracy. As is evident from table 1, the accuracy baseline for the most frequent label (*telic-artifact*) is already quite high.

Looking at results with various scaling methods and learners on single features (table 1), we found that the SVM$_{acc}$ learner consistently yields better accuracy and macro-averaged F-measure than the other two learners. For the weighting functions, we found that none of the measures was consistently better than the others; results for the single features in table 1 are reported for a weighting function that works best for either accuracy or macro-averaged F-measure using. (For space reasons, table 1 shows numbers only for the w12 feature and L_1-norm scaling; other features and settings show a similar relation between the scores for different learners).

As in the investigation by Ó Séaghdha and Copestake (2007), dependency triples from the path between the two target words are the most effective feature representation and yields both the greatest accuracy value (with L_1 scaling and quantile-based setting of thresholds) and the greatest F-measure macroaverage (with G^2 scaling and setting of thresholds based on average and standard deviation). Combination of the `triples` feature with

curring together about $\exp(1) \approx 2.7$ times as often as would be expected from the marginal distribution for that co-occurrence relation.

	agentive	beh-anim	beh-artif	beh-body	beh-env	grooming	location	telic-artif	telic-body	telic-role
count	14	94	13	2	5	17	12	425	24	35
w12	0.105	0.513	0.000	0.000	0.000	0.000	0.154	0.834	0.214	0.255
triples	0.125	0.601	0.000	0.000	0.000	0.000	0.153	0.853	0.153	0.238
attr1+pl2	0.333	0.826	**0.258**	0.000	0.000	**0.500**	0.421	0.874	0.636	0.754
w1+w2	0.385	0.834	0.222	0.000	0.000	0.400	0.571	0.877	0.619	0.767
GermaNet	**0.480**	**0.859**	0.190	0.000	0.000	0.451	**0.636**	0.909	**0.773**	0.857
GWN+w12	0.400	0.857	0.133	0.000	**0.333**	0.384	0.600	**0.916**	0.600	**0.873**

Table 3: Results by relation

other features based on paired co-occurrences does not lead to further improvements, especially with those features that also express information from the dependency path (`rel`,`relsat`).

In comparison, the accuracy of the GermaNet hypernyms feature (which includes combinations of the hypernyms of first and second word) is much higher than the versions that do not make use of hand-crafted taxonomic knowledge, which is surprising since it uses only taxonomic and no relational information. The pairwise feature combination for GermaNet features yields another small improvement over these already very good results. Distributional information on single words, both the strictly window-based `w1+w2` feature and the one that is based on more elaborated distributional modeling (`attr1+pl2`) show quite good results that show further (but relatively small) improvements when combined with the `triples` feature.

The importance of taxonomic (or, alternatively, distributional semantic) information for the task proposed here - namely, the supervised classification of qualia-like relations - partly mirrors results for the supervised classification of relations between nominals, where Ó Séaghdha and Copestake (2007) find that their best system for distributional similarity based on the BNC performs at about the same level as a (somewhat simpler) approach using WordNet-based classification (Ó Séaghdha, 2007), with only much more sophisticated approaches such as the one of Ó Séaghdha and Copestake (2009), which also makes use of a considerably larger textual basis to improve results over the level of the WordNet-based approach.

Another reason for the importance of taxonomic information in this task may lie in the fact that the different relations have relatively strong selectional restrictions (for animate objects, roles/professions, body parts, or artifacts on the noun side, and certain types of actions or events on the verb side).

Looking at the results for each relation in table 3, we see that both *telic-artifact* and *behaviour-animate*, the two relations with the largest counts, are classified quite reliably, while *behaviour-bodypart* and *behaviour-environment*, the two relations with very few examples, are never found by the system. Among the other relations, taxonomical information for nouns and verbs seems to be instrumental for adequate classification of the *grooming* relation and possibly also for *location*, *telic-bodypart* and *telic-role*.

7 Summary

In this paper, we have presented a dataset containing cross-part-of-speech relations between concrete nouns and human verb associates and demonstrated a state-of-the-art approach for the supervised multiclass classification of the qualia relations in this dataset.[3] Our results show that taxonomic information from GermaNet is much superior to all other features, while corpus-based dependency triples are still visibly superior to shallow surface-based features.

Important questions for future research would include a more direct comparison to other languages (ideally using a similar data set and information sources) to tease apart the influences of word order, taxonomic organization, and data sparsity, respectively.

[3]The dataset and future corrected/improved versions, are available on request. Please feel free to send an email to the author if you want to use it or produce a create a version for another language.

Acknowledgements The work described in this paper was funded by the Deutsche Forschungsgemeinschaft (DFG) as part of Collaborative Research Centre (SFB) 833. The author gratefully acknowledges Melike Heubach's help with the annotation of the dataset.

References

Bergsma, S., Lin, D., and Goebel, R. (2008). Discriminative learning of selectional preference from unlabeled text. In *EMNLP 2008*.

Berland, M. and Charniak, E. (1999). Finding parts in very large corpora. In *Proceedings of ACL-1999*.

Boyd-Graber, J., Fellbaum, C., Osherson, D., and Schapire, R. (2006). Adding dense, weighted connections to WordNet. In *Proceedings of the Global WordNet Conference*.

Cassel, S. (2009). MaltParser and LIBLINEAR - transition-based dependency parsing with linear classification for feature model optimization. Master's thesis, Uppsala University.

Chaffin, R. and Herrmann, D. J. (1987). Relation element theory: A new account of the representation and processing of semantic relations. In Gorfein, D. S., editor, *Memory and Learning: the Ebbinghaus Centennial Conference*. Erlbaum.

Chklovski, T. and Pantel, P. (2004). VerbOcean: Mining the web for fine-grained semantic verb relations. In *Proc. EMNLP 2004*.

Cimiano, P. and Wenderoth, J. (2005). Automatically learning qualia structures from the web. In *Proceedings of the ACL'05 Workshop on Deep Lexical Acquisition*.

Dumais, S. (1991). Improving the retrieval of information from external sources. *Behavior Research Methods, Instruments and Computers*, 23(2):229–236.

Dunning, T. (1993). Accurate methods for the statistics of surprise and coincidence. *Computational Linguistics*, 19(1):61–74.

Erk, K., Padó, S., and Padó, U. (2010). A flexible, corpus-driven model of regular and inverse selectional preferences. *Computational Linguistics*, 36(4):723–761.

Girju, R., Badulescu, A., and Moldovan, D. (2003). Learning semantic constraints for the automatic discovery of part-whole relations. In *NAACL-HLT 2003*.

Girju, R., Nakov, P., Nastase, V., Szpakowicz, S., and Turney, P. (2009). Classification of semantic relations between nominals. *Language Resources and Evaluation*, 43(2):105–121.

Hare, M., Jones, M., Thomson, C., Kelly, S., and McRae, K. (2009). Activating event knowledge. *Cognition*, 111:151–167.

Hearst, M. (1992). Automatic acquisition of hyponyms from large text corpora. In *Proc. of the 14th International Conference on Computational Linguistics (COLING 92)*.

Hearst, M. (1998). Automated discovery of wordnet relations. In *WordNet: An Electronic Lexical Database*. MIT Press, Cambridge (MA), USA.

Hendrickx, I., Kim, S. N., Kozareva, Z., Nakov, P., Séaghdha, D. O., Padó, S., Pennacchiotti, M., Romano, L., and Szpakowicz, S. (2010). Semeval-2010 task 8: Multi-way classification of semantic relations between pairs of nominals. In *SemEval 2010*.

Henrich, V. and Hinrichs, E. (2010). GernEdiT - the GermaNet editing tool. In *Proceedings of the Seventh Conference on International Language Resources and Evaluation (LREC 2010)*, pages 2228–2235.

Herdağdelen, A. and Baroni, M. (2009). BagPack: A general framework to represent semantic relations. In *ACL09 Workshop on Geometric Models of Natural Language Semantics (GEMS09)*.

Joachims, T. (2005). A support vector method for multivariate performance measures. In *Proceedings of the International Conference on Machine Learning (ICML)*.

Katrenko, S. and Adriaans, P. (2008a). Qualia structures and their impact on the concrete noun categorization task. In *ESSLLI 2008 workshop on Distributional Lexical Semantics*.

Katrenko, S. and Adriaans, P. (2008b). Semantic types of some generic relation arguments: Detection and evaluation. In *ACL/HLT 2008*.

Katrenko, S. and Adriaans, P. (2010). Finding constraints for semantic relations via clustering. In *CLIN 2010*.

Kurc, R. and Piasecki, M. (2008). Automatic acquisition of wordnet relations by the morpho-syntactic patterns extracted from the corpora in Polish. In *Proceedings of the International Multiconference on Computer Science and Information Technology - Third International Symposium Advances in Artificial Intelligence and Applications (IMCSIT 2008)*.

Lenci, A., Calzolari, N., and Zampolli, A. (2003). SIMPLE: Plurilingual semantic lexicons for natural language processing. *Linguistica Computatazionale*, 16–17:323–352.

McRae, K., Cree, G., Seidenberg, M., and McNorgan, C. (2005). Semantic feature production norms for a large set of living and nonliving things. *Behaviour Research Methods*, 37:547–559.

Melinger, A., Schulte im Walde, S., and Weber, A. (2006). Characterizing response types and revealing noun ambiguity in german association norms. In *Workshop on Making Sense of Sense: Bringing Psycholinguistics and Computational Linguistics Together*.

Miller, G. A. and Fellbaum, C. (1991). Semantic networks of English. *Cognition*, 41:197–229.

Miyao, Y. and Tsujii, J. (2002). Maximum entropy estimation for feature forests. In *HLT 2002*.

Morris, J. and Hirst, G. (2004). Non-classical lexical semantic relations. In *HLT/NAACL Workshop on Computational Lexical Semantics*.

Nakov, P. and Kozareva, Z. (2011). Combining relational and attributional similarity for semantic relation classification. In *RANLP 2011*.

Ó Séaghdha, D. and Copestake, A. (2009). Using lexical and relational similarity to classify semantic relations. In *EACL 2009*.

Ó Séaghdha, D. (2007). Annotating and learning compound noun semantics. In *Proceedings of the ACL07 Student Research Workshop*.

Ó Séaghdha, D. (2010). Latent variable models of selectional preference. In *ACL 2010*.

Ó Séaghdha, D. and Copestake, A. (2007). Co-occurrence contexts for noun compound interpretation. In *ACL 2007 Workshop on A Broader Perspective on Multiword Expressions*.

Ó Séaghdha, D. and Copestake, A. (2009). Using lexical and relational similarity to classify semantic relations. In *12th Conference of the European Chapter of the Association for Computational Linguistics (EACL)*.

Padó, S. and Lapata, M. (2007). Dependency-based construction of semantic space models. *Computational Linguistics*, 33(2):161–199.

Pantel, P. and Lin, D. (2002). Discovering word senses from text. In *Proceedings of ACM Conference on Knowledge Discovery and Data Mining (KDD-02)*, pages 613–619.

Pantel, P. and Pennachiotti, M. (2006). Espresso: Leveraging generic patterns for automatically harvesting semantic relations. In *COLING/ACL 2006*.

Pustejovsky, J. (1991). The generative lexicon. *Computational Linguistics*, 17(4):409–441.

Regneri, M. (2006). VerbOzean - maschinelles Lernen von semantischen Relationen zwischen deutschen Verben. Bachelorarbeit, Universität des Saarlandes.

Rüd, S. and Zarcone, A. (2011). Covert events and qualia structures for German verbs. In *Metonymy 2011*.

Schmid, H., Fitschen, A., and Heid, U. (2004). SMOR: A German computational morphology covering derivation, composition and inflection. In *Proceedings of LREC 2004*.

Schmid, H. and Laws, F. (2008). Estimation of conditional probabilities with decision trees and an application to fine-grained POS tagging. In *COLING 2008*.

Snow, R., Jurafsky, D., and Ng, A. Y. (2005). Learning syntactic patterns for automatic hypernym discovery. In *NIPS 2005*.

Tjong Kim Sang, E. and Hofmann, K. (2009). Lexical patterns or dependency patterns: Which is better for hypernym extraction. In *CoNLL-2009*.

Turney, P. (2008). A uniform approach to analogies, synonyms, antonyms and associations. In *Coling 2008*.

Turney, P. and Littman, M. (2003). Learning analogies and semantic relations. Technical Report ERB-1103, National Research Council, Institute for Information Technology.

Turney, P. and Pantel, P. (2010). From frequency to meaning: Vector space models of semantics. *Journal of Artificial Intelligence Research*, 37:141–188.

Versley, Y. (2007). Using the Web to resolve coreferent bridging in German newspaper text. In *Proceedings of GLDV-Frühjahrstagung 2007*, Tübingen. Narr.

Versley, Y., Beck, A. K., Hinrichs, E., and Telljohann, H. (2010). A syntax-first approach to high-quality morphological analysis and lemma disambiguation for the TüBa-D/Z treebank. In *Proceedings of the 9th Conference on Treebanks and Linguistic Theories (TLT9)*.

Versley, Y. and Panchenko, Y. (2012). Not just bigger: Towards better-quality Web corpora. In *Proceedings of the 7th Web as Corpus Workshop (WAC-7)*, pages 44–52.

Verspoor, C. M. (1997). *Contextually-Dependent Lexical Semantics*. PhD thesis, University of Edinburgh.

Vigliocco, G., Vinson, D., Lewis, W., and Garrett, M. (2004). Representing the meanings of object and action words: The featural and unitary semantic space hypothesis. *Cognitive Psychology*, 48:422–488.

Weeds, J., Weir, D., and McCarthy, D. (2004). Characterizing measures of lexical distributional similarity. In *CoLing 2004*.

Wellner, B., Pustejovsky, J., Havasi, C., Rumshisky, A., and Sauri, R. (2006). Classification of discourse coherence relations: An exploratory study using multiple knowledge sources. In *Proc. 7th SIGdial Workshop on Discourse and Dialogue*.

Yamada, I. and Baldwin, T. (2004). Automatic discovery of telic and agentive roles from corpus data. In *Proceedings of the 18th Pacific Asia Conference on Language, Information and Computation (PACLIC 18)*.

Building an Arabic Multiword Expressions Repository

Abdelati Hawwari, Kfir Bar, Mona Diab
Center for Computational Learning Systems
Columbia University
{ah3019,kfir,mdiab}@ccls.columbia.edu

Abstract

We introduce a list of Arabic multiword expressions (MWE) collected from various dictionaries. The MWEs are grouped based on their syntactic type. Every constituent word in the expressions is manually annotated with its full context-sensitive morphological analysis. Some of the expressions contain semantic variables as place holders for words that play the same semantic role. In addition, we have automatically annotated a large corpus of Arabic text using a pattern-matching algorithm that considers some morpho-syntactic features as expressed by a highly inflected language, such as Arabic. A sample part of the corpus is manually evaluated and the results are reported in this paper.

1 Introduction

A multiword expression (MWE) refers to a multiword unit or a collocation of words that co-occur together statistically more than chance. A MWE is a cover term for different types of collocations, which vary in their transparency and fixedness. MWEs are pervasive in natural language, especially in web based texts and speech genres. Identifying MWEs and understanding their meaning is essential to language understanding, hence they are of crucial importance for any Natural Language Processing (NLP) applications that aim at handling robust language meaning and use. In fact, the seminal paper (Sag et al., 2002) refers to this problem as a key issue for the development of high-quality NLP applications. MWEs are classified based on their syntactic constructions. Among the various classes, one can find the Verb Noun Constructions (VNC), Noun Noun Construction (NNC) and others. A MWE typically has an idiosyncratic meaning that is more or different from the meaning of its component words. In this paper we focus on MWEs in Arabic. Like many other Semitic languages, Arabic is highly inflected; words are derived from a root and a pattern (template), combined with prefixes, suffixes and circumfixes. As opposed to English equivalents, Arabic MWEs can be expressed in a large number of forms, expressing various inflections and derivations of the words while maintaining the exact same meaning, for example, *>gmD [flAn] Eynyh En [Al>mr]* [1], "[one] disregarded/overlooked/ignored [the issue]", literally, closed one's eyes, vs. *>**gmDt** [flAnp]* ***EynyhA*** *En [Al>mr]*, "[one_*fem*] disregarded/overlooked/ignored_*fem* [the issue]", where the predicate takes on the feminine inflection. However, in many cases, there are morphological features that cannot be changed in different contexts, for example, *mkrh >xAk lA bTl*, "forced with no choice", in this example, regardless of context, the words of the MWE do not agree in number and gender with the surrounding context. These are considered frozen expressions. One of the challenges in building MWE list for Arabic is to identify those features and document them in every MWE. Our resource is available for download.[2]

We have manually collected a large number of MWEs from various Arabic dictionaries, which are based on MSA corpora, and then filtered by Arabic

[1] We use the Buckwalter transliteration for rendering Arabic script in Romanization through out the paper (Buckwalter, 2002).

[2] To get a direct access, please send a request to one of the authors

native linguists. We then classified them based on their syntactic constructions, considering the relevant syntactic phenomena expressed in Arabic. The MWEs were manually annotated with the context-sensitive SAMA (Maamouri, 2010) morphological analysis for each word to assist an automated identification of MWEs in a large corpus of text. Part of the Arabic Gigaword 4.0 (Parker, 2009) is processed accordingly and the MWEs are annotated based on a deterministic algorithm considering different variants of every MWE in our list. There are diverse tasks that require a corpus with annotated MWEs, which have not been addressed in Arabic due to the lack of such a resource. However, a lot of attention is put on those tasks when implemented in English and other languages. Among those tasks, classifying MWEs in a running text is the most common one. Diab and Bhutada (2009) applied a supervised learning framework to the problem of classifying token level English MWEs in context. They used the annotated corpus provided by Cook (2008), a resource of almost 3000 English sentences annotated with VNC usage at the token level. Katz and Giesbrecht (2006) carried out a vector similarity comparison between the context of an English MWE and that of the constituent words using Latent Semantic Analysis to determine if the expression is idiomatic or not. In work by Hashimoto and Kawahara (2008), they addressed token classification into idiomatic versus literal for Japanese MWEs of all types. They annotated a corpus of 102K sentences, and used it to train a supervised classifier for MWEs. Using MWEs in machine translation is another application. Carpuat and Diab (2010) studied the effect of integrating English MWEs with a statistical translation system. They used the WordNet 3.0 lexical database (Fellbaum, 1998) as the main source for MWEs. Attia et al., in 2010, extracted Arabic MWEs from various resources. They focused only on nominal MWEs and used diverse techniques for automatic MWE extraction from cross-lingual parallel Wikipedia titles, machine-translated English MWEs taken from the English WordNet and the Arabic Gigaword 4.0 corpus. They found a large number of MWEs, however only a few of them were evaluated.

In this paper, we describe the process of manually creating a relatively comprehensive Arabic MWE list. We use the resulting list to tag MWE occurrences in context in a corpus.

The paper is organized as follows: In Section 2 we describe the process of creating the Arabic MWE list. Section 3 discusses the algorithm for automatic deterministic tagging of MWEs in running text, based on pattern matching. Sections 4 and 5 summarize the results of applying the pattern-matching algorithm on a corpus. Finally, we conclude in Section 6.

2 Arabic MWE List

Our Arabic MWE list is created based on a collection of about 5,000 expressions, which is manually extracted from various Arabic dictionaries (Abou Saad, 1987; Seeny et al., 1996; Dawod, 2003; Fayed, 2007). Each MWE is preprocessed by the following steps: 1) cleaning punctuations and unnecessary characters, 2) breaking alternative expressions into individual entries, and 3) running MADA (Habash and Rambow, 2005; Roth et al, 2008) on each MWE individually for finding the context-sensitive morphological analysis for every word. Some of the extracted MWEs are originally enriched with placeholder generic words that play the same semantic role in the context of the MWE. That set of generic words is manually normalized and reduced to a group of types, as shown in Table 2.

Generic Type	Semantic Role	Example
flAn "so-and-so" a person	Agent/Patient	*qr* ***flAn*** *EynA* "pleased **someone**"
*k*A* "something" an object	Goal	*ElY HsAb* ***k*A*** "at the expense of **that/this**"
<mr "something" an issue	Source	***<mr*** *Abn ywmh* "**something** very new"

Table 1 – Generic Types

Generic words are sometimes provided with or without additional clitics. For example, in the MWE *lEbt* [***bflAn***] *AldnyA*, literally, "the world played-passive with so-and-so:", which could be translated as "life played havoc with so-and-so", the word *bflan* "to so-and-so" has the preposition *b* "with" cliticized to it. Every word that substitutes a generic word (an instantiation) has to comply with the morphological features of the context surrounding it.

The automatic preprocessing steps we ran on the list are followed by a series of manual ones. We found that the short context we had for every MWE was not sufficient for MADA to return the correct analysis with reasonable precision. Therefore, we had to go over the results and manually select the correct analysis for each word in every MWE. Generic words are also assigned with their correct analysis in context.

The class of each MWE is assigned manually. Arabic is highly inflected; therefore many MWE classes can be identified. However, in this paper, we focus only on the major ones. The following classes are used: Verb-Verb Construction (VVC) as in *>xZ [flAn] w>ETY* "give and take"; Verb-Noun Construction (VNC), for example, *md [flAn] Aljswr* "[someone] built bridges" as in *extending the arms of peace*; Verb-Particle Construction (VPC) as in *mDY [flAn] fy* "[someone] continues working on"; Noun-Noun Construction (NNC) as in *Enq {lzjAjp* "bottleneck"; Adjective Noun Construction (ANC) as in *[flAn] wAsE {l&fq* "[someone] broad-minded".

The final list comprises 4,209 MWE types. Table 2 presents the total number of MWE types for each category.

MWE Category Type	Number
VVC	41
VNC	1974
VPC	670
NNC	1239
ANC	285

Table 2 – Arabic MWEs by category types

3 Deterministic Identification of Arabic MWEs

We developed a pattern-matching algorithm for discovering MWEs in Arabic running text. The main goal of this algorithm is to deterministically identify instances of MWEs from the list in a large Arabic corpus, considering some morphological as well as syntactic phenomena. We use the Arabic Gigaword 4.0 (AGW). [3] To capture the large number of morpho-syntactic variations of the MWEs in context, the pattern-matching algorithm is designed to use some of the information available from the selected morphological analysis for every MWE word, as well as shallow-syntactic information that we automatically assigned for every word in the corpus.

One of our immediate intentions is to use the list of MWEs for learning how to statistically classify new ones in running text. Therefore, we begin here with annotating a large part of the AGW corpus with all the occurrences a MWE given in the list. In order to make some shallow-syntactic features available for the pattern-matching algorithm, we pre-processed the AGW with AMIRAN, an updated version of the AMIRA tools (Diab et al., 2004, 2007). AMIRAN is a tool for finding the context-sensitive morpho-syntactic information. AMIRAN combines AMIRA output with morphological analyses provided by SAMA. AMIRAN is also enriched with Named-Entity-Recognition (NER) class tags provided by (Benajiba et al., 2008). For every word, AMIRAN is capable of identifying the clitics, diacritized lemma, stem, full part-of-speech tag excluding case and mood, base-phrase chunks and NER tags. Part of this information was used in previous work for processing English MWEs.

When looking for Arabic MWEs in the pre-processed corpus, there are two important issues that the pattern-matching algorithm is addressing: morphological variations and gaps. We now elaborate further on each one of them.

Morphological variations: As mentioned above, Arabic is highly inflected; clitics may be attached to reflect definiteness, conjunction, possessive pronouns and prepositions. This fact forces the pattern-matching algorithm to match words on a more abstract level then their surface form. The algorithm considers different levels of representation for each of the words. Those levels are matched based on the information provided by AMIRAN on corpus words, on the one hand, and the morphological analyses that are selected manually for every MWE word on the other hand. In the experiment reported here, we match words on the lemma level. The lemma provided by AMIRAN and the one manually chosen by MADA/SAMA analyses are taken from the same pool, hence matching is enabled. It is worth noting

3 http://www.ldc.upenn.edu/Catalog/catalogEntry.jsp?catalogId=LDC2009T30

that in Arabic, the lemma is a generic name for a group of words that can be derived from one of its underlying stems, sharing the same meaning. For instance, the noun *bnt* "girl" and its plural form *bnAt* "girls" are reduced to the same lemma form *bnt*. Obviously, perfect and imperfect forms of a verb are also assigned to the same lemma. A lemma form does not include the clitics; for every corpus word, this information is recorded by AMIRAN. Since clitics are in many cases important for matching MWES, the pattern-matching algorithm considers them. For example, in the MWE: *<x* [flAn] bAlv<r*, "[so-and-so] requited", the proclitic *b* "with" expressed in the last word, is important for matching.

Gaps: Sometimes a MWE can be found with additional words such as modifiers that are not part of the original MWE expression words. For instance, the MWE: *wDEt AlHrb <wzArhA*, "the war is over", is found in the text: *wDEt AlHrb* ***AlEAlmyp AlvAnyp*** *<wzArhA*, "the second world war is over". The nominal modifiers *AlEAlmyp AlvAnyp* ("second world...") are not present in the original MWE taken from the list, and therefore considered as gap fillers. To be able to identify gaps of MWEs in context, the pattern-matching algorithm uses the part-of-speech and base-phrase tags provided for every word by AMIRAN. In the reported experiment, we allowed an MWE to be matched over gaps of noun-phrases complementing MWE words. In other words, we allowed every MWE noun to be matched with a complete non-recursive noun-phrase that appears in the text. The matching is performed only on the first noun of the containing noun-phrase, restricting our approach using only noun-phrases expressing the head noun in the beginning of a phrase. For instance, in the previous example *AlHrb AlEAlmyp AlvAnyp*, "the Second World War", is a noun-phrase with a first noun word *AlHrb* "the war". This noun-phrase matches the word *AlHrb* "the war" from the list MWE *wDEt AlHrb <wzArhA* "the war is over", hence allowing the entire MWE to be found. Obviously, allowing gaps of any types would have increased the recall but on the other hand a large number of false positive MWEs would have been identified. Currently, only noun-phrases are considered as potential gap fillers. Considering other phrase types is left for future work. We plan on identifying the types of potential gap fillers and correlating them with the various MWE types.

One of the remaining problems with identifying MWEs deterministically in a running text is that the exact MWE words can be found in a text, however given the context, in some cases they are not idiomatic. This is the case for many VNCs for instance. Hence, they are not a unified concept – a word with gaps -- as in our definition of a MWE usage. Accordingly a token MWE classifier is required to identify such cases, teasing idiomatic from literal MWEs apart.

4 Building MWE Annotated Corpus

We ran the pattern-matching algorithm on a large part of the AGW after we pre-processed the documents with AMIRAN. Overall, we had 250 million tokens and found 481,131 MWE instances. Table 3 summarizes the exact number of MWEs that we found, grouped by their class type.

The matching was performed on the lemma level constraining the search with clitic matching. Gaps are restricted only to noun-phrases at this time, as mentioned above. The output of this process follows the Inside Outside Beginning (IOB) annotation scheme. In fact, the output files are based on the same input AMIRAN files, enriched with O, B/I-MWE tags as found by the pattern-matching algorithm. Figure 1 shows how a complete sentence, containing a MWE, is annotated by the pattern-matching algorithm.

MWE Category Type	Number
VVC	576
VNC	64,504
VPC	75,844
NNC	316,393
ANC	23,814

Table 3 – Annotated MWEs by class

5 Evaluation

The annotations are manually evaluated by a native speaker of Arabic. We sub sampled the corpus and examined each MWE instance that is identified by the pattern-matching algorithm. Table 4 shows our findings. Each row represents one category type. The middle column shows the number of instances evaluated, followed by the number of unique MWE types. In the last column, the number of correct instances as it was examined in context, is reported. The correctness of an instance is determined by its context. Remember that MWEs are not only matched statically; generic words, gaps and inflections may cause the pattern-matching algorithm to annotate expressions with an MWE type, incorrectly.

Word	Lemma	POS	NER	MWE
swlAnA	suwlAnA	NN	I-OR	O
:	:	PUNC	O	O
AlAtHAd	<it~iHAd	NN	B-GP	O
AlAwrwby	Auwrub~iy	NN	I-GP	O
w+	wa+	CC	O	O
wA$nTn	wA$inoTuwn	NNP	B-GP	O
ysEyAn	saEaY-a	VBPMD3	O	O
l+	li+	IN	O	O
AyjAd	AiyjAd	NN	O	O
Alyp	|liy~ap	NNFS	O	O
l+	li+	IN	O	O
wqf	waqof	NN	O	O
ATlAq	**Talaq**	**NN**	**O**	**B-MW**
Al+	**Al+**	**DET**	**O**	**I-MW**
nAr	**nAr**	**NN**	**O**	**I-MW**

Figure 1 – Annotated sentence example

MWE Type	Evaluated Instances	Correct Instances
VVC	111 (**2** types)	2
VNC	157 (**34** types)	154
VPC	161 (**32** types)	125
NNC	155 (**26** types)	154

Table 4 – Evaluation Results

The evaluation set is relatively small. Nevertheless, one can see that in most cases the annotations are correct. For the VNC, the pattern matching algorithm achieves an accuracy of 98%, for VPC, we get an accuracy of 77.6%, and NNC we achieve an accuracy of 99%. It is worth noting that NNCs are the only category that employs the gapping. The VVC category contains only a few MWE types, in the sampled set we evaluated 111 instances of merely two different types from which, one was constantly identified incorrectly by the algorithm and it constitutes the majority of the instances (109 instances).

6 Conclusions

In this paper we have introduced a list of MWEs in Arabic. The MWEs are enriched with morphological information that was carefully assigned to every word. A large part of the Arabic Gigaword 4.0 was deterministically annotated using a pattern-matching algorithm, considering morphological variations as expressed by Arabic and some potential gaps. A sample of the corpus was manually evaluated with encouraging results. Building both resources is a first step toward our research in the field of Arabic MWEs. Classifying the level of idiomaticity of the part of the MWE classes is one direction we are currently exploring.

Acknowledgment

This paper is based upon work supported by the Defense Advanced Research Projects Agency (DARPA) under Contract No. HR0011-12-C-0014. Any opinions, findings and conclusions or recommendations expressed in this paper are those of the authors and do not necessarily reflect the views of DARPA.

References

Attia, Mohammed, Antonio Toral, Lamia Tounsi, Pavel Pecina and Josef van Genabith. 2010. Automatic extraction of Arabic multiword expressions. In *Proceedings of the 7th Conference on Language Resources and Evaluation, LREC-2010*, Valletta, Malta.

Abou Saad, Ahmed. 1987. A Dictionary of Arabic Idiomatic Expressions (mu'jm altrakib wala'barat alastlahiah ala'rbiah alkdim mnha walmould). *Dar El Ilm Lilmalayin*.

Benajiba, Yassine, Mona Diab and Paolo Rosso. 2008. Arabic Named Entity Recognition: An SVM-based approach. In *Proceedings of the Arab International Conference on Information Technology, ACIT-2008*, Tunisia.

Buckwalter, Tim. 2002. Buckwalter Arabic Morphological Analyzer Version 1.0. LDC catalog number LDC2002L49, ISBN 1-58563-257-0.

Carpuat, Marine and Mona Diab. 2010. Task-based Evaluation of Multiword Expressions: a Pilot Study in Statistical Machine Translation. *HLT-NAACL*.

Cook, Paul, Afsaneh Fazly, and Suzanne Stevenson. 2008. The VNC-Tokens Dataset. In *Proceedings of the LREC Workshop on Towards a Shared Task for Multiword Expressions (MWE 2008)*, Marrakech, Morocco.

Dawood, Mohammed. 2003. A Dictionary of Arabic Contemporary Idioms (mu'jm alta'bir alastlahiat). *Dar Ghareeb.*

Diab, Mona and Pravin Bhutada. 2009. Verb noun construction MWE token supervised classification. In *Workshop on Multiword Expressions (ACL-IJCNLP)*, pp. 17–22.

Diab, Mona. 2009. Second Generation Tools (AMIRA 2.0): Fast and Robust Tokenization, POS tagging, and Base Phrase Chunking. *MEDAR 2nd International Conference on Arabic Language Resources and Tools*, Cairo, Egypt.

Fayed, Wafaa Kamel. 2007. A Dictionary of Arabic Contemporary Idioms (mu'jm alta'bir alastlahiat). *Abu Elhoul.*

Fellbaum, Christiane. 1998. WordNet: An Electronic Lexical Database. *MIT Press.*

Habash, Nizar and Owen Rambow. 2005. Arabic Tokenization, Morphological Analysis, and Part-of-Speech Tagging in One Fell Swoop. In *Proceedings of the Conference of American Association for Computational Linguistics*, Ann Arbor, MI, 578-580.

Hashimoto, Chikara and Daisuke Kawahara. 2008. Construction of an idiom corpus and its application to idiom identification based on WSD incorporating idiom-specific features. In *Proceedings of the 2008 Conference on Empirical Methods in Natural Language Processing*, Honolulu, Hawaii, pages 992–1001.

Katz, Graham and Eugenie Giesbrecht. 2006. Automatic identification of non-compositional multiword expressions using latent semantic analysis. In *Proceedings of the Workshop on Multiword Expressions: Identifying and Exploiting Underlying Properties*, Sydney, Australia, pages 12–19.

Maamouri, Mohamed, et al. 2010. Standard Arabic Morphological Analyzer (SAMA) Version 3.1. *Linguistic Data Consortium*, Philadelphia

Parker, Robert, et al. 2009. Arabic Gigaword Fourth Edition LDC2009T30, ISBN 1-58563-532-4. *Linguistic Data Consortium (LDC)*, Philadelphia

Roth, R., Rambow, O., Habash, N., Diab, M. and Rudin, C. 2008. Arabic Morphological Tagging, Diacritization, and Lemmatization Using Lexeme Models and Feature Ranking. In *Proceedings of Association for Computational Linguistics (ACL)*, Columbus, Ohio.

Sag, Ivan A. and Timothy Baldwin, Francis Bond, Ann A. Copestake, and Dan Flickinger. 2002. Multiword expressions: A pain in the neck for nlp. In *Proceedings of the Third International Conference on Computational Linguistics and Intelligent Text Processing*, London, UK, pp. 1–15.

Sieny, Mahmoud Esmail, Mokhtar A. Hussein and Sayyed A. Al-Doush. 1996. A contextual Dictionary of Idioms (almu'jm alsyaqi lelta'birat alastlahiah). *Librairie du Liban Publishers.*

Unsupervised frame based semantic role induction: application to French and English

Alejandra Lorenzo
Lorraine University/LORIA Nancy
alejandra.lorenzo@loria.fr

Christophe Cerisara
CNRS/LORIA Nancy
christophe.cerisara@loria.fr

Abstract

This paper introduces a novel unsupervised approach to semantic role induction that uses a generative Bayesian model. To the best of our knowledge, it is the first model that jointly clusters syntactic verbs arguments into semantic roles, and also creates verbs classes according to the syntactic frames accepted by the verbs. The model is evaluated on French and English, outperforming, in both cases, a strong baseline. On English, it achieves results comparable to state-of-the-art unsupervised approaches to semantic role induction.

1 Introduction and background

Semantic Role Labeling (SRL) is a major task in Natural Language Processing which provides a shallow semantic parsing of a text. Its primary goal is to identify and label the semantic relations that hold between predicates (typically verbs), and their associated arguments (Màrquez et al., 2008).

The extensive research carried out in this area resulted in a variety of annotated resources, which, in time, opened up new possibilities for supervised SRL systems. Although such systems show very good performance, they require large amounts of annotated data in order to be successful. This annotated data is not always available, very expensive to create and often domain specific (Pradhan et al., 2008). There is in particular no such data available for French. To bypass this shortcoming, "annotation-by-projection" approaches have been proposed (Pado and Lapata, 2006) which in essence, (i) project the semantic annotations available in one language (usually English), to text in another language (in this case French); and (ii) use the resulting annotations to train a semantic role labeller. Thus Pado and Pitel (2007) show that the projection-based annotation framework permits bootstrapping a semantic role labeller for FrameNet which reaches an F-measure of 63%; and van der Plas et al. (2011) show that training a joint syntactic-semantic parser based on the projection approach permits reaching an F-measure for the labeled attachment score on PropBank annotation of 65%.

Although they minimize the manual effort involved, these approaches still require both an annotated source corpus and an aligned target corpus. Moreover, they assume a specific role labeling (e.g., PropBank, FrameNet or VerbNet roles) and are not generally portable from one framework to another.

These drawbacks with supervised approaches motivated the need for unsupervised methods capable of exploiting large amounts of unannotated data. In this context several approaches have been proposed. Swier and Stevenson (2004) were the first to introduce unsupervised SRL in an approach that used the VerbNet lexicon to guide unsupervised learning. Grenager and Manning (2006) proposed a directed graphical model for role induction that exploits linguistic priors for syntactic and semantic inference. Following this work, Lang and Lapata (2010) formulated role induction as the problem of detecting alternations and mapping non-standard linkings to cannonical ones, and later as a graph partitioning problem in (Lang and Lapata, 2011b). They also proposed an algorithm that uses successive splits and merges of semantic roles clusters in order to improve their quality in (Lang and Lapata, 2011a). Finally, Titov and Klementiev (2012), introduce two new Bayesian models that treat unsupervised role induction as the clustering of syntactic argument signatures, with clusters corresponding to semantic roles, and achieve the best state-of-the-art results.

In this paper, we propose a novel unsupervised approach to semantic role labeling that differs from previous work in that it integrates the notion of verb classes into the model (by analogy with VerbNet, we call these verb classes, frames). We show that this approach gives good results both on the English PropBank and on a French corpus annotated with VerbNet style semantic roles. For the English PropBank, although the model is more suitable for a framework that uses a shared set of role labels such as VerbNet, we obtain results comparable to the state-of-the-art. For French, the model is shown to outperform a strong baseline by a wide margin.

2 Probabilistic Model

As mentioned in the introduction, semantic role labeling comprises two sub-tasks: argument identification and role induction. Following common practice (Lang and Lapata, 2011a; Titov and Klementiev, 2012), we assume oracle argument identification and focus on argument labeling. The approach we propose is an unsupervised generative Bayesian model that clusters arguments into classes each of which can be associated with a semantic role. The model starts by generating a frame assignment to each verb instance where a frame is a clustering of verbs and associated roles. Then, for each observed verb argument, a semantic role is drawn conditioned on the frame. Finally, the word and dependency label of this argument are generated. The model admits a simple Gibbs algorithm where the number of latent variables is proportional to the number of roles and frames to be clustered.

There are two key benefits of this model architecture. First, it directly encodes linguistic intuitions about semantic frames: the model structure reflects the subcategorisation property of the frame variable, which also groups verbs that share the same set of semantic roles, something very close to the VerbNet notion of frames. Second, by ignoring the "verb-specific" nature of PropBank labels, we reduce the need for a large amount of data and we better share evidence across roles.

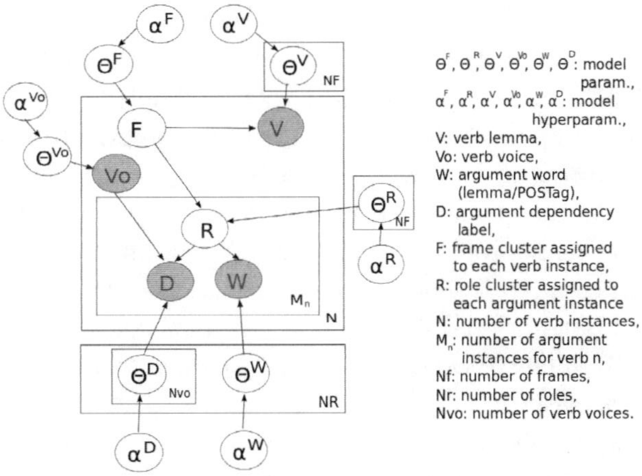

Figure 1: Plate diagram of the proposed directed Bayesian model.

In addition, because it is unsupervised, the model is independent both of the language and of the specific semantic framework (since no inventory of semantic role is a priori chosen).

2.1 Model description

The goal of the task is to assign argument instances to clusters, such that each argument cluster represents a specific semantic role, and each role corresponds to one cluster. The model is represented in the form of a plate diagram in Figure 1. The observed random variables are the verb V (lemma), its voice Vo (active or passive), the words W (lemma) that are arguments of this verb, and the syntactic dependency labels D that link the argument to its head. There are two latent variables: the frame F that represents the class of the verb, and the role R assigned to each of its arguments. The parameters θ of all multinomial distributions are Dirichlet distributed, with fixed symmetric concentration hyper-parameter α. The frame plays a fundamental role in this setting, since it intends to capture classes of verbs that share similar distributions of role arguments.

The model's generative story is described next, followed by a description of the inference algorithm used to apply the model to an unannotated corpus.

2.2 Generative story

For each verb instance, the proposed model first generates a frame cluster, a voice (active or passive), and then a verb lemma from the distribution of verbs in this frame. The number of arguments is assumed fixed. For each argument, a role is sampled conditioned on the frame. Then, a word is sampled from the distribution of words associated to this role, and finally a dependency label is generated, conditioned both on the role and the voice. All multinomial parameters are collapsed, and thus not sampled. All Dirichlet hyper-parameters are assumed constant.

To identify words, we use either word lemmas or part-of-speech tags. In order to avoid data sparseness issues, we consider the word lemma only in cases where there are more than 9 instances of the word lemma in the corpus. Otherwise, if the number of word lemma instances is less than 10, we use the part-of-speech tags.

2.3 Learning and Inference

A collapsed Gibbs sampler is used to perform posterior inference on the model. Initially, all frames F_i are sampled randomly from a uniform distribution, while the roles $R_{i,j}$ are assigned either randomly or following the deterministic syntactic function baseline, which simply clusters predicate arguments according to their syntactic function. This function is described in detail in Section 3.

The Gibbs sampling algorithm samples each latent variable (F_i and $R_{i,j}$) in turn according to its posterior distribution conditioned on all other instances of this variable (noted $F_{\neg i}$ and $R_{\neg(i,j)}$ respectively) and all other variables. These posteriors are detailed next.

In the following, $R_{i,j}$ represents the random variable for the jth role of the ith verb in the corpus: its value is $R_{i,j} = r_{i,j}$ at a given iteration of the sampling algorithm. $nr_{f,r}$ is the count of occurrences of $(F_i = f, R_{i,j} = r)$ in the whole corpus, excluding the ith instance when the superscript $^{-i}$ is used. A star $*$ matches any possible value. The joint probability over the whole corpus with collapsed multinomial parameters is:

$$
\begin{aligned}
&p(F,R,V,W,D,Vo|\alpha)\\
&= \frac{\prod_{i=1}^{N_f}\Gamma(nf_i+\alpha^F)}{\Gamma(\sum_{i=1}^{N_f} nf_i+\alpha^F)}\frac{\Gamma(\sum_{i=1}^{N_f}\alpha^F)}{\prod_{i=1}^{N_f}\Gamma(\alpha^F)}\times\\
&\prod_{i=1}^{N_f}\frac{\prod_{j=1}^{N_v}\Gamma(nv_{i,j}+\alpha^V)}{\Gamma(\sum_{j=1}^{N_v} nv_{i,j}+\alpha^V)}\frac{\Gamma(\sum_{j=1}^{N_v}\alpha^V)}{\prod_{j=1}^{N_v}\Gamma(\alpha^V)}\times\\
&\prod_{i=1}^{N_f}\frac{\prod_{j=1}^{N_r}\Gamma(nr_{i,j}+\alpha^R)}{\Gamma(\sum_{j=1}^{N_r} nr_{i,j}+\alpha^R)}\frac{\Gamma(\sum_{j=1}^{N_r}\alpha^R)}{\prod_{j=1}^{N_r}\Gamma(\alpha^R)}\times\\
&\prod_{i=1}^{N_{vo}}\prod_{j=1}^{N_r}\frac{\prod_{k=1}^{N_d}\Gamma(nd_{i,j,k}+\alpha^D)}{\Gamma(\sum_{k=1}^{N_d} nd_{i,j,k}+\alpha^D)}\frac{\Gamma(\sum_{k=1}^{N_d}\alpha^D)}{\prod_{k=1}^{N_d}\Gamma(\alpha^D)}\times\\
&\prod_{i=1}^{N_r}\frac{\prod_{j=1}^{N_w}\Gamma(nw_{i,j}+\alpha^W)}{\Gamma(\sum_{j=1}^{N_w} nw_{i,j}+\alpha^W)}\frac{\Gamma(\sum_{j=1}^{N_w}\alpha^W)}{\prod_{j=1}^{N_w}\Gamma(\alpha^W)}\times\\
&\frac{\prod_{i=1}^{N_{vo}}\Gamma(nvo_i+\alpha^{Vo})}{\Gamma(\sum_{i=1}^{N_{vo}} nvo_i+\alpha^{Vo})}\frac{\Gamma(\sum_{i=1}^{N_{vo}}\alpha^{Vo})}{\prod_{i=1}^{N_{vo}}\Gamma(\alpha^{Vo})}
\end{aligned}
$$

The posterior from which the frame is sampled is derived from the joint distribution as follows:

$$
\begin{aligned}
&p(F_i=y|F_{\neg i},R,V,W,Vo) \qquad (1)\\
&\propto \frac{p(F,R,V,W,D,Vo)}{p(F_{\neg i},R_{\neg i},V_{\neg i},W_{\neg i},D_{\neg i},Vo_{\neg i})}\\
&= \frac{(nf_y^{-i}+\alpha^F)}{(\sum_{z=1}^{N_f} nf_z^{-i}+\alpha^F)}\times\frac{(nv_{y,v_i}^{-i}+\alpha^V)}{(\sum_{j=1}^{N_v} nv_{y,j}^{-i}+\alpha^V)}\times\\
&\frac{\prod_{r\in r_{i,*}}\prod_{x=0}^{nr_r^{+i}-1}(nr_{y,r}^{-i}+\alpha^R+x)}{\prod_{x=0}^{M_i}(\sum_{r=1}^{N_r} nr_{y,r}^{-i}+\alpha^R+x)}
\end{aligned}
$$

where nr_r^{+i} is the count of occurrences of role r in the arguments of verb instance i ($M_i = \sum_r nr_r^{+i}$).

The update equation for sampling the role becomes:

$$
\begin{aligned}
&p(R_{i,j}=y|R_{\neg(i,j)},F,V,W,D,Vo) \qquad (2)\\
&\propto \frac{p(F,R,V,W,D,Vo)}{p(F_{\neg i},V_{\neg i},R_{\neg(i,j)},W_{\neg(i,j)},D_{\neg(i,j)},Vo_{\neg(i,j)})}\\
&= \frac{(nr_{f_i,y}^{-(i,j)}+\alpha^R)}{(\sum_{k=1}^{N_r} nr_{f_i,k}^{-(i,j)}+\alpha^R)}\times\frac{(nd_{vo_i,y,d_{i,j}}^{-(i,j)}+\alpha^D)}{(\sum_{k=1}^{N_d} nd_{vo_i,y,k}^{-(i,j)}+\alpha^D)}\times\\
&\frac{(nw_{y,w_{i,j}}^{-(i,j)}+\alpha^W)}{(\sum_{k=1}^{N_w} nw_{y,k}^{-(i,j)}+\alpha^W)}
\end{aligned}
$$

After T iterations, the process is stopped and the expected value of the sampled frames and roles after the burn-in period (20 iterations) is computed. With deterministic (syntactic) initialization, T is set to 200, while it is set to 2000 with random initialization because of slower convergence.

3 Evaluations and results

We evaluate our model both on English to situate our approach with respect to the state of the art; and on French to demonstrate its portability to other languages.

3.1 Common experimental setup

The model's parameters have been tuned with a few rounds of trial-and-error on the English development corpus: For the hyper-parameters, we set

$\alpha^F = 0.5$, $\alpha^R = 1.e^{-3}$, $\alpha^V = 1.e^{-7}$, $\alpha^{Vo} = 1.e^{-3}$, $\alpha^D = 1.e^{-8}$ and $\alpha^W = 0.5$. For the evaluation on French, we only changed the α^F and α^W parameters. In order to reflect the rather uniform distribution of verb instances across verb classes we set α^F to 1. Moreover, we set α^W to 0.001 because of the smaller number of words and roles in the French corpus. The number of roles and frames were chosen based on the properties of each corpus. We set number of roles to 40 and 10, and the number of frames to 300 and 60 for English and French respectively. As done in (Lang and Lapata, 2011a) and (Titov and Klementiev, 2012), we use purity and collocation measures to assess the quality of our role induction process. For each verb, the purity of roles' clusters is computed as follows:

$$PU = \frac{1}{N} \sum_i \max_j |G_j \cap C_i|$$

where C_i is the set of arguments in the ith cluster found, G_j is the set of arguments in the jth gold class, and N is the number of argument instances. In a similar way, the collocation of roles' clusters is computed as follows:

$$CO = \frac{1}{N} \sum_j \max_i |G_j \cap C_i|$$

Then, each score is averaged over all verbs. In the same way as (Lang and Lapata, 2011a), we use the micro-average obtained by weighting the scores for individual verbs proportionally to the number of argument instances for that verb. Finally the F1 measure is the harmonic mean of the aggregated values of purity and collocation:

$$F1 = \frac{2 * CO * PU}{CO + PU}$$

3.2 Evaluations on French

To evaluate our model on French, we used a manually annotated corpora consisting on sentences from the Paris 7 Treebank (Abeillé et al., 2000), containing verbs extracted from the gold standard V-GOLD (Sun et al., 2010)[1]. For each verb, at most 25 sentences from the Paris 7 Treebank were randomly selected and annotated with VerbNet-style thematic roles. In some cases, the annotated roles were obtained by merging some of the VerbNet roles (e.g., Actor, Actor1 and Actor2 are merged); or by grouping together classes sharing the same thematic grids. The resulting roles assignment groups 116 verbs into 12 VerbNet classes, each associated with a unique thematic grid. Table 1 shows the set of roles used and their relation to VerbNet roles. This constitutes our gold evaluation corpus.

Role	VerbNet roles
Agent	Agent, Actor, Actor1, Actor2
Experiencer	Experiencer
Theme	Stimulus, Theme, Theme1, Theme2
Topic	Proposition, Topic
PredAtt	Predicate, Attribute
Patient	Patient, Patient1, Patient2
Start	Material, Source
End	Product, Destination, Recipient
Location	Location
Instrument	Instrument
Cause	Cause
Beneficiary	Beneficiary
Extent	Asset, Extent, Time, Value

Table 1: VerbNet role groups (French).

The baseline model is the "syntactic function" used for instance in (Lang and Lapata, 2011a), which simply clusters predicate arguments according to the dependency relation to their head. This is a standard baseline for unsupervised SRL, which, although simple, has been shown difficult to outperform. As done in previous work, it is implemented by allocating a different cluster to each of the 10 most frequent syntactic relations, and one extra cluster for all the other relations. Evaluation results are shown in Table 2. The proposed model significantly outperforms the deterministic baseline, which validates the unsupervised learning process.

	PU	CO	F1
Synt.Func. (baseline)	78.9	73.4	76.1
Proposed model - rand. init	74.6	82.9	78.5

Table 2: Comparison of the Syntactic Function baseline with the proposed system initialized randomly, evaluated with gold parses and argument identification (French).

3.3 Evaluations on English

We made our best to follow the setup used in previous work (Lang and Lapata, 2011a; Titov and Kle-

[1] V-GOLD consists of 16 fine grained Levin classes with 12 verbs each (translated to French) whose predominant sense in English belong to that class.

mentiev, 2012), in order to compare with the current state of the art.

The data used is the standard CoNLL 2008 shared task (Surdeanu et al., 2008) version of Penn Treebank WSJ and PropBank. Our model is evaluated on gold generated parses, using the gold PropBank annotations. In PropBank, predicates are associated with a set of roles, where roles A2-A5 or AA are verb specific, while adjuncts roles (AM) are consistent across verbs. Besides, roles A0 and A1 attempt to capture Proto-Agent and Proto-Patient roles (Dowty, 1991), and thus are more valid across verbs and verb instances than A2-A5 roles.

Table 3 reports the evaluation results of the proposed model along with those of the baseline system and of some of the latest state-of-the-art results.

	PU	CO	F1
Synt.Func.(LL)	81.6	77.5	79.5
Split Merge	88.7	73.0	80.1
Graph Part.	88.6	70.7	78.6
TK-Bay.1	88.7	78.1	83.0
TK-Bay.2	89.2	74.0	80.9
Synt.Func.	79.6	84.6	82.0
Proposed model - rand. init	82.2	83.4	82.8
Proposed model - synt. init	83.4	84.1	83.7

Table 3: Comparison of the proposed system (last 2 rows) with other unsupervised semantic role inducers evaluated on gold parses and argument identification.

We can first note that, despite our efforts to reproduce the same baseline, there is still a difference between our baseline (Synt.Func.) and the baseline reported in (Lang and Lapata, 2011a) (Synt.Func.(LL)) [2].

The other results respectively correspond to the Split Merge approach presented in (Lang and Lapata, 2011a) (Split Merge), the Graph Partitioning algorithm (Graph Part.) presented in (Lang and Lapata, 2011b), and two Bayesian approaches presented in (Titov and Klementiev, 2012), which achieve the best current unsupervised SRL results. The first such model (TK-Bay.1) clusters argument fillers and directly maps some syntactic labels to semantic roles for some adjunct like modifiers that are explicitly represented in the syntax, while the second model (TK-Bay.2) does not include these two features.

[2] We identified afterwards a few minor differences in both experimental setups that partly explain this, e.g., evaluation on the test vs. train sets, finer-grained gold classes in our case...

Two versions of the proposed model are reported in the last rows of Table 3: one with random (uniform) initialization of all variables, and the other with deterministic initialization of all R_i from the syntactic function. Indeed, although many unsupervised system are very sensitive to initialization, we observe that in the proposed model, unsupervised inference reaches reasonably good performances even with a knowledge-free initialization. Furthermore, when initialized with the strong deterministic baseline, the model still learns new evidences and improves over the baseline to give comparable results to the best unsupervised state-of-the-art systems.

4 Conclusions and future work

We have presented a method for unsupervised SRL that is based on an intuitive generative Bayesian model that not only clusters arguments into semantic roles, but also explicitly integrates the concept of frames in SRL. Previous approaches to semantic role induction proposed some clustering of roles without explicitly focusing on the verb classes generated. Although there has been work on verb clustering, this is, to the best of our knowledge, the first approach that jointly considers both tasks.

In this work in progress, we focused on the role induction task and we only evaluated this part, leaving the evaluation of verb classes as future work. We successfully evaluated the proposed model on two languages, French and English, showing, in both cases, consistent performances improvement over the deterministic baseline. Furthermore, its accuracy reaches a level comparable to that of the best state-of-the-art unsupervised systems.

The model could be improved in many ways, and in particular by including some penalization term for sampling the same role for several arguments of a verb instance (at least for core roles). Moreover, we believe that our model better fits within a framework that allows roles sharing between verbs (or frames), such as VerbNet, and we would like to carry out a deeper evaluation on this concept.

Acknowledgments

The authors wish to thank Claire Gardent for her valuable suggestions and Ingrid Falk for providing the data for the evaluation on French.

References

A. Abeillé, L. Clément, and A. Kinyon. 2000. Building a treebank for French. In *Proceedings of the LREC 2000*.

David Dowty. 1991. Thematic proto-roles and argument selection. *Language*, 67:547–619.

Trond Grenager and Christopher D. Manning. 2006. Unsupervised discovery of a statistical verb lexicon. In *Proceedings of the 2006 Conference on Empirical Methods in Natural Language Processing*, EMNLP '06, pages 1–8, Stroudsburg, PA, USA. Association for Computational Linguistics.

Joel Lang and Mirella Lapata. 2010. Unsupervised induction of semantic roles. In *Human Language Technologies: The 2010 Annual Conference of the North American Chapter of the Association for Computational Linguistics*, HLT '10, pages 939–947, Stroudsburg, PA, USA. Association for Computational Linguistics.

Joel Lang and Mirella Lapata. 2011a. Unsupervised semantic role induction via split-merge clustering. In *ACL*, pages 1117–1126. Association for Computer Linguistics.

Joel Lang and Mirella Lapata. 2011b. Unsupervised semantic role induction with graph partitioning. In *EMNLP*, pages 1320–1331. Association for Computer Linguistics.

Lluís Màrquez, Xavier Carreras, Kenneth C. Litkowski, and Suzanne Stevenson. 2008. Semantic role labeling: an introduction to the special issue. *Comput. Linguist.*, 34(2):145–159, June.

Sebastian Pado and Mirella Lapata. 2006. Optimal constituent alignment with edge covers for semantic projection. In *Proceedings of ACL-COLING 2006*, pages 1161–1168, Sydney, Australia.

Sebastian Pado and Guillaume Pitel. 2007. Annotation précise du franais en sémantique de rôles par projection cross-linguistique. In *Proceedings of TALN-07*, Toulouse, France.

Sameer S. Pradhan, Wayne Ward, and James H. Martin. 2008. Towards robust semantic role labeling. *Comput. Linguist.*, 34(2):289–310, June.

L. Sun, A. Korhonen, T. Poibeau, and C. Messiant. 2010. Investigating the cross-linguistic potential of VerbNet-style classification. In *Proceedings of the 23rd International Conference on Computational Linguistics*, COLING '10, pages 1056–1064, Stroudsburg, PA, USA. Association for Computational Linguistics.

Mihai Surdeanu, Richard Johansson, Adam Meyers, Lluís Màrquez, and Joakim Nivre. 2008. The conll-2008 shared task on joint parsing of syntactic and semantic dependencies. In *Proceedings of the Twelfth Conference on Computational Natural Language Learning*, CoNLL '08, pages 159–177, Stroudsburg, PA, USA. Association for Computational Linguistics.

Robert S. Swier and Suzanne Stevenson. 2004. Unsupervised Semantic Role Labelling. In *EMNLP*, pages 95–102. Association for Computational Linguistics.

Ivan Titov and Alexandre Klementiev. 2012. A bayesian approach to unsupervised semantic role induction. In *Proceedings of the Conference of the European Chapter of the Association for Computational Linguistics*, Avignon, France, April.

Lonneke van der Plas, Paola Merlo, and James Henderson. 2011. Scaling up cross-lingual semantic annotation transfer. In *Proceedings of ACL/HLT*, pages 299–304.

Using Nominal Compounds for Word Sense Discrimination

Yannick Versley
University of Tübingen
Department of Linguistics
versley@sfs.uni-tuebingen.de

Verena Henrich
University of Tübingen
Department of Linguistics
verena.henrich@uni-tuebingen.de

Abstract

In many morphologically rich languages, conceptually independent morphemes are glued together to form a new word (a compound) with a meaning that is often at least in part predictable from the meanings of the contributing morphemes. Assuming that most compounds express a subconcept of exactly one sense of its nominal head, we use compounds as a higher-quality alternative to simply using general second-order collocate terms in the task of word sense discrimination. We evaluate our approach using lexical entries from the German wordnet GermaNet (Henrich and Hinrichs, 2010).

1 Introduction

In several morphologically rich languages such as German and Dutch, compounds are usually written as one word: In a process where nouns, verbs and other prefixes combine with a head noun (called the *simplex* when it occurs on its own), a novel word can be formed which is typically interpretable by considering its parts and the means of combination. The process of compounding is both highly productive and subject to lexicalization (i.e., the creation of non-transparent compounds that can only be interpreted as a whole rather than as a combination of parts). The analysis of compounds have been subject to interest in machine translation as well as in the semantic processing of morphologically rich languages. The analysis of compounds is generally challenging for many reasons. In particular, compounds leave us with the dilemma of either modeling them as complete units, yielding a more accurate picture for lexicalized compounds but creating a more severe sparse data problem in general, or trying to separate out their parts and ending up with problems of wrongly split lexicalized compounds, or of incurring mis-splits where spurious ambiguities occur.

The purpose of this paper is to address the question of whether semantic information of compound occurrences can be used to learn more about the sense distribution of the simplex head, with respect to a text collection. Specifically, this paper focuses on the task of *word sense discrimination*, where the goal is to find different senses of a word without assuming a hand-crafted lexical resource as training material (in contrast to word sense *disambiguation*, where the exact sense inventory to be tagged is known at training and inference time, and where making effective use of a resource such as WordNet (Miller and Fellbaum, 1991) or GermaNet (Henrich and Hinrichs, 2010) is an important part of the problem to be solved).

While the present paper focuses on nominal compounds in German, the method as such can also be applied to other languages where compounds are written as one word.

2 Related Work

Automatic word sense discrimination (WSD) is a task that consists of the automatic discovery of a sense inventory for a word and of associated examples for each sense.

To evaluate systems performing word sense discrimination, earlier research such as Schütze (1998) uses either *pseudowords* – two words that have been artificially conflated to yield an ambiguous concept such as *wide range/consulting firm* – or use (expensive) manually annotated data. Subsequently, the contexts of these occurrences are clustered into groups that correspond to training examples for each postulated sense.

A different approach to the idea of word sense discrimination can be found in the work of Pantel and Lin (2002): they retrieve a set of most-similar items to the target word, and then cluster these similar items according to distributional semantic properties. In Pantel and Lin's approach, the output of the word sense induction algorithm is not a group of contexts with the target word that will be used to represent a sense, but instead one or more words that are (hopefully) related to one particular sense. The contexts in which the related words occur could then be used as positive examples for that particular sense of the target word.

Pantel and Lin aim at a principled approach to compare the soft-clustering approaches they propose, in conjunction with a fixed set of related words. While the main interest of this paper lies in comparing different methods for generating the candidate set of related words, the exact clustering method is only of marginal interest. In this paper, a simpler hard clustering method is used and only the assignment for the tight center of a cluster is considered since the non-central items can be different or even incomparable for the different methods.

3 Our Approach

Our approach to word sense discrimination is based on the idea that different compounds that have the same simplex word as their head (e.g. *Blütenblatt* 'petal', and *Revolverblatt* 'tabloid rag') are less ambiguous than the simplex (*Blatt* 'leaf', 'newspaper') itself. This assumption is along the lines with what the "one sense per collocation" heuristic of Yarowsky (1993) would predict.

Yarowsky noted that in a corpus of homographs/homophones/near-homographs, translation distinctions, and pseudo-words, a single collocation (such as "foreign" or "presidential") is often enough to disambiguate the occurrence of a near-homograph such as aid/aide. While Yarowsky claims that most of the problems of such an approach would be due to absent or unseen collocates, it is easily imaginable that collocates such as *old* or *big* can occur with multiple senses of a word.

In German, noun compounds usually involve at least a minimum degree of lexicalization: In English, 'red flag' and 'red beet' are lexicalized (i.e., denote something more specific than the compositional interpretation would suggest), but 'red rag' or 'red box' are purely compositional. In German, *Rotwein* 'red wine' is a compound, but the more compositional *roter Apfel/*Rotapfel* 'red apple' is not a compound and points to the fact that 'red apple' only has a compositional interpretation. Because of this minimal required degree of lexicalization, we would expect that German nominal compounds (as well as any compounds in a language that has a similar distinction between affixating and non-affixating compounds) are, for the largest portion, compositional enough to be interpretable, but lexicalized enough that a compound is always specific to only one sense of its head simplex.

3.1 Finding Committees

The method of finding committees that form sense clusters is illustrated in Figure 1 using the target word example *Blatt*. To generate a candidate list of related terms, our method first retrieves all words (compounds) that have the target word as a suffix (step 3 in Figure 1). This candidate set is then sorted according to distributional similarity with the target word and cut off after N items (step 2 in Figure 1) to reduce the influence of spurious matches and non-taxonomic compounds and to avoid too much noise in the candidate list.

In order to evaluate the method of selecting compounds as candidate words, we first cluster the set of candidate words into as many clusters as there are target word senses represented in the candidate words (step 3 in Figure 1, again using the distributional similarity vectors of the words described in the following subsection 3.2).

To avoid biasing our method towards any particular method of choosing the candidate words, we simply assume that it is possible to produce a 'reasonable' number of clusters. In the next step, the most central items of each cluster (the 'committee') are determined, purely by closeness to the cluster's

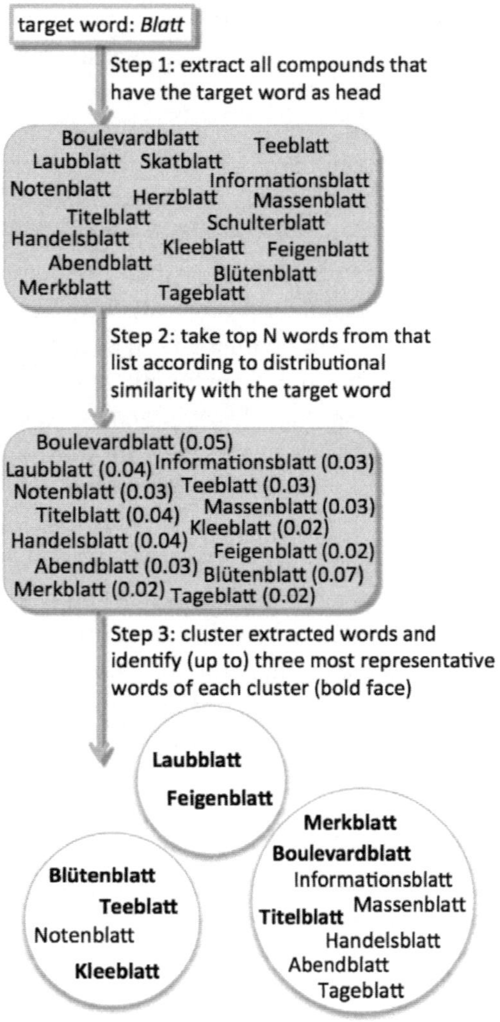

Figure 1: Steps in the clustering method

centroid and disregarding similarity with the target word. The committee words are rendered in bold face in the circles in Figure 1. The quality of the approach is then evaluated according to whether the committees form a suitable representation for the set of senses that the target word possesses.

An advantage of only including compounds in the candidate list of related terms, instead of all words, is that the related words generated by such an approach are conceptually considerably closer to the target word than those using all words as candidates: Using all words, the top candidates include the coordinate terms *Frucht* 'fruit' and *Blüte* 'flower', as well as more faraway terms such as *Tuch* 'cloth' or *Haar* 'hair'; using only compounds of the simplex, the candidate list contains mostly hyponyms such as *Laubblatt* 'leaf', *Titelblatt* 'title page' or *Notenblatt* 'sheet of music'.

3.2 Distributional Similarity and Clustering

Both for the initial selection of candidate words (where the list is cut off after the top-N similar terms) and for the subsequent clustering step, frequency profiles from a large corpus are used to create a semantic vector from the target word and each (potential or actual) candidate word.

To construct these frequency profiles, the *webnews* corpus of Versley and Panchenko (2012) is used, which contains 1.7 billion words of text from various German online newspapers. The text is parsed using MALTParser (Hall et al., 2006) and the frequency of collocates with the `ATTR` (premodifying adjective) and `OBJA` (accusative object) relations is recorded. Vectors are weighted using the conservative pointwise mutual information estimate from Pantel and Lin (2002). For selecting most-similar words in candidate selection, we use a kernel based on the Jensen-Shannon Divergence across both grammatical relations, similar to the method proposed by Ó Séaghdha and Copestake (2008).

The resulting vector representations of words are then clustered using average-link hierarchical agglomerative clustering using the CLUTO toolkit (Zhao and Karypis, 2005), which uses cosine similarity to assess the similarity of two vectors. In the study of Pantel and Lin (2002), agglomerative clustering was among the best-performing off-the-shelf clustering methods.

As we initially found that many features that were used in clustering were less relevant to the different senses of the head word that were targeted, we also introduce a method to enforce a focus on target word compatible aspects of those words. In the basic approach (**raw**), the normal vector representation of each word is used. In the modified approach (**intersect**), only the features that are relevant for the target word are selected, by using for each feature the minimum value of (i) that feature's value in the candidate word's vector and (ii) that feature's value in the target word's vector.

3.3 Competing and Upper Baselines

To see how well our method performs in relation to other approaches for finding related terms describing each sense of a synset, two lower baselines and one upper baseline have been implemented.

One lower baseline uses general distributionally similar items. This is an intelligent (but realistic) **general** baseline method – close in spirit to Pantel and Lin (2002). It simply consists in retrieving the distributionally most similar words for the clustering task. Effectively, this resembles our own method, but without the compound filtering step.

The second lower baseline assumes that it should always be possible to find one word that is related to one of the senses (yielding poor coverage but trivializing the clustering problem). This trivial baseline is called **one-cluster**.

The upper baseline (called **profile**) assumes that it knows which senses of the word should be modeled and that errors can only be introduced by the clustering step not reproducing the original sense. This baseline retrieves the synsets corresponding to each sense of the word from GermaNet, and, among the terms in the neighbouring synsets (synonyms, hypernyms, hyponyms as well as sibling synsets), select those that are both unambiguous (i.e., do not have other synsets corresponding to that word) and are distributionally most similar to the (ambiguous) target word.

4 Evaluation Framework

Our evaluation framework is based on retrieving a set of words related to the target item (the candidate set), and then using collocate vectors extracted from a corpus to cluster the candidate set into multiple subsets.

Once we have a clustering of the generated terms, we want a **quantitative evaluation** of the clustering. The underlying idea for this is that we would like to have, for each sense of the target word, a cluster that has one or several words describing it. (We should not assume that it is always possible to find many related words for a particular sense).

4.1 Evaluation Data

As target items, we used a list of simplexes that are most productive in terms of compounding, using a set of gold-standard compound splits that were created by Henrich and Hinrichs (2011); candidate words (both compounds and general neighbours) were selected using a frequency list extracted from the TüPP-D/Z corpus (Müller, 2004). For the experiments themselves, no information about correct splits of the compounds was assumed and potential compounds were simply retrieved as lemma forms that have the target word as a suffix.

The subsets from clustering the candidate set are then evaluated according to whether the most-central related words in that cluster are related to the same sense of the target word, and how many senses of the target word are covered by the clusters.

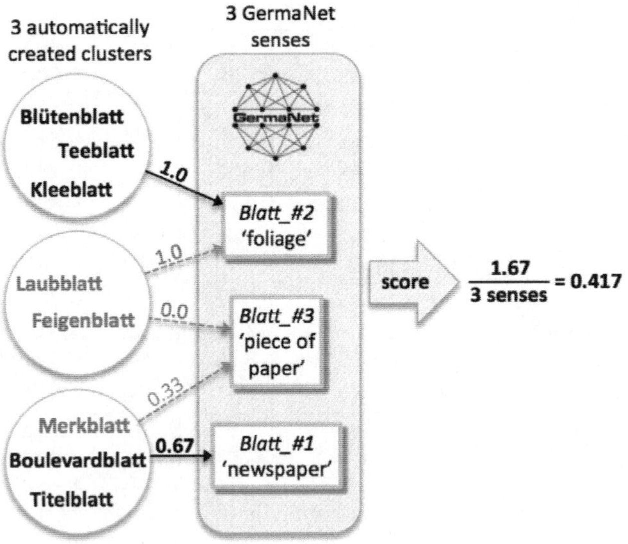

Figure 2: Evaluation procedure for the committees of related words

4.2 Evaluation Metric

Given the committee lists that are output by the candidate selection and output, we calculate an evaluation score by creating a mapping between senses of the target word and the committees that are the output of the clustering algorithm, choosing that mapping according to a quality measure that describes how well the committee members match that synset (the *precision* of that possible pairing between a committee and a sense of the target word), as shown in figure 2. Each candidate word is assigned a sense of the target word, either because it is a hyponym of that sense (for the compound-based method) or because its path distance in GermaNet's taxonomy is less than four (for the general terms method). If a candidate word is not near any of the target word's sense synsets, it is assigned no sense (and always

candidates	num	vectors	score	quality	coverage
compound	5	intersect	0.399	0.882	0.468
compound	30	intersect	0.489	0.721	0.702
compound	100	intersect	0.419	0.586	0.769
general	5	intersect	0.433	0.882	0.510
general	30	intersect	0.528	0.696	0.784
general	100	intersect	**0.573**	0.650	**0.896**
compound	5	raw	0.406	0.898	0.468
compound	30	raw	0.479	0.712	0.702
compound	100	raw	0.422	0.591	0.769
general	5	raw	0.441	**0.902**	0.510
general	30	raw	0.526	0.694	0.784
general	100	raw	0.551	0.630	0.896
profile	10n	intersect	0.737	0.781	0.945
profile	10n	raw	0.753	**0.801**	**0.946**
one-cluster	1	—	0.325	1.000	0.325

Table 1: Evaluation scores for the different methods and baselines

counted wrong).[1]

Given a committee C of these (at most) k most-central candidate words in a cluster, we can calculate a measure $P(C,s) = \frac{|w \in C : \text{sense}(w)=s|}{|C|}$ that describes how well this cluster corresponds to a given sense. (Ideally, the committee would contain words only related to one sense).

Using the Kuhn-Munkres algorithm (Kuhn, 1955), we compute a mapping between each represented synset s and a cluster C_s such that $\sum_s P(C_s, s)$ is maximized. The final score for one target word is this sum divided by the total number of synsets for the target word – this means that a method that yields a less representative set of candidate words will normally not get a better score, unless the clusters are of higher enough quality, than one that has candidate terms for each cluster.

In addition to the *score* metric, we calculated a *quality* metric that divides the raw sum by the number of senses covered in the candidate set, and a *coverage* metric that corresponds to the fraction of senses covered by the candidate set in the first place (see Table 1).

5 Results and Discussion

Table 1 contains quantitative results for the different methods and also evaluation statistics for some lower and upper baselines: Selecting exactly one related word as a candidate (and putting it in a cluster of its own) would yield a quality of 1.0, since that cluster is related to exactly one synset, but a very poor coverage of 0.325. For the *profile* upper baseline, which takes related terms from GermaNet and uses imperfect information only in clustering, we see that our clustering approach is able to reconstruct committees of sense-identical terms out of the candidate list fairly well: given related terms for each sense, distributional similarity yields fairly good quality (0.801) and, unsurprisingly, near-perfect coverage for all senses (0.946).

For the actual methods using compounds of a word (*compound* rows in Table 1) or distributionally similar words (*general* rows), we find that the compound-based candidate selection only reaches very limited coverage numbers and furthermore gives the best results with a smaller number of candidate words (30 for compounds versus 100 for general). Whether this effect is due to minority senses being less productive in compounding or whether compounds of the minority senses are not represented in GermaNet is left to be investigated in future work.

6 Conclusion

We used compounds in the selection of candidate words for representing a target word's senses in a word sense discrimination approach. Because compounds are less-frequent overall than the similar-frequency coordinate terms that are retrieved in the general baseline approach, the proposed approach does less well in covering all senses encoded in the gold standard and gets lower results in our evaluation metric. In contrast to previous work by Pantel and Lin, our evaluation approach allows a principled comparison between approaches to generate candidate lemmas in such a task and would be applicable also to other alternative methods to do so.

Acknowledgements We would like to thank Anne Brock, as well as several anonymous reviewers, for helpful comments of an earlier version of this paper. The research in this paper was partially funded by the Deutsche Forschungsgemeinschaft as part of Collaborative Research Centre (SFB) 833.

[1] If a candidate word is not represented in GermaNet at all, it is discarded before the committee-building step, so that all committee words are in fact GermaNet-represented terms.

References

Agirre, E., Aldezabal, I., and Pociello, E. (2006). Lexicalization and multiword expression in the Basque WordNet. In *Proceedings of the first International WordNet Conference*.

Bentivogli, L. and Pianta, E. (2004). Extending WordNet with syntagmatic information. In *Proceedings of the Second Global WordNet Conference (GWC 2004)*.

Hall, J., Nivre, J., and Nilsson, J. (2006). Discriminative classifiers for deterministic dependency parsing. In *Proceedings of the COLING/ACL 2006 Main Conference Poster Sessions*.

Henrich, V. and Hinrichs, E. (2010). GernEdiT - the GermaNet editing tool. In *LREC 2010*.

Henrich, V. and Hinrichs, E. (2011). Determining immediate constituents of compounds in GermaNet. In *Proc. International Conference Recent Advances in Language Processing (RANLP 2011)*.

Kuhn, H. W. (1955). The hungarian method for the assignment problem. *Naval Research Logistics Quarterly*, 2:83–97.

Miller, G. A. and Fellbaum, C. (1991). Semantic networks of English. *Cognition*, 41:197–229.

Müller, F. H. (2004). Stylebook for the Tübingen partially parsed corpus of written German (TüPP-D/Z). Technischer Bericht, Seminar für Sprachwissenschaft, Universität Tübingen.

Ó Séaghdha, D. and Copestake, A. (2008). Semantic classification with distributional kernels. In *Proceedings of the 22nd International Conference on Computational Linguistics (COLING 2008)*.

Pantel, P. and Lin, D. (2002). Discovering word senses from text. In *Proceedings of ACM Conference on Knowledge Discovery and Data Mining (KDD-02)*.

Schütze, H. (1998). Automatic word sense discrimination. *Computational Linguistics*, 24(1):97–123.

Versley, Y. and Panchenko, Y. (2012). Not just bigger: Towards better-quality Web corpora. In *Proceedings of the 7th Web as Corpus Workshop (WAC-7)*.

Yarowsky, D. (1993). One sense per collocation. In *HUMAN LANGUAGE TECHNOLOGY: Proceedings of a Workshop Held at Plainsboro*.

Zhao, Y. and Karypis, G. (2005). Hierarchical clustering algorithms for document datasets. *Data Mining and Knowledge Discovery*, 10:141–168.

Machine Learning of Syntactic Attachment from Morphosyntactic and Semantic Co-occurrence Statistics

Adam Slaski and **Szymon Acedański** and **Adam Przepiórkowski**
University of Warsaw
and
Institute of Computer Science
Polish Academy of Sciences

Abstract

The paper presents a novel approach to extracting dependency information in morphologically rich languages using co-occurrence statistics based not only on lexical forms (as in previously described collocation-based methods), but also on morphosyntactic and wordnet-derived semantic properties of words. Statistics generated from a corpus annotated only at the morphosyntactic level are used as features in a Machine Learning classifier which is able to detect which heads of groups found by a shallow parser are likely to be connected by an edge in the complete parse tree. The approach reaches the precision of 89% and the recall of 65%, with an extra 6% recall, if only words present in the wordnet are considered.

1 Introduction

The practical issue handled in this paper is how to connect syntactic groups found by a shallow parser into a possibly complete syntactic tree, i.e., how to solve the attachment problem. To give a well-known example from English, the task is to decide whether in *I shot an elephant in my pajamas*[1], the group *in my pajamas* should be attached to *an elephant* or to *shot* (or perhaps to *I*).

The standard approach to this problem relies on finding collocation strengths between syntactic objects, usually between lexical items which are heads of these objects, and resolve attachment ambiguities on the basis of such collocation information. The current work extends this approach in two main ways. First, we consider a very broad range of features: not only lexical, but also lexico-semantic, lexico-grammatical, and grammatical. Second, and more importantly, we train classifiers based not on these features directly, but rather on various association measures calculated for each of the considered features. This way the classifier selects which types of features are important and which association measures are most informative for any feature type.

The proposed method is evaluated on Polish, a language with rich inflection (and relatively free word order), which exacerbates the usual data sparseness problem in NLP.

In this work we assume that input texts are already part-of-speech tagged and chunked, the latter process resulting in the recognition of basic syntactic groups. A syntactic group may, e.g., consist of a verb with surrounding adverbs and particles or a noun with its premodifiers. We assume that all groups have a syntactic head and a semantic head. In verbal and nominal groups both heads are the same word, but in prepositional and numeral groups they usually differ: the preposition and the numeral are syntactic heads of the respective constituents, while the semantic head is the head noun within the nominal group contained in these constituents.

To simplify some of the descriptions below, by *syntactic object* we will understand either a shallow group or a word. We will also uniformly talk about syntactic and semantic heads of all syntactic objects; in case of words, the word itself is its own syntactic and semantic head. In effect, any syntactic object may be represented by a pair of words (the two

[1] `http://www.youtube.com/watch?v=NfN_gcjGoJo`

heads), and each word is characterised by its base form and its morphosyntactic tag.

2 Algorithm

The standard method of solving the PP-attachment problem is based on collocation extraction (cf., e.g., (Hindle and Rooth, 1993)) and consists of three main steps: first a training corpus is scanned and frequencies of co-occurrences of pairs of words (or more general: syntactic objects) are gathered; then the collected data are normalised to obtain, for each pair, the strength of their connection; finally, information about such collocation strengths is employed to solve PP-attachment in new texts. An instance of the PP-attachment problem is the choice between two possible edges in a parse tree: (n_1, pp) and (n_2, pp), where pp is the prepositional phrase, and n_1 and n_2 are nodes in the tree (possible attachment sites). This is solved by choosing the edge with the node that has a stronger connection to the pp.

On this approach, collocations (defined as a relation between lexemes that co-occur more often than would be expected by chance) are detected by taking pairs of syntactic objects and only considering the lemmata of their semantic heads. The natural question is whether this could be generalised to other properties of syntactic objects. In the following, the term *feature* will refer to any properties of linguistic objects taken into consideration in the process of finding collocation strengths between pairs of objects.

2.1 Lexical and Morphosyntactic Features

To start with an example of a generalised collocation, let us consider morphosyntactic valence. In order to extract valence links between two objects, we should consider the lemma of one object (potential predicate) and the morphosyntactic tag, including the value of case, etc., of the other (potential argument). This differs from standard (lexical) collocation, where the same properties of both objects are considered, namely, their lemmata.

Formally, we define a feature f to be a pair of functions $l_f \colon \mathsf{so} \rightarrow L_f$ and $r_f \colon \mathsf{so} \rightarrow R_f$, where so stands for the set of syntactic objects and L_f, R_f are the investigated properties. For example, to learn dependencies between verbs and case values of their objects, we can take $l_f(\mathsf{w}) = \mathsf{base}(\mathsf{semhead}(\mathsf{w}))$ (the lemma of the semantic head of w) and $r_f(\mathsf{w}) = \mathsf{case}(\mathsf{synhead}(\mathsf{w}))$ (the case value of the syntactic head of w). On the other hand, in order to obtain the usual collocations, it is sufficient to take both functions as mapping a syntactic object to a base form of its semantic head.

What features should be considered in the task of finding dependencies between syntactic objects? The two features mentioned above, aimed at finding lexical collocations and valence relations, are obviously useful. However, in a morphologically rich language, like Polish, taking the full morphosyntactic tag as the value of a feature function leads to the data sparsity problem. Clearly, the most important valence information a tag may contribute is part of speech and grammatical case. Hence, we define the second function in the "valence" feature more precisely to be the base form and grammatical case (if any), if the syntactic object is a preposition, or part of speech and grammatical case (if any), otherwise. For example, consider the sentence *Who cares for the carers?* and assume that it has already been split into basic syntactic objects in the following way: [*Who*] [*cares*] [*for the carers*] [*?*]. The syntactic head of the third object is *for* and the lemma of the semantic head is CARER. So, the valence feature for the pair *care* and *for the carers* (both defined below via their syntactic and semantic heads) will give:

$$l_{val}(\langle \text{CARE:verb, 3s; CARE:verb, 3s}\rangle) = \text{CARE}$$
$$r_{val}(\langle \text{FOR:prep, obj; CARER:noun, pl}\rangle) = \langle \text{FOR, obj}\rangle,$$

where 3s stands for the "3rd person singular" property of verbs and obj stands for the objective case in English.

Additionally, 7 morphosyntactic features are defined by projecting both syntactic objects onto any (but the same of the two objects) combination of grammatical case, gender and number. For example one of those features is defined in the following way:

$$l_f(\mathsf{w}) = r_f(\mathsf{w}) = \\ = \langle \mathsf{case}(\mathsf{synhead}(\mathsf{w})), \mathsf{gender}(\mathsf{synhead}(\mathsf{w}))\rangle.$$

Another feature relates the two objects' syntactic heads, by looking at the part of speech of the first one and the case of the other one. The final feature records information about syntactic (number, gender, case) agreement between the objects.

2.2 Lexico-Semantic Features

Obviously, the semantics of syntactic objects is important in deciding which two objects are directly connected in a syntactic tree. To this end, we utilise a wordnet.

Ideally, we would like to represent a syntactic object via its semantic class. In wordnets, semantic classes are approximated by synsets (synonym sets) which are ordered by the hyperonymy relation. We could represent a syntactic object by its directly corresponding synset, but in terms of generalisation this would hardly be an improvement over representing such an object by its semantic head. In most cases we need to represent the object by a hypernym of its synset. But how far up should we go along the hypernymy path to find a synset of the right granularity? This is a difficult problem, so we leave it to the classifier. Instead, lexico-semantic features are defined in such a way that, for a given lexeme, all its hypernyms are counted as observations.

After some experimentation, three features based on this idea are defined:

1. $l_f(\mathsf{w}) = \mathsf{base}(\mathsf{semhead}(\mathsf{w}))$
   $r_f(\mathsf{w}) = \mathsf{sset}(\mathsf{w})$
   (for all $\mathsf{sset}(\mathsf{w}) \in \mathsf{hypernyms}(\mathsf{w})$),
2. $l_f(\mathsf{w}) = \mathsf{base}(\mathsf{semhead}(\mathsf{w}))$
   $r_f(\mathsf{w}) = \langle \mathsf{sset}(\mathsf{w}), \mathsf{case}(\mathsf{synhead}(\mathsf{w})) \rangle$
   (for all $\mathsf{sset}(\mathsf{w}) \in \mathsf{hypernyms}(\mathsf{w})$),
3. $l_f(\mathsf{w}) = \mathsf{sset}(\mathsf{w})$
   $r_f(\mathsf{w}) = \mathsf{sset}(\mathsf{w})$

In the last feature, where both objects are represented by synsets, only those minimally general hypernyms of the two objects are considered that co-occur in the training corpus more than T (threshold) times. In the experiments described below, performed on a 1-million-word training corpus, the threshold was set to 30.

2.3 Association Measures

For any two syntactic objects in the same sentence the strength of association is computed between them using each of the 14 features (standard collocations, 10 morphosyntactic features, 3 lexico-semantic features) defined above. In fact, we use not 1 but 6 association measures most suitable for language analysis according to (Seretan, 2011): log likehood ratio, chi-squared, t-score, z-score, pointwise mutual information and raw frequency. The last choice may seem disputable, but as was shown in (Krenn and Evert, 2001) (and reported in various works on valence acquisition), in some cases raw frequency behaves better than more sophisticated measures.

We are well aware that some of the employed measures require the distribution of frequencies to meet certain conditions that are not necessarily fulfilled in the present case. However, as explained in the following subsection, the decision which measures should ultimately be taken into account is left to a classifier.

2.4 Classifiers

Let us first note that no treebank is needed for computing the features and measures presented in the previous section. These measures represent co-occurrence strengths of syntactic objects based on different grouping strategies (by lemma, by part of speech, by case, gender, number, by wordnet synsets, etc.). Any large, morphosyntactically annotated (and perhaps chunked) corpus is suitable for computing such features. A treebank is only needed to train a classifier which uses such measures as input signals.[2]

In order to apply Machine Learning classifiers, one must formally define what counts as an instance of the classification problem. In the current case, for each pair of syntactic objects in a sentence, a single instance is generated with the following signals:

- absolute distance (in terms of the number of sytnactic objects in between),
- ordering (the sign of the distance),
- 6 measures (see § 2.3) of lexical collocation,
- $10 \times 6 = 60$ values of morphosyntactic co-occurrence measures,
- $3 \times 6 = 18$ values of lexico-semantic (wordnet-based) co-occurrence measures,
- a single binary signal based on 14 high-precision low-recall handwritten syntactic de-

[2] We use the term *signal* instead of the more usual *feature* in order to avoid confusion with features defined in § 2.1 and in § 2.2.

cision rules which define common grammatical patterns like verb-subject agreement, genitive construction, etc.; the rules look only at the morphosyntactic tags of the heads of syntactic objects,
- the classification target from the treebank: a binary signal describing whether the given pair of syntactic objects form an edge in the parse tree.

The last signal is used for training the classifier and then for evaluation. Note that lexical forms of the compared syntactic objects or their heads are not passed to the classifier, so the size of the training treebank can be kept relatively small.

An inherent problem that needs to be addressed is the imbalance between the sizes of two classification categories. Of course, most of the pairs of the syntactic objects do not form an edge in the parse tree, so a relatively high classification accuracy may be achieved by the trivial classifier which finds no edges at all. We experimented with various well-known classifiers, such as decision trees, Support Vector Machines and clustering algorithms, and also tried subsampling[3] of the imbalanced data. Finally, satisfactory results were achieved by employing a Balanced Random Forest classifier.

Random Forest (Breiman, 2001) is a set of unpruned C4.5 (Quinlan, 1993) decision trees. When building a single tree in the set, only a random subset of all attributes is considered at each node and the best is selected for splitting the data set. Balanced Random Forest (BRF, (Chen et al., 2004)) is a modified version of the Random Forest. A single tree of BRF is built by first randomly subsampling the more frequent instances in the training set to match the number of less frequent ones and then creating a decision tree from this reduced data set.

3 Experiments and Evaluation

The approach presented above has been evaluated on Polish.

First, a manually annotated 1-million-word subcorpus of the National Corpus of Polish (Przepiórkowski et al., 2010), specifically, its morphosyntactic and shallow syntactic annotation, was used to compute the co-occurrence statistics. The wordnet used for lexico-semantic measures was *Słowosieć* (Piasecki et al., 2009; Maziarz et al., 2012), the largest Polish wordnet.

Then a random subset of sentences from this corpus was shallow-parsed by Spejd (Buczyński and Przepiórkowski, 2009) and given to linguists, who added annotation for the dependency links between syntactic objects. Each sentence was processed by two linguists, and in case of any discrepancy, the sentence was simply rejected. The final corpus contains 963 sentences comprising over 8000 tokens.

From this data we obtained over 23 500 classification problem instances. Then we performed the classification using a BRF classifier written for Weka (Witten and Frank, 2005) as part of the research work on definition extraction with BRFs (Kobyliński and Przepiórkowski, 2008). The results were 10-fold cross-validated. A similar experiment was performed taking into account only those instances which describe syntactic objects with semantic heads present in the wordnet. The results were measured in terms of precision and recall over edges in the syntactic tree: what percentage of found edges are correct (precision) and what percentage of correct edges were found by the algorithm (recall). The obtained measures are presented in Table 1.

Expected YES	Expected NO	Classified
2674	319	YES
1781	21250	NO
	Precision:	0.89
	Recall:	0.60
	F-measure:	0.72

Expected YES	Expected NO	Classified
1933	241	YES
1008	13041	NO
	Precision:	0.89
	Recall:	0.66
	F-measure:	0.76

Table 1: Confusion matrix (# of instances) and measures for the full data set and for data present in wordnet.

[3]Removing enough negative instances in the training set to balance the numbers of instances representing both classes.

We also looked at the actual decision trees that were generated during the training. We note that the signal most frequently observed near the tops of decision trees was the one from handwritten rules. The second one was the distance. By looking at the trees, we could not see any clear preferences for other types of signals. This suggests that both morphosyntactic and lexico-semantic signals contribute to the accuracy of the classification.

Based on this inspection of decision trees, we performed another experiment to learn how much improvement we get from generalised collocation signals. We evaluated – on the same data – a not so trivial baseline algorithm which, for each syntactic object, creates an edge to its nearest neighbour accepted by the handwritten rules, if any. Note that this baseline builds on the fact that a node in a parse tree has at most one parent, whereas the algorithm described above does not encode this property, yet; clearly, there is still some room for improvement. The baseline reaches 0.78 precision and 0.47 recall (F-measure is 0.59). Therefore, the improvement from co-occurrence signals over this strong baseline is 0.13, which is rather high. Also, given the high precision, our algorithm may be suitable for using in a cascade of classifiers.

4 Related Work

There is a plethora of relevant work on resolving PP-attachment ambiguities in particular and finding dependency links in general, and we cannot hope to do it sufficient justice here.

One line of work, exemplified by the early influential paper (Hindle and Rooth, 1993), posits the problem of PP-attachment as the problem of choosing between a verb v and a noun n_1 when attaching a prepositional phrase defined by the syntactic head p and the semantic head n_2. Early work, including (Hindle and Rooth, 1993), concentrated on lexical associations, later also using wordnet information, e.g., (Clark and Weir, 2000), in a way similar to that described above. Let us note that this scenario was criticised as unrealistic by (Atterer and Schütze, 2007), who argue that "PP attachment should not be evaluated in isolation, but instead as an integral component of a parsing system, without using information from the gold-standard oracle", as in the approach proposed here.

Another rich thread of relevant research is concerned with valence acquisition, where shallow parsing and association measures based on morphosyntactic features are often used at the stage of collecting evidence, (Manning, 1993; Korhonen, 2002), also in work on Polish, (Przepiórkowski, 2009). However, the aim in this task is the construction of a valence dictionary, rather than disambiguation of attachment possibilities in a corpus.

A task more related to the current one is presented in (Van Asch and Daelemans, 2009), where a PP-attacher operates on top of a shallow parser. However, this memory-based module is fully trained on a treebank (Penn Treebank, in this case) and is concerned only with finding anchors for PPs, rather than with linking any dependents to their heads.

Finally, much work has been devoted during the last decade to probabilistic dependency parsing (see (Kübler et al., 2009) for a good overview). Classifiers deciding whether – at any stage of dependency parsing – to perform *shift* or *reduce* typically rely on lexical and morphosyntactic, but not lexico-semantic information (Nivre, 2006). Again, such classifiers are fully trained on a treebank (converted to parser configurations).

5 Conclusion

Treebanks are very expensive, morphosyntactically annotated corpora are relatively cheap. The main contribution of the current paper is a novel approach to factoring out syntactic training in the process of learning of syntactic attachment. All the fine-grained lexical training data were collected from a relatively large morphosyntactically annotated and chunked corpus, and only less than 100 signals (although many of them continuous) were used for training the final classifier on a treebank. The advantage of this approach is that reasonable results can be achieved on the basis of tiny treebanks (here, less than 1000 sentences).

We are not aware of work fully analogous to ours, either for Polish or for other languages, so we cannot fully compare our results to the state of the art. The comparison with a strong baseline algorithm which uses handwritten rules shows a significant improvement – over 0.13 in terms of F-measure.

Acknowledgments

This research is supported by the POIG.01.01.02-14-013/09 project which is co-financed by the European Union under the European Regional Development Fund.

References

Michaela Atterer and Hinrich Schütze. 2007. Prepositional phrase attachment without oracles. *Computational Linguistics*, 33(4):469–476.

Leo Breiman. 2001. Random forests. *Machine Learning*, 45:5–32.

Aleksander Buczyński and Adam Przepiórkowski. 2009. Spejd: A shallow processing and morphological disambiguation tool. In Zygmunt Vetulani and Hans Uszkoreit, editors, *Human Language Technology: Challenges of the Information Society*, volume 5603 of *Lecture Notes in Artificial Intelligence*, pages 131–141. Springer-Verlag, Berlin.

Chao Chen, Andy Liaw, and Leo Breiman. 2004. Using random forest to learn imbalanced data. Technical Report 666, University of California, Berkeley.

Stephen Clark and David Weir. 2000. A class-based probabilistic approach to structural disambiguation. In *In Proceedings of the 18th International Conference on Computational Linguistics*, pages 194–200.

Donald Hindle and Mats Rooth. 1993. Structural ambiguity and lexical relations. *Computational Linguistics*, 19(1):103–120.

Łukasz Kobyliński and Adam Przepiórkowski. 2008. Definition extraction with balanced random forests. In Bengt Nordström and Aarne Ranta, editors, *Advances in Natural Language Processing: GoTAL 2008, Gothenburg, Sweden*, volume 5221 of *Lecture Notes in Artificial Intelligence*, pages 237–247, Berlin. Springer-Verlag.

Anna Korhonen. 2002. *Subcategorization Acquisition*. PhD Thesis, University of Cambridge.

Brigitte Krenn and Stefan Evert. 2001. Can we do better than frequency? A case study on extracting PP-verb collocations. In *Proceedings of the ACL Workshop on Collocations*, Toulouse, France.

Sandra Kübler, Ryan McDonald, and Joakim Nivre. 2009. *Dependency Parsing*. Morgan & Claypool.

Christopher D. Manning. 1993. Automatic acquisition of a large subcategorization dictionary from corpora. In *Proceedings of the 31st Annual Meeting of the Association for Computational Linguistics*, pages 235–242, Columbus, OH.

Marek Maziarz, Maciej Piasecki, and Stanisław Szpakowicz. 2012. Approaching plWordNet 2.0. In *Proceedings of the 6th Global Wordnet Conference*, Matsue, Japan.

Joakim Nivre. 2006. *Inductive Dependency Parsing*. Springer-Verlag, Berlin.

Maciej Piasecki, Stanisław Szpakowicz, and Bartosz Broda. 2009. *A Wordnet from the Ground Up*. Oficyna Wydawnicza Politechniki Wroclawskiej, Wrocław.

Adam Przepiórkowski, Rafał L. Górski, Marek Łaziński, and Piotr Pęzik. 2010. Recent developments in the National Corpus of Polish. In *Proceedings of the Seventh International Conference on Language Resources and Evaluation, LREC 2010*, Valletta, Malta. ELRA.

Adam Przepiórkowski. 2009. Towards the automatic acquisition of a valence dictionary for Polish. In Małgorzata Marciniak and Agnieszka Mykowiecka, editors, *Aspects of Natural Language Processing*, volume 5070 of *Lecture Notes in Computer Science*, pages 191–210. Springer-Verlag, Berlin.

John Ross Quinlan. 1993. *C4.5 Programs for Machine Learning*. Morgan Kaufmann.

Violeta Seretan. 2011. *Syntax-Based Collocation Extraction*. Text, Speech and Language Technology. Springer, Dordrecht.

Vincent Van Asch and Walter Daelemans. 2009. Prepositional phrase attachment in shallow parsing. In *Proceedings of the International Conference RANLP-2009*, pages 12–17, Borovets, Bulgaria, September.

Ian H. Witten and Eibe Frank. 2005. *Data Mining: Practical machine learning tools and techniques*. Morgan Kaufmann, San Francisco, CA, 2nd edition.

Combining Rule-Based and Statistical Syntactic Analyzers

María Jesús Aranzabe[*], Arantza Díaz de Ilarraza, Nerea Ezeiza, Kepa Bengoetxea, Iakes Goenaga, Koldo Gojenola,
Department of Computer Languages and Systems / [*] Department of Basque Philology
University of the Basque Country UPV/EHU
{maxux.aranzabe@ehu.es, kepa.bengoetxea, jipdisaa@si.ehu.es, n.ezeiza@ehu.es, koldo.gojenola@ehu.es, iakes@gmail.com}

Abstract

This paper presents the results of a set of preliminary experiments combining two knowledge-based partial dependency analyzers with two statistical parsers, applied to the Basque Dependency Treebank. The general idea will be to apply a stacked scheme where the output of the rule-based partial parsers will be given as input to MaltParser and MST, two state of the art statistical parsers. The results show a modest improvement over the baseline, although they also present interesting lines for further research.

1. Introduction

In this paper we present a set of preliminary experiments on the combination of two knowledge-based partial syntactic analyzers with two state of the art data-driven statistical parsers. The experiments have been performed on the Basque Dependency Treebank (Aduriz et al., 2003).

In the last years, many attempts have been performed trying to combine different parsers (Surdeanu and Manning, 2010), with significant improvements over the best individual parser's baseline. The two most successful approaches have been stacking (Martins et al., 2008) and voting (Sagae and Lavie, 2006, Nivre and McDonald, 2008, McDonald and Nivre, 2011). In this paper we will experiment the use of the stacking technique, giving the tags obtained by the rule-based syntactic partial parsers as input to the statistical parsers.

Morphologically rich languages present new challenges, as the use of state of the art parsers for more configurational and non-inflected languages like English does not reach similar performance levels in languages like Basque, Greek or Turkish (Nivre et al., 2007a). As it was successfully done on part of speech (POS) tagging, where the use of rule-based POS taggers (Tapanainen and Voutilainen, 1994) or a combination of a rule-based POS tagger with a statistical one (Aduriz et al., 1997, Ezeiza et al., 1998) outperformed purely statistical taggers, we think that exploring the combination of knowledge-based and data-driven systems in syntactic processing can be an interesting line of research.

Most of the experiments on combined parsers have relied on different types of statistical parsers (Sagae and Lavie, 2006, Martins et al., 2008, McDonald and Nivre, 2011), trained on an automatically annotated treebank. Yeh (2000) used the output of several baseline diverse parsers to increase the performance of a second transformation-based parser. In our work we will study the use of two partial rule-based syntactic analyzers together with two data-driven parsers:

- A rule-based chunker (Aduriz et al., 2004) that marks the beginning and end of noun phrases, postpositional phrases and verb chains, in the IOB (Inside/ Outside/Beginning of a chunk) style.
- A shallow dependency relation annotator (Aranzabe et al., 2004), which tries to detect dependency relations by assigning a

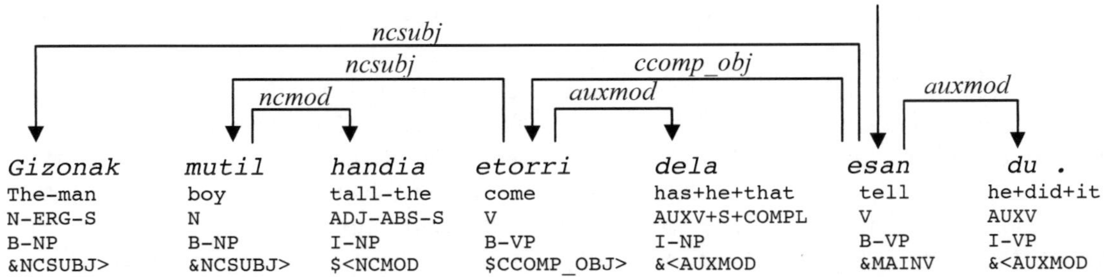

Figure 1. Dependency tree for the sentence *Gizonak mutil handia etorri dela esan du* (the man told that the tall boy has come). The two last lines show the tags assigned by the rule-based chunker and the rule-based dependency analyzer, respectively.

(V = main verb, N = noun, AUXV = auxiliary verb, COMPL = completive, ccomp_obj = clausal complement object, ERG = ergative, S: singular, auxmod = auxiliary, ncsubj = non-clausal subject, B-NP = beginning of NP, I-NP = inside an NP, &MAINV = main verb, &<AUXMOD = verbal auxiliary modifier).

set of predefined tags to each word, where each tag gives both the name of a dependency relation (e.g. subject) together with the direction of its head (left or right).

- We will use two statistical dependency parsers, MaltParser (Nivre et al., 2007b) and MST (McDonald et al, 2005).

In the rest of this paper, section 2 will first present the corpus and the different parsers we will combine, followed by the experimental results in section 3, and the main conclusions of the work.

2. Resources

This section will describe the main resources that have been used in the experiments. First, subsection 2.1 will describe the Basque Dependency Treebank, and then subsection 2.2 will explain the main details of the analyzers that have been employed. The analyzers are a rule-based chunker, a rule-based shallow dependency parser and two state of the art data-driven dependency parsers, MaltParser and MST.

2.1 Corpora

Our work will make use the second version of the Basque dependency Treebank (BDT II, Aduriz et al., 2003), containing 150,000 tokens (11,225 sentences). Figure 1 presents an example of a syntactically annotated sentence. Each word contains its form, lemma, category or coarse part of speech (CPOS), POS, morphosyntactic features such as case, number of subordinate relations, and the dependency relation (headword + dependency). The information in figure 1 has been simplified due to space reasons, as typically each word contains many morphosyntactic features (case, number, type of subordinated sentence, ...), which are relevant for parsing. The last two lines of the sentence in figure 1 do not properly correspond to the treebank, but are the result of the rule-based partial syntactic analyzers (see subsection 2.2). For evaluation, we divided the treebank in three sets, corresponding to training, development, and test (80%, 10%, and 10%, respectively). The experiments were performed on the development set, leaving the best system for the final test.

2.2 Analyzers

This subsection will present the four types of analyzers that have been used. The rule-based analyzers are based on the Contraint Grammar (CG) formalism (Karlsson et al., 1995), based on the assignment of morphosyntactic tags to words using a formalism that has the capabilities of finite state automata or regular expressions, by means of a set of rules that examine mainly local contexts of words to determine the correct tag assignment.

The rule-based chunker (RBC henceforth, Aranzabe et al., 2009) uses 560 rules, where 479 of the rules deal with noun phrases and the rest with verb phrases. The chunker delimits the chunks with three tags, using a standard IOB marking style (see figure 1). The first one is to mark the beginning of the phrase (B-VP if it is a verb phrase and B-NP whether it's a noun phrase) and the other one to mark the continuation of the phrase (I-NP or I-VP, meaning that the word is inside an NP or VP). The last tag marks words that are outside a chunk. The evaluation of the chunker on the BDT gave a result of 87% precision and 85% recall over all chunks. We must take into account that this evaluation was performed on the gold POS tags, rather than on automatically assigned POS tasks, as in the present experiment. For that reason, the results can serve as an upper bound on the real results.

The rule-based dependency analyzer (RBDA, Aranzabe et al., 2004) uses a set of 505 CG rules that try to assign dependency relations to wordforms. As the CG formalism only allows the assignment of tags, the rules only aim at marking the name of the dependency relation together with the direction of the head (left or right). For example, this analyzer assigns tags of the form &NCSUBJ> (see figure 1), meaning that the corresponding wordform is a non-clausal syntactic subject and that its head is situated to its right (the ">" or "<" symbols mark the direction of the head). This means that the result of this analysis is on the one hand a partial analysis and, on the other hand, it does not define a dependency tree, and can also be seen as a set of constraints on the shape of the tree. The system was evaluated on the BDT, obtaining f-scores between 90% for the *auxmod* dependency relation between the auxiliary and the main verb and 52% for the *subject* dependency relation, giving a (macro) average of 65%.

Regarding the data-driven parsers, we have made use of MaltParser (Nivre et al., 2007b) and MST Parser (McDonald et al., 2006), two state of the art dependency parsers representing two dominant approaches in data-driven dependency parsing, and that have been successfully applied to typologically different languages and treebanks (McDonald and Nivre, 2007).

MaltParser (Nivre, 2006) is a representative of local, greedy, transition-based dependency parsing models, where the parser obtains deterministically a dependency tree in a single pass over the input using two data structures: a stack of partially analyzed items and the remaining input sequence. To determine the best action at each step, the parser uses history-based feature models and discriminative machine learning. The learning configuration can include any kind of information (such as word-form, lemma, category, subcategory or morphological features). Several variants of the parser have been implemented, and we will use one of its standard versions (MaltParser version 1.4). In our experiments, we will use the Stack-Lazy algorithm with the *liblinear* classifier.

The MST Parser can be considered a representative of global, exhaustive graph-based parsing (McDonald et al., 2005, 2006). This algorithm finds the highest scoring directed spanning tree in a dependency graph forming a valid dependency tree. To learn arc scores, it uses large-margin structured learning algorithms, which optimize the parameters of the model to maximize the score margin between the correct dependency graph and all incorrect dependency graphs for every sentence in a training set. The learning procedure is global since model parameters are set relative to classifying the entire dependency graph, and not just over single arc attachments. This is in contrast to the local but richer contexts used by transition-based parsers. We use the freely available version of MSTParser[1]. In the following experiments we will make use of the second order non-projective algorithm.

3. Experiments

We will experiment the effect of using the output of the knowledge-based analyzers as input to the data-driven parsers in a stacked learning scheme. Figure 1 shows how the two last lines of the example sentence contain the tags assigned by the rule-based chunker (B-NP, I-NP, B-VP and I-VP) and the rule-based partial dependency analyzer (&NCSUBJ, &<NCMOD, &<AUXMOD, &CCOMP_OBJ and &MAINV) .

The first step consisted in applying the complete set of text processing tools for Basque, including:

- Morphological analysis. In Basque, each word can receive multiple affixes, as each lemma can generate thousands of word-forms by means of morphological properties, such as case, number, tense, or different types of subordination for verbs. Consequently, the morphological analyzer for Basque (Aduriz et al. 2000) gives a high ambiguity. If only categorial (POS) ambiguity is taken into account, there is an average of 1.55 interpretations per word-form, which rises to 2.65 when the full morphosyntactic information is taken into account, giving an overall 64% of ambiguous word-forms.
- Morphological disambiguation. Disambiguating the output of morphological analysis, in order to obtain a single interpretation for each word-form,

[1] http://mstparser.sourceforge.net

	MaltParser		MST Parser	
	LAS	UAS	LAS	UAS
Baseline	76.77%	82.09%	77.96%	84.04%
+ RBC	77.10% (+0.33)	82.29% (+0.20)	77.99% (+0.03)	83.99% (-0.05)
+ RBDA	*77.15% (+0.38)	82.27% (+0.18)	78.03% (+0.07)	83.76% (-0.28)
+ RBC + RBDA	*77.25% (+0.48)	82.18% (+0.09)	78.00% (+0.04)	83.34% (-0.70)

Table 1. Evaluation results

(RBC = rule-based chunker, RBDA = rule-based dependency analyzer, LAS: Labeled Attachment Score, UAS: Unlabeled Attachment Score, *: statistically significant in McNemar's test, $p < 0.05$)

can pose an important problem, as determining the correct interpretation for each word-form requires in many cases the inspection of local contexts, and in some others, as the agreement of verbs with subject, object or indirect object, it could also suppose the examination of elements which can be far from each other, added to the free constituent order of the main sentence elements in Basque. The erroneous assignment of incorrect part of speech or morphological features can difficult the work of the parser.

- Chunker
- Partial dependency analyzer

When performing this task, we found the problem of matching the treebank tokens with those obtained from the analyzers, as there were divergences on the treatment of multiword units, mostly coming from Named Entities, verb compounds and complex postpositions (formed with morphemes appearing at two different words). For that reason, we performed a matching process trying to link the multiword units given by the morphological analysis module and the treebank, obtaining a correct match for 99% of the sentences.

Regarding the data-driven parsers, they are trained using two kinds of tags as input:

- POS and morphosyntactic tags coming from the automatic morphological processing of the dependency treebank. Disambiguation errors, such as an incorrect POS category or morphological analyses (e.g. the assignment of an incorrect case) can harm the parser, as tested in Bengoetxea et al. (2011).
- The output of the rule-based partial syntactic analyzers (two last lines of the example in figure 1). These tags contain errors of the CG-based syntactic taggers. As the analyzers are applied after morphological processing, the errors can be propagated and augmented.

Table 1 shows the results of using the output of the knowledge-based analyzers as input to the statistical parsers. We have performed three experiments for each statistical parser, trying with the chunks provided by the chunker, the partial dependency parser, and both. The table shows modest gains, suggesting that the rule-based analyzers help the statistical ones, giving slight increases over the baseline, which are statistically significant when applying MaltParser to the output of the rule-based dependency parser and a combination of the chunker and rule-based parsers. As table 1 shows, the parser type is relevant, as MaltParser seems to be sensitive when using the stacked features, while the partial parsers do not seem to give any significant improvement to MST.

3.1 Error analysis

Looking with more detail at the errors made by the different versions of the parsers, we observe significant differences in the results for different dependency relations, seeing that the statistical parsers behave in a different manner regarding to each relation, as shown in table 2. The table shows the differences in f-score[2] corresponding to five local dependency relations, (determination of verbal modifiers, such as subject, object and indirect object).

McDonald and Nivre (2007) examined the types of errors made by the two data-driven parsers used in this work, showing how the greedy algorithm of MaltParser performed better with local dependency relations, while the graph-based algorithm of MST was more accurate for global relations. As both the chunker and the partial dependency analyzer are based on a set of local rules in the CG formalism, we could expect that the stacked parsers could benefit mostly on the local dependency relations.

[2] f-score = 2 * precision * recall / (precision + recall)

	MaltParser				MST Parser			
Dependency relation	**Baseline**	**+ RBC**	**+ RBDA**	**+ RBC + RBDA**	**Baseline**	**+ RBC**	**+ RBDA**	**+ RBC + RBDA**
ncmod	75,29	75,90	76,08	**76,40**	77,15	**77,44**	76,39	76,92
ncobj	67,34	68,49	**69,67**	69,54	64,85	64,86	65,56	**66,18**
ncpred	61,37	61,92	61,26	**63,50**	**60,37**	57,55	58,44	59,27
ncsubj	61,92	61,90	**63,96**	63,91	59,19	59,26	62,23	**61,61**
nciobj	75,76	76,53	**77,16**	76,29	74,23	**74,47**	72,16	69,08

Table 2. Comparison of the different parsers' f-score with regard to specific dependency relations (ncmod = non-clausal modifier, ncobj = non-clausal object, ncpred = non-clausal predicate, ncsubj = non-clausal subject, nciobj = non-clausal indirect object)

Table 2 shows how the addition of the rule-based parsers' tags performs in accord with this behavior, as MaltParser gets f-score improvements for the local relations. Although not shown in Table 2, we also inspected the results on the long distance relations, where we did not observe noticeable improvements with respect to the baseline on any parser. For that reason, MaltParser, seems to mostly benefit of the local nature of the stacked features, while MST does not get a significant improvement, except for some local dependency relations, such as ncobj and ncsubj.

We performed an additional test using the partial dependency analyzer's gold dependency relations as input to MaltParser. As could be expected, the gold tags gave a noticeable improvement to the parser's results, reaching 95% LAS. However, when examining the scores for the output dependency relations, we noticed that the gold partial dependency tags are beneficial for some relations, although negative for some others. For example the non-clausal modifier (ncmod) relation's f-score increases 3.25 points, while the dependency relation for clausal subordinate sentences functioning as indirect object decreases 0.46 points, which is surprising in principle.

For all those reasons, the relation between the input dependency tags and the obtained results seems to be intricate, and we think that it deserves new experiments in order to determine their nature. As each type of syntactic information can have an important influence on the results on specific relations, their study can shed light on novel schemes of parser combination.

4. Conclusions

We have presented a preliminary effort to integrate different syntactic analyzers, with the objective of getting the best from each system. Although the potential gain is in theory high, the experiments have shown very modest improvements, which seem to happen in the set of local dependency relations. We can point out some avenues for further research:

- Development of the rule-based dependency parser using the dependencies that give better improvements on the gold dependency tags, as this can measure the impact of each kind of shallow dependency tag on the data-driven parsers.
- Development of rules that deal with the phenomena where the statistical parsers perform worse. This requires a careful error analysis followed by a redesign of the manually developed CG tagging rules.
- Application of other types of combining schemes, such as voting, trying to get the best from each type of parser.

Finally, we must also take into account that the rule-based analyzers were developed mainly having linguistic principles in mind, such as coverage of diverse linguistic phenomena or the treatment of specific syntactic constructions (Aranzabe et al., 2004), instead of performance-oriented measures, such as precision and recall. This means that there is room for improvement in the first-stage knowledge-based parsers, which will have, at least in theory, a positive effect on the second-phase statistical parsers, allowing us to test whether knowledge-based and machine learning-based systems can be successfully combined.

Acknowledgements

This research was supported by the Department of Industry of the Basque Government (IT344-10, S-PE11UN114), the University of the Basque Country (GIU09/19) and the Spanish Ministry of

Science and Innovation (MICINN, TIN2010-20218).

References

Itziar Aduriz, José María Arriola, Xabier Artola, Arantza Díaz de Ilarraza, Koldo Gojenola and Montse Maritxalar. 1997. Morphosyntactic disambiguation for Basque based on the Constraint Grammar Formalism. Conference on *Recent Advances in Natural Language Processing* (RANLP), Bulgaria.

Itziar Aduriz, Eneko Agirre, Izaskun Aldezabal, Iñaki Alegria, Xabier Arregi, Jose Mari Arriola, Xabier Artola, Koldo Gojenola, Montserrat Maritxalar, Kepa Sarasola, and Miriam Urkia. 2000. A word-grammar based morphological analyzer for agglutinative languages. *Coling 2000*, Saarbrucken.

Itziar Aduriz, José María Arriola, Arantza Díaz de Ilarraza, Koldo Gojenola, Maite Oronoz and Larraitz Uria. 2004. A cascaded syntactic analyser for Basque. In *Computational Linguistics and Intelligent Text Processing*, pages 124-135. LNCS Series. Springer Verlag. Berlin. 2004

Itziar Aduriz, Maria Jesus Aranzabe, Jose Maria Arriola, Aitziber Atutxa, Arantza Diaz de Ilarraza, Aitzpea Garmendia and Maite Oronoz. 2003. Construction of a Basque dependency treebank. *Treebanks and Linguistic Theories*.

María Jesús Aranzabe, José María Arriola and Arantza Díaz de Ilarraza. 2004. Towards a Dependency Parser for Basque. In *Proceedings of the Workshop on Recent Advances in Dependency Grammar*, Geneva, Switzerland.

Maria Jesus Aranzabe, Jose Maria Arriola and Arantza Díaz de Ilarraza. 2009. Theoretical and Methodological issues of tagging Noun Phrase Structures following Dependency Grammar Formalism. In Artiagoitia, X. and Lakarra J.A. (eds) Gramatika Jaietan. Patxi Goenagaren omenez. Donostia: Gipuzkoako Foru Aldundia-UPV/EHU.

Kepa Bengoetxea and Koldo Gojenola. 2010. Application of Different Techniques to Dependency Parsing of Basque. Proceedings of the *1st Workshop on Statistical Parsing of Morphologically Rich Languages* (SPMRL), NAACL-HLT Workshop.

Kepa Bengoetxea, Arantza Casillas and Koldo Gojenola. 2011. Testing the Effect of Morphological Disambiguation in Dependency Parsing of Basque. Proceedings of the *International Conference on Parsing Technologies (IWPT). 2nd Workshop on Statistical Parsing Morphologically Rich Languages (SPMRL)*, Dublin, Ireland.

Gülsen Eryiğit, Joakim Nivre and Kemal Oflazer. 2008. Dependency Parsing of Turkish. *Computational Linguistics*, Vol. 34 (3).

Nerea Ezeiza, Iñaki Alegria, José María Arriola, Rubén Urizar and Itziar Aduriz. 1998. Combining Stochastic and Rule-Based Methods for Disambiguation in Agglutinative Languages. *COLING-ACL'98*, Montreal.

Fred Karlsson, Atro Voutilainen, Juka Heikkila and Arto Anttila. 1995. *Constraint Grammar: A Language-independent System for Parsing Unrestricted Text*. Mouton de Gruyter.

André F. T. Martins, Dipanjan Das, Noah A. Smith and Eric P. Xing. 2008. Stacking Dependency Parsing. *Proceedings of EMNLP-2008*.

Ryan McDonald, Kevin Lerman and Fernando Pereira. 2005. Online large-margin training of dependency parsers. In *Proceedings of ACL*.

Ryan McDonald, Kevin Lerman and Fernando Pereira. 2006. Multilingual dependency analysis with a two-stage discriminative parser. In Proc. CoNLL.

Ryan McDonald and Joakim Nivre. 2007. Characterizing the Errors of Data-Driven Dependency Parsing Models. Proceedings of the 2007 *Joint Conference on Empirical Methods in Natural Language Processing and Computational Natural Language Learning*, EMNLP/CoNLL.

Ryan McDonald and Joakim Nivre. 2011. Analyzing and Integrating Dependency Parsers. *Computational Linguistics*, Vol. 37(1), 197-230.

Joakim Nivre. 2006. *Inductive Dependency Parsing*. Springer.

Joakim Nivre, Johan Hall, Sandra Kübler, Ryan McDonald, Jens Nilsson, Sebastian Riedel and Deniz Yuret. 2007a. The CoNLL 2007 Shared Task on Dependency Parsing. *Proceedings of EMNLP-CoNLL*.

Joakim Nivre, Johan Hall, Jens Nilsson, Atanas Chanev, Gülsen Eryiğit, Sandra Kübler, S. Marinov and Edwin Marsi. 2007b. MaltParser: A language-independent system for data-driven dependency parsing. *Natural Language Engineering*.

Joakim Nivre and Ryan McDonald. 2008. Integrating graph-based and transition-based dependency parsers. *Proceedings* of ACL-2008.

Kenji Sagae and Alon Lavie. 2006. Parser Combination by Reparsing. *Proceedings of the Human Language*

Technology Conference of the North American Chapter of the ACL, pages 129–132, New York.

Mihai Surdeanu and Christopher D. Manning. 2010. Ensemble Models for Dependency Parsing: Cheap and Good? *Proceedings of the Human Language Technology Conference of the North American Chapter of the ACL.*

Pasi Tapanainen and Atro Voutilainen. 1994. Tagging Accurately-Don´t guess if you know. *Proceedings of the Conference on Applied Natural Language Processing*, ANLP´94.

Alexander Yeh. 2000. Using existing systems to supplement small amounts of annotated grammatical relations training data. *Proceedings of ACL* 2000.

Statistical Parsing of Spanish and Data Driven Lemmatization

Joseph Le Roux[†] **Benoît Sagot**[⋆] **Djamé Seddah**[⋆,◇]
[†] Laboratoire d'Informatique Paris Nord, Université Paris Nord, UMR CNRS 7030
[⋆]Alpage, INRIA & Université Paris Diderot
[◇] Université Paris Sorbonne
leroux@univ-paris13.fr, benoit.sagot@inria.fr, djame.seddah@paris-sorbonne.fr

Abstract

Although parsing performances have greatly improved in the last years, grammar inference from treebanks for morphologically rich languages, especially from small treebanks, is still a challenging task. In this paper we investigate how state-of-the-art parsing performances can be achieved on Spanish, a language with a rich verbal morphology, with a non-lexicalized parser trained on a treebank containing only around 2,800 trees. We rely on accurate part-of-speech tagging and data-driven lemmatization to provide parsing models able to cope lexical data sparseness. Providing state-of-the-art results on Spanish, our methodology is applicable to other languages with high level of inflection.

1 Introduction

Grammar inference from treebanks has become the standard way to acquire rules and weights for parsing devices. Although tremendous progress has been achieved in this domain, exploiting small treebanks is still a challenging task, especially for languages with a rich morphology. The main difficulty is to make good generalizations from small example sets exhibiting data sparseness. This difficulty is even greater when the inference process relies on semi-supervised or unsupervised learning techniques which are known to require more training examples, as these examples do not explicitly contain all the information.

In this paper we want to explore how we can cope with this difficulty and get state-of-the-art syntactic analyses with a non-lexicalized parser that uses modern semisupervised inference techniques. We rely on accurate data-driven lemmatization and part-of-speech tagging to reduce data sparseness and ease the burden on the parser. We try to see how we can improve parsing structure predictions solely by modifying the terminals and/or the preterminals of the trees. We keep the rest of the tagset as is.
In order to validate our method, we perform experiments on the Cast3LB constituent treebank for Spanish (Castillan). This corpus is quite small, around 3,500 trees, and Spanish is known to have a rich verbal morphology, making the tag set quite complex and difficult to predict. Cowan and Collins (2005) and Chrupała (2008) already showed interesting results on this corpus that will provide us with a comparison for this work, especially on the lexical aspects as they used lexicalized frameworks while we choose PCFG-LAs.

This paper is structured as follows. In Section 2 we describe the Cast3LB corpus in details. In Section 3 we present our experimental setup and results which we discuss and compare in Section 4. Finally, Section 5 concludes the presentation.

2 Data Set

The Castillan 3LB treebank (Civit and Martì, 2004) contains 3,509 constituent trees with functional annotations. It is divided in training (2,806 trees), development (365 trees) and test (338 trees).

We applied the transformations of Chrupała (2008) to the corpus where CP and SBAR nodes are added to the subordinate and relative clauses but we did not perform any other transformations, like the coordination modification applied by Cowan and Collins (2005).

The Cast3LB tag set is rich. In particular part-of-speech (POS) tags are fine-grained and encode precise morphological information while non-terminal tags describe subcategorization and function labels.

Without taking functions into account, there are 43 non-terminal tags. The total tag set thus comprises 149 symbols which makes the labeling task challenging.

The rich morphology of Spanish can be observed in the treebank through word form variation. Table 1 shows some figures extracted from the corpus (training, development and test). In particular the word form/lemma ratio is 1.54, which is similar to other Romance language treebanks (French FTB and Italian ITB).

# of tokens	94 907
# of unique word forms	17 979
# of unique lemmas	11 642
ratio word form/lemma	1.54

Table 1: C3LB properties

Thus, we are confronted with a small treebank with a rich tagset and a high word diversity. All these conditions make the corpus a case in point for building a parsing architecture for morphologically-rich languages.

3 Experiments

We conducted experiments on the Cast3LB development set in order to test various treebank modifications, that can be divided in two categories: (i) modification of the preterminal symbols of the treebank by using simplified POS tagsets; (ii) modification of the terminal symbols of the treebank by replacing word tokens by lemmas.

3.1 Experimental Setup

In this section we describe the parsing formalism and POS tagging settings used in our experiments.

PCFG-LAs To test our hypothesis, we use the grammatical formalism of Probabilistic Context-Free Grammars with Latent Annotations (PCFG-LAs) (Matsuzaki et al., 2005; Petrov et al., 2006). These grammars depart from the standard PCFGs by automatically refining grammatical symbols during the training phase, using unsupervised techniques. They have been applied successfully to a wide range of languages, among which French (Candito and Seddah, 2010), German (Petrov and Klein, 2008), Chinese and Italian (Lavelli and Corazza, 2009).

For our experiments, we used the LORG PCFG-LA parser implementing the CKY algorithm. This software also implements the techniques from Attia et al. (2010) for handling out-of-vocabulary words, where interesting suffixes for part-of-speech tagging are collected on the training set, ranked according to their information gain with regards to the part-of-speech tagging task. Hence, all the experiments are presented in two settings. In the first one, called *generic*, unknown words are replaced with a dummy token `UNK`, while in the second one, dubbed *IG*, we use the collected suffixes and typographical information to type unknown words.[1] We retained the 30 best suffixes of length 1, 2 and 3.

The grammar was trained using the algorithm of Petrov and Klein (2007) using 3 rounds of split/merge/smooth[2]. For lexical rules, we applied the strategy dubbed *simple lexicon* in the Berkeley parser. Rare words – words occurring less than 3 times in the training set – are replaced by a special token, which depends on the OOV handling method (*generic* or *IG*), before collecting counts.

POS tagging We performed parsing experiments with three different settings regarding POS information provided as an input to the parser: (i) with no POS information, which constitutes our baseline; (ii) with gold POS information, which can be considered as a topline for a given parser setting; (iii) with POS information predicted using the MElt POS-tagger (Denis and Sagot, 2009), using three different tagsets that we describe below.

MElt is a state-of-the-art sequence labeller that is trained on both an annotated corpus and an external lexicon. The standard version of MElt relies on Maximum-Entropy Markov models (MEMMs). However, in this work, we have used a multiclass perceptron instead, as it allows for much faster training with very small performance drops (see Table 2). For training purposes, we used the training section of the Cast3LB (76,931 tokens) and the Le*ff*e lexicon (Molinero et al., 2009), which contains almost 800,000 distinct (form, category) pairs.[3]

We performed experiments using three different

[1]Names *generic* and *IG* originally come from Attia et al. (2010).

[2]We tried to perform 4 and 5 rounds but 3 rounds proved to be optimal on this corpus.

[3]Note that MElt does not use information from the exter-

TAGSET	baseline	reduced2	reduced3
Nb. of tags	106	42	57
Multiclass Perceptron			
Overall Acc.	96.34	97.42	97.25
Unk. words Acc.	91.17	93.35	92.30
Maximum-Entropy Markov model (MEMM)			
Overall Acc.	96.46	97.42	97.25
Unk. words Acc.	91.57	93.76	92.87

Table 2: MElt POS tagging accuracy on the Cast3LB development set for each of the three tagsets. We provide results obtained with the standard MElt algorithm (MEMM) as well as with the multiclass perceptron, used in this paper, for which training is two orders of magnitude faster. Unknown words represent as high as 13.5 % of all words.

tagsets: (i) a *baseline tagset* which is identical to the tagset used by Cowan and Collins (2005) and Chrupała (2008); with this tagset, the training corpus contains 106 distinct tags;
(ii) the *reduced2* tagset, which is a simplification of the baseline tagset: we only retain the first two characters of each tag from the baseline tagset; with this tagset, the training corpus contains 42 distinct tags;
(iii) the *reduced3* tagset, which is a variant of the reduced2 tagset: contrarily to the reduced2 tagset, the reduced3 tagset has retained the mood information for verb forms, as it proved relevant for improving parsing performances as shown by (Cowan and Collins, 2005); with this tagset, the training corpus contains 57 distinct tags.

Melt POS tagging accuracy on the Cast3LB development set for these three tagsets is given in Table 2, with overall figures together with figures computed solely on unknown words (words not attested in the training corpus, i.e., as high as 13.5 % of all tokens).

3.2 Baseline

The first set of experiments was conducted with the baseline POS tagset. Results are summarized in Table 3. This table presents parsing statistics on the Cast3LB development set in the 3 POS settings introduced above (i) no POS provided, (ii) gold POS provided and (iii) predicted POS provided. For each POS tagging setting it shows labeled precision, labeled recall, labeled F1-score, the percentage of exact match and the POS tagging accuracy. The latter needs not be the same as presented in Section 3.1 because (i) punctuation is ignored and (ii) if the parser cannot use the information provided by the tagger, it is discarded and the parser performs POS-tagging on its own.

MODEL	LP	LR	F1	EXACT	POS
Word Only					
Generic	81.42	81.04	**81.23**	**14.47**	**90.89**
IG	80.15	79.60	79.87	14.19	85.01
Gold POS					
Generic	87.83	87.49	**87.66**	**30.59**	99.98
IG	86.78	86.53	86.65	27.96	99.98
Pred. POS					
Generic	84.47	84.39	**84.43**	**22.44**	95.82
IG	83.60	83.66	83.63	21.78	95.82

Table 3: Baseline PARSEVAL scores on Cast3LB dev. set ($\leq$ 40 words)

As already mentioned above, this tagset contains 106 distinct tags. On the one hand it means that POS tags contain useful information. On the other hand it also means that the data is already sparse and adding more sparseness with the IG suffixes and typographical information is detrimental. This is a major difference between this POS tagset and the two following ones.

3.3 Using simplified tagsets

We now turn to the modified tagsets and measure their impact on the quality of the syntactic analyses. Results are summarized in Table 4 for the *reduced2* tagset and in Table 5 for *reduced3*. In these two settings, we can make the following remarks.

- Parsing results are better with *reduced3*, which indicates that verbal mood is an important feature for correctly categorizing verbs at the syntactic level.
- When POS tags are not provided, using suffixes and typographical information improves OOV word categorization and leads to a better tagging accuracy and F1 parsing score (78.94 vs. 81.81 for *reduced2* and 79.69 vs. 82.44 for *reduced3*).

nal lexicon as constraints, but as features. Therefore, the set of categories in the external lexicon need not be identical to the tagset. In this work, the Leffe categories we used include some morphological information (84 distinct categories).

- When providing the parser with POS tags, whether gold or predicted, both settings show an interesting difference w.r.t. to unknown words handling. When using *reduced2*, the IG setting is better than the generic one, whereas the situation is reversed in *reduced3*. This indicates that *reduced2* is too coarse to help finely categorizing unknown words and that the refinement brought by IG is beneficial, however the added sparseness. For *reduced3* it is difficult to say whether it is the added richness of the POS tagset or the induced OOV sparseness that explains why IG is detrimental.

MODEL	LP	LR	F1	EXACT	POS
Word Only					
Generic	78.86	79.02	78.94	15.23	88.18
IG	81.89	81.72	**81.81**	**16.17**	**92.19**
Gold POS					
Generic	86.56	85.90	86.23	26.64	100.00
IG	86.90	86.63	**86.77**	**29.28**	100.00
Pred. POS					
Generic	84.16	83.81	83.99	21.05	96.76
IG	84.57	84.32	**84.45**	**21.38**	96.76

Table 4: PARSEVAL scores on Cast3LB development set with *reduced2* tagset ($\leq$ 40 words)

MODEL	LP	LR	F1	EXACT	POS
Word Only					
Generic	79.61	79.78	79.69	**14.90**	87.29
IG	82.57	82.31	**82.44**	14.24	**91.63**
Gold POS					
Generic	88.08	87.69	**87.89**	**30.59**	100.00
IG	87.56	87.31	87.43	29.61	100.00
Pred. POS					
Generic	85.56	85.38	**85.47**	23.03	96.56
IG	85.32	85.24	85.28	**23.36**	96.56

Table 5: PARSEVAL scores on Cast3LB development set with *reduced3* tagset ($\leq$ 40 words)

3.4 Lemmatization Impact

Being a morphologically rich language, Spanish exhibits a high level of inflection similar to several other Romance languages, for example French and Italian (gender, number, verbal mood). Furthermore, Spanish belongs to the pro-drop family and clitic pronouns are often affixed to the verb and carry functional marks. This makes any small treebank of this language an interesting play field for statistical parsing. In this experiment, we want to use lemmatization as a form of morphological clustering. To cope with the loss of information, we provide the parser with predicted POS. Lemmatization is carried out by the morphological analyzer MORFETTE, (Chrupała et al., 2008) while POS tagging is done by the MElt tagger. Lemmatization performances are on a par with previously reported results on Romance languages (see Table 6)

TAGSET	ALL	SEEN	UNK (13.84%)
baseline	98.39	99.01	94.55
reduced2	98.37	98.88	95.18
reduced3	98.24	98.88	94.23

Table 6: Lemmatization performance on the Cast3LB.

To make the parser less sensitive to lemmatization and tagging errors, we train both tools on a 20 jackknifed setup[4]. Resulting lemmas and POS tags are then reinjected into the train set. The test corpora is itself processed with tools trained on the unmodified treebank. Results are presented Table 7. They show an overall small gain, compared to the previous experiments but provide a clear improvement on the richest tagset, which is the most difficult to parse given its size (106 tags).

First, we remark that POS tagging accuracy with the baseline tagset when no POS is provided is lower than previously observed. This can be easily explained: it is more difficult to predict POS with morphological information when morphological information is withdrawn from input.

Second, and as witnessed before, reduction of the POS tag sparseness using a simplified tagset and increase of the lexical sparseness by handling OOV words using typographical information have adverse effects. This can be observed in the generic Predicted POS section of Table 7 where the *baseline* tagset is the best option. On the other hand, in IG Predicted POS, using the *reduced3* is better than *baseline* and *reduced2*. Again this tagset is a tradeoff between rich information and data sparseness.

[4]The training set is split in 20 chunks and each one is processed with a tool trained on the 19 other chunks. This enables the parser to be less sensitive to lemmatization and/or pos tagging errors.

TAGSET	LR	LP	F1	EX	POS
Word Only – Generic					
baseline	79.70	80.51	**80.1**	15.23	74.04
reduced2	79.19	79.78	79.48	**15.56**	**89.25**
reduced3	79.92	80.03	79.97	13.16	87.67
Word Only – IG					
baseline	80.67	81.32	**80.99**	**15.89**	75.02
reduced2	80.54	81.3	80.92	15.13	**90.93**
reduced3	80.52	80.94	80.73	15.13	88.53
Pred. POS – Generic					
baseline	85.03	85.57	**85.30**	**23.68**	95.68
reduced2	83.98	84.73	84.35	23.36	**96.78**
reduced3	84.93	85.19	85.06	21.05	96.60
Pred. POS – IG					
baseline	84.60	85.06	84.83	23.68	95.68
reduced2	84.29	84.82	84.55	21.71	**96.78**
reduced3	84.86	85.39	**85.12**	**22.70**	96.60

Table 7: Lemmmatization Experiments

In all cases *reduced2* is below the other tagsets wrt. to Parseval F1 although tagging accuracy is better. We can conclude that it is too poor from an informational point of view.

4 Discussion

There is relatively few works actively pursued on statistical constituency parsing for Spanish. The initial work of Cowan and Collins (2005) consisted in a thorough study of the impact of various morphological features on a lexicalized parsing model (the Collins Model 1) and on the performance gain brought by the reranker of Collins and Koo (2005) used in conjunction with the feature set developed for English. Direct comparison is difficult as they used a different test set (approximately, the concatenation of our development and test sets). They report an F-score of 85.1 on sentences of length less than 40.[5]

However, we are directly comparable with Chrupała (2008)[6] who adapted the Collins Model 2 to Spanish. As he was focusing on wide coverage LFG grammar induction, he enriched the non terminal annotation scheme with functional paths rather than trying to obtain the optimal tagset with respect to pure parsing performance. Nevertheless, using the same split and providing gold POS, our system provides better performance (around 2.3 points better, see Table 8).

It is of course not surprising for a PCFG-LA model to outperform a Collins' model based lexicalized parser. However, it is a fact that, on such small treebank configurations, PCFG-LA are crucially lacking annotated data. It is only by greatly reducing the POS tagset and using either a state-of-the-art tagger or a lemmatizer (or both), that we can boost our system performance.
The sensitivity of PCFG-LA models to lexical data sparseness was also shown on French by Seddah et al. (2009). In fact they showed that performance of state-of-the-art lexicalized parsers (Charniak, Collins models, etc.) were crossing that of Berkeley parsers when the training set contains around 2500–3000 sentences. Here, with around 2,800 sentences of training data, we are probably in a setting where both parser types exhibit similar performances, as we suspect French and Spanish to behave in the same way. It is therefore encouraging to notice that our approach, which relies on accurate POS tagging and lemmatization, provides state-of-the-art performance. Let us add that a similar method, involving only MORFETTE, was applied with success to Italian within a PCFG-LA framework and French with a lexicalized parser, both leading to promising results (Seddah et al., 2011; Seddah et al., 2010).

5 Conclusion

We presented several experiments reporting the impact of lexical sparseness reduction on non lexicalized statistical parsing. We showed that, by using state-of-the-art lemmatization and POS tagging on a reduced tagset, parsing performance can be on a par with lexicalized models that manage to extract more information from a small corpus exhibiting a rich lexical diversity. It remains to be seen whether applying the same kind of simplifications to the rest of the tagset, i.e. on the internal nodes, can further improve parse structure quality. Finally, the methods we presented in this paper are not language specific and can be applied to other languages if similar resources exist.

[5]See `http://pauillac.inria.fr/~seddah/spmrl-spanish.html` for details on comparison with that work.

[6]We need to remove CP and SBAR nodes to be fairly comparable.

TAGSET	MODE	TOKENS	ALL	≤ 70	≤ 40
reduced3	Gen.	pred. POS	83.92	84.27	85.08
	eval. w/o CP/SBAR		*84.02*	*84.37*	*85.24*
baseline	IG	pred. lemma & POS	84.15	84.40	85.26
	eval. w/o CP/SBAR		*84.34*	*84.60*	*85.45*
reduced3	Gen.	gold POS	86.21	86.63	87.84
	eval. w/o CP/SBAR		*86.35*	*86.77*	*88.01*
baseline		gold POS	83.96	84.58	–
	(Chrupała, 2008)				

Table 8: PARSEVAL F-score results on the Cast3LB test set

Acknowledgments

Thanks to Grzegorz Chrupała and Brooke Cowan for answering our questions and making data available to us. This work is partly funded by the French Research Agency (EDyLex, ANR-09-COORD-008).

References

Mohammed Attia, Jennifer Foster, Deirdre Hogan, Joseph Le Roux, Lamia Tounsi, and Josef van Genabith. 2010. Handling unknown words in statistical latent-variable parsing models for arabic, english and french. In *Proceedings of the NAACL/HLT Workshop on Statistical Parsing of Morphologically Rich Languages (SPMRL 2010)*, Los Angeles, CA.

Marie Candito and Djamé Seddah. 2010. Parsing word clusters. In *Proceedings of the NAACL/HLT Workshop on Statistical Parsing of Morphologically Rich Languages (SPMRL 2010)*, Los Angeles, CA.

Grzegorz Chrupała, Georgiana Dinu, and Josef van Genabith. 2008. Learning morphology with morfette. In *In Proceedings of LREC 2008*, Marrakech, Morocco. ELDA/ELRA.

Grzegorz Chrupała. 2008. *Towards a machine-learning architecture for lexical functional grammar parsing*. Ph.D. thesis, Dublin City University.

M. Civit and M. A. Martì. 2004. Building cast3lb: A spanish treebank. *Research on Language and Computation*, 2(4):549 – 574.

Michael Collins and Terry Koo. 2005. Discriminative reranking for natural language parsing. *Computational Linguistics*, 31(1):25–69.

B. Cowan and M. Collins. 2005. Morphology and reranking for the statistical parsing of spanish. In *Proceedings of the conference on Human Language Technology and Empirical Methods in Natural Language Processing*, pages 795–802. Association for Computational Linguistics.

Pascal Denis and Benoît Sagot. 2009. Coupling an annotated corpus and a morphosyntactic lexicon for state-of-the-art pos tagging with less human effort. In *Proceedings of PACLIC 2009*, Hong-Kong, China.

Alberto Lavelli and Anna Corazza. 2009. The berkeley parser at the evalita 2009 constituency parsing task. In *EVALITA 2009 Workshop on Evaluation of NLP Tools for Italian*.

Takuya Matsuzaki, Yusuke Miyao, and Jun'ichi Tsujii. 2005. Probabilistic cfg with latent annotations. In *Proceedings of the 43rd Annual Meeting of the Association for Computational Linguistics (ACL)*, pages 75–82.

Miguel A. Molinero, Benoît Sagot, and Lionel Nicolas. 2009. A morphological and syntactic wide-coverage lexicon for spanish: The leffe. In *Proceedings of the International Conference RANLP-2009*, pages 264–269, Borovets, Bulgaria, September. Association for Computational Linguistics.

Slav Petrov and Dan Klein. 2007. Improved inference for unlexicalized parsing. In *Human Language Technologies 2007: The Conference of the North American Chapter of the Association for Computational Linguistics; Proceedings of the Main Conference*, pages 404–411, Rochester, New York, April. Association for Computational Linguistics.

Slav Petrov and Dan Klein. 2008. Parsing german with latent variable grammars. In *Proceedings of the ACL Workshop on Parsing German*.

Slav Petrov, Leon Barrett, Romain Thibaux, and Dan Klein. 2006. Learning accurate, compact, and interpretable tree annotation. In *Proceedings of the 21st International Conference on Computational Linguistics and 44th Annual Meeting of the Association for Computational Linguistics*, Sydney, Australia, July. Association for Computational Linguistics.

Djamé Seddah, Marie Candito, and Benoit Crabbé. 2009. Cross parser evaluation and tagset variation: A French Treebank study. In *Proceedings of the 11th International Conference on Parsing Technologies (IWPT'09)*, pages 150–161, Paris, France, October. Association for Computational Linguistics.

Djamé Seddah, Grzegorz Chrupała, Ozlem Cetinoglu, Josef van Genabith, and Marie Candito. 2010.

Lemmatization and statistical lexicalized parsing of morphologically-rich languages. In *Proceedings of the NAACL/HLT Workshop on Statistical Parsing of Morphologically Rich Languages (SPMRL 2010)*, Los Angeles, CA.

Djamé Seddah, Joseph Le Roux, and Benoît Sagot. 2011. Towards using data driven lemmatization for statistical constituent parsing of italian. In *Working Notes of EVALITA 2011*, Rome, Italy, December.

Assigning Deep Lexical Types Using Structured Classifier Features for Grammatical Dependencies

João Silva
University of Lisbon
Dept. Informatics, Faculty of Sciences
Campo Grande, Lisboa, Portugal
jsilva@di.fc.ul.pt

António Branco
University of Lisbon
Dept. Informatics, Faculty of Sciences
Campo Grande, Lisboa, Portugal
antonio.branco@di.fc.ul.pt

Abstract

Deep linguistic grammars are able to provide rich and highly complex grammatical representations of sentences, capturing, for instance, long-distance dependencies and returning a semantic representation. These grammars lack robustness in the sense that they do not gracefully handle words missing from their lexicon. Several approaches have been explored to handle this problem, many of which consist in pre-annotating the input to the grammar with shallow processing machine-learning tools. Most of these tools, however, use features based on a fixed window of context, such as n-grams. We investigate whether the use of features that encode discrete structures, namely grammatical dependencies, can improve the performance of a machine learning classifier that assigns deep lexical types. In this paper we report on the design and evaluation of this classifier.

1 Introduction

Parsing is one of the fundamental tasks in Natural Language Processing and a critical step in many applications. Many of the most commonly used parsers rely on probabilistic approaches. These parsers are obtained through data-driven approaches, by inferring a probabilistic language model over a dataset of annotated sentences. Though these parsers always produce some analysis of their input sentences, they do not go into deep linguistic analysis.

Deep grammars, also referred to as precision grammars, seek to make explicit information about highly detailed linguistic phenomena and produce complex grammatical representations for their input sentences. For instance, they are able to capture long-distance dependencies and produce the semantic representation of a sentence. Although there is a great variety of parsing methods (see (Mitkov, 2004) for an overview), all CKY-based algorithms require a lexical look-up initialization step that, for each word in the input, returns all its possible categories.

From this it follows that if any of the words in a sentence is not present in the lexicon—an *out-of-vocabulary* (OOV) word—a full parse of that sentence is impossible to obtain. Given that novelty is one of the defining characteristics of natural languages, unknown words will eventually occur. Hence, being able to handle OOV words is of paramount importance if one wishes to use a grammar to analyze unrestricted texts.

Another important issue is that of lexical ambiguity. That is, words that may bear more than one lexical category. The combinatorial explosion of lexical and syntactic ambiguity may hinder parsing due to increased requirements in terms of parsing time and memory usage. Thus, even if there were no OOV words in the input, being able to assign syntactic categories to words prior to parsing may be desirable for efficiency reasons.

For the shallower parsing approaches, such as plain constituency parsing, it suffices to determine the part-of-speech of words, so pre-processing the input with a POS tagger is a common and effective way to tackle either of these problems. However, the linguistic information contained in the lexicon of a deep grammar is much more fine-grained, including, in particular, the subcategorization frame (SCF) of the word, which further constraints what can be taken as a well-formed sentence by imposing several restrictions on co-occurring expressions.

Thus, what for a plain POS tagger corresponds to a single category is often expanded into hundreds of different distinctions, and hence tags, when at the level of detail required by a deep grammar. For instance, the particular grammar we will be using for the study reported in this paper—a grammar following the HPSG framework—has in its current version a lexicon with roughly 160 types for verbs and nearly 200 types for common nouns.

While the deep grammar may proceed with the analysis knowing only the base POS category of a word, it does so at the cost of vastly increased ambiguity[1] which may even allow the grammar to accept ungrammatical sentences as valid. This has lead to research that specifically targets annotating words with a tagset suitable for deep grammars.

Current approaches tend to use shallow features with limited context (e.g. n-grams). However, given that the SCF is one of the most relevant pieces of information that is associated with a word in the lexicon of a deep grammar, one would expect that features describing the inter-word dependencies in a sentence would be highly discriminative and help to accurately assign lexical types. Accordingly, in this paper we investigate the use of structured features that encode grammatical dependencies in a machine-learning classifier and how it compares with state-of-the-art approaches.

Our study targets Portuguese, a Romance language with a rich morphology, in particular in what concerns verb inflection (see for instance, (Mateus et al., 2003) for a detailed account of Portuguese grammar and (Branco et al., 2008) for an assessment of the issues raised by verbal ambiguity).

Paper outline: Section 2 provides an overview of related work, with a focus on supertagging, and introduces tree kernels as a way of handling structured classifier features. Section 3 introduces the particular deep grammar that is used in this work and how it supports the creation of the corpus that provides the data for training and evaluation of the classifier. The classifier itself, and the features it uses, are described in Section 4. Section 5 covers empirical evaluation and comparison with other approaches. Finally, Section 6 concludes with some final remarks.

[1]For instance, a common noun POS tag could be taken as being any of the nearly 200 common noun types existing in the lexicon of the grammar we use in this paper.

2 Background and Related Work

The construction of a hand-crafted lexicon for a deep grammar is a time-consuming task requiring trained linguists. More importantly, such lexica are invariably incomplete since they often do not cover specialized domains and are slow to incorporate new words.

Accordingly, much research in this area has been focused on automatic lexical acquisition (Brent, 1991; Briscoe and Carroll, 1997; Baldwin, 2005). That is, approaches that try to discover all the lexical types a given unknown word may occur with, thus effectively creating a new lexical entry. However, at run-time, it is still up to the grammar using the newly acquired lexical entry to choose which of those lexical types is the correct one for each particular occurrence of that word; and, ultimately, one can only acquire the lexicon entries for those words that are present in the corpus. Thus, any system that is constantly exposed to new text—e.g. parsing text from the Web—will eventually come across some unknown word that has not yet been acquired. Moreover, such words must be dealt with on-the-fly, since it is unlikely that the system can afford to wait until it has accumulated enough occurrences of the unknown word to be able to apply offline lexicon acquisition methods.

In the work reported in the present paper we use a different approach, closer to what is known as supertagging, where we assign on-the-fly a single lexical type to a word.

2.1 Supertagging

POS tagging is a task that relies only on local information (e.g. the word and a small window of context) to achieve a form of syntactic disambiguation. As such, POS tags are commonly assigned prior to parsing as a way of reducing parsing ambiguity by restricting words to a certain syntactic category. Less ambiguity leads to a greatly reduced search space and, as a consequence, faster parsing.

Supertagging, first introduced by Bangalore and Joshi (1994), can be seen as a natural extension of this idea to a richer tagset, in particular to one that includes information on subcategorization frames.

In (Bangalore and Joshi, 1994) supertagging was applied to the Lexicalized Tree Adjoining Grammar (LTAG) formalism. As the name indicates, this is a lexicalized grammar, like HPSG, but in LTAG each lexical item is associated with one or more trees, the elementary structures, which localize information on dependencies, even long-range ones, by requiring that all and only the dependents be present in the structure.

The supertagger in (Bangalore and Joshi, 1994) assigns an elementary structure to each word using a simple trigram model. The data for training was obtained by taking the sentences of length under 15 words in the Wall Street Journal together with some other minor corpora, and parsing them with XTAG, a wide-coverage grammar for English based on LTAG. In addition, and due to data-sparseness, POS tags were used in training instead of words.

Evaluation was performed over 100 held-out sentences from the Wall Street Journal. For a tagset of 365 elementary trees, this supertagger achieved 68% accuracy, which is far too low to be useful for parsing.

In a later experiment, the authors improved the supertagger by smoothing model parameters and adding additional training data (Bangalore and Joshi, 1999). The larger dataset was obtained by extending the corpus from the previous experiment with Penn Treebank parses that were automatically converted to LTAG. The conversion process relied on several heuristics, and though it is not perfect, the authors found that the issues concerning conversion were far outweighed by the benefit of increased training data.

The improved supertagger increased accuracy to 92% (Bangalore and Joshi, 1999). The supertagger can also assign the n-best tags, which increases the chances of it assigning the correct supertag at the cost of leaving more unresolved ambiguity. With 3-best tagging, it achieved 97% accuracy.

A supertagger was also used by Clark and Curran (2007), in their case for a Combinatory Categorial Grammar (CCG). This formalism uses a set of logical combinators to manipulate linguistic construction tough, for our purposes here, it matters only that lexical items receive complex tags that describe the constituents they require to create a well-formed construction.

The set of 409 lexical categories to be assigned was selected by taking those categories that occur at least 10 times in sections 02–21 of a CCG automatic annotation of Penn Treebank (CCGBank).

Evaluation was performed over section 00 of CCGBank, and achieved 92% per word accuracy.

As with the LTAG supertagger, assigning more than one tag can greatly increase accuracy. However, instead of a fixed n-best number of tags—which might be to low, or too high, depending on the case at hand—the CCG supertagger assigns all tags with a likelihood within a factor β of the best tag. A value for β as small as 0.1, which results in an average of 1.4 tags per word, is enough to boost accuracy up to 97%.

Supertagging for HPSG: There has been some work on using supertagging together with the HPSG framework. As with other works on supertagging, it is mostly concerned with restricting the parser search space in order to increase parsing efficiency, and not specifically with the handling of OOV words.

Prins and van Noord (2003) present an HMM-based supertagger for the Dutch Alpino grammar. An interesting feature of their approach is that the supertagger is trained over the output of the parser itself, thus avoiding the need for a hand-annotated dataset.

The supertagger was trained over 2 million sentences of newspaper text parsed by Alpino. A gold standard was created by having Alpino choose the best parse for a set of 600 sentences. The supertagger, when assigning a single tag (from a tagset with 2,392 tags), achieves a token accuracy close to 95%.

It is not clear to what extent these results can be affected by some sort of bias in the disambiguation module of Alpino, given that both the sequence of lexical types in the training dataset and in the gold standard are taken from the best parse produced by Alpino.

Matsuzaki et al. (2007) use a supertagger with the Enju grammar for English. The novelty in their work comes from the use of a context-free grammar (CFG) to filter the tag sequences produced by the supertagger before running the HPSG parser. In this approach, a CFG approximation of the HPSG is created. The key property of this approximation is that the language it recognizes is a superset of the parsable supertag sequences. Hence, if the CFG is unable to parse a sequence, it can be safely discarded, thus further reducing the amount of sequences the HPSG parser has to deal with.

The provided evaluation is mostly concerned with showing the improvement in parsing speed. Nevertheless, the quality of the supertagging process can be inferred from the accuracy of the parse results, which achieved a labeled precision and recall for predicate-argument relations of 90% and 86%, respectively, over 2,300 sentences with up to 100 words in section 23 of the Penn Treebank.

Dridan (2009) tests two supertaggers, one induced using the TnT tagger (Brants, 2000) and another using the C&C supertagger (Clark and Curran, 2007), over different datasets. For simplicity, we will only refer to the results of TnT over a dataset of 814 sentences of tourism data.

The author experiments with various tag granularities in order to find a balance between tag expressiveness and tag predictability. For instance, assigning only POS—a tagset with only 13 tags—is the easiest task, with 97% accuracy, while a highly granular supertag formed by the lexical type concatenated with any selectional restriction present in the lexical entry increases the number of possible tags to 803, with accuracy dropping to 91%.

2.2 Support-Vector Machines and Tree Kernels

Support-vector machines (SVM) are a well known supervised machine-learning algorithm for linear binary classification. They are part of the family of kernel-based methods where a general purpose learning algorithm is coupled with a problem-specific kernel function (Cristianini and Shawe-Taylor, 2000).

For the work presented in this paper we wish to apply the learning algorithm over discrete tree-like structures that encode grammatical dependencies (see Figure 1 for an example). A suitable kernel for such a task is the tree kernel introduced by Collins and Duffy (2002), which uses a representation that implicitly tracks all subtrees seen in the training data.

This representation starts by implicitly enumerating all subtrees that are found in the training data. A given tree, T, is then represented by a (huge) vector where the n-th position counts the number of occurrences of the n-th subtree in T.

Under this representation, the inner product of two trees gives a measure of their similarity. However, explicitly calculating such an operation is prohibitively expensive due to the high dimensions of the feature space. Fortunately, the inner product can be replaced by a rather simple kernel function that sums over the subtrees that are common to both trees (see (Collins and Duffy, 2002) for a proof).

3 Grammar and Base Dataset

The deep linguistic grammar used in this study is LXGram, a hand-built HPSG grammar for Portuguese (Branco and Costa, 2008; Branco and Costa, 2010).

We used this grammar to support the annotation of a corpus. That is, the grammar is used to provide the set of possible analyses for a sentence (the parse forest). Human annotators then perform manual disambiguation by picking the correct analysis from among all those that form the parse forest.[2] This grammar-supported approach to corpus annotation ensures that the various linguistic annotation layers—morphological, syntactic and semantic—are consistent.

The corpus that was used is composed mostly by a subset of the sentences in CETEMPúblico, a corpus of plain text excerpts from the Público newspaper.

After running LXGram and manually disambiguating the parse forests, we were left with a dataset consisting of 5,422 sentences annotated with all the linguistic information provided by LXGram.

4 Classifier and Feature Extraction

For training and classification we use SVM-light-TK (Moschitti, 2006), an extension to the widely-used SVM-light (Joachims, 1999) software for SVMs that adds a function implementing the tree kernel introduced in Section 2.2. With SVM-light-TK one can

[2] In our setup, two annotators work in a double-blind scheme, where those cases where they disagree are adjudicated by a third annotator. Inter-annotator agreement is 0.86.

directly provide one or more tree structures as features (using the standard parenthesis representation of trees) together with the numeric feature vectors that are already accepted by SVM-light.

Given that the task at stake is a multi-class classification problem but an SVM is a binary classifier, the problem must first be binarized (Galar et al., 2011). For this work we have chosen a one-vs-one binarization scheme, where multiple classifiers are created, each responsible for discriminating between a pair of classes. This divides a problem with n classes into $n(n-1)/2$ separate binary problems (i.e. one classifier for each possible class pairing). Each classifier then performs a binary decision, voting for one of the two classes it is tasked with discriminating, and the class with the overall largest number of votes is chosen.

The dataset, having been produced with the help of a deep grammar, contains a great deal of linguistic information. The first step is thus to extract from each sentence the relevant features in a format that can be used by SVM-light-TK.

Since we are aiming at discriminating between deep lexical types, which, among other information, encode the SCF of a word, the dependency structure associated with a word is expected to be a piece of highly relevant information. We start by extracting the dependency representation of a sentence from the output of LXGram.[3] The dependency representation that is obtained through this process consists of a list of tuples, each relating a pair of words in the sentence through a grammatical relation.

The example in Figure 1 shows the dependency representation of the sentence "a o segundo dia de viagem encontrámos os primeiros golfinhos" (Eng.: by the second day of travel we found the first dolphins).[4] Note that each word is also annotated with its lexical type, POS tag and lemma, though this is not shown in the example for the sake of readability.

For a one-vs-one classifier tasked with discriminating between types A and B we are concerned with finding instances of type A to be taken as positive examples and instances of type B to be taken as negative examples.

Take, for instance, the word "encontrámos" from the example in Figure 1. Its lexical type in this particular occurrence is verb-dir_trans-lex, the type assigned to transitive verbs by LXGram. A one-vs-one classifier tasked with recognizing this type (against some other type) will take this instance as a positive example.

However, the full dependency representation of the sentence has too many irrelevant features for learning how to classify this word. Instead, we focus more closely on the information that is relevant to determining the SCF of the word by looking only at its immediate neighbors in the dependency graph: its dependents and the word it depends on.

This information is encoded in two trees, shown in Figure 2, which are the actual features given to SVM-light-TK.

One tree, labeled with H as root, is used to represent the word and its dependents. The target word is marked by being under an asterisk "category" while the dependents fall under a "category" corresponding to the relation between the target word and the dependent. The words appears as the leafs of the tree, with their POS tags as the pre-terminal nodes.[5]

The second feature tree, labeled with D as root, encodes the target word—again marked with an asterisk—and the word it is dependent on. In the example shown in Figure 2, since the target word is the main verb of the sentence, the feature tree has no other nodes apart from that of the target word.

5 Evaluation

The following evaluation results were obtained following a standard 10-fold cross-validation approach, where the folds were taken from a random shuffle of the sentences in the corpus.

We compare the performance of our tree kernel (TK) approach with two other automatic annotators, TnT (Brants, 2000) and SVMTool (Giménez and Màrquez, 2004).

TnT is a statistical POS tagger, well known for its efficiency—in terms of training and tagging speed—and for achieving state-of-the-art results despite having a quite simple underlying

[3]The details of this process are outside the scope of the current paper and will be reported elsewhere.

[4]Relations in the example: ADV (adverb), C (complement), DO (direct object), PRED (predicate), SP (specifier) and TMP (temporal modifier).

[5]POS tags in the example: V (verb), PREP (preposition) and CN (common noun).

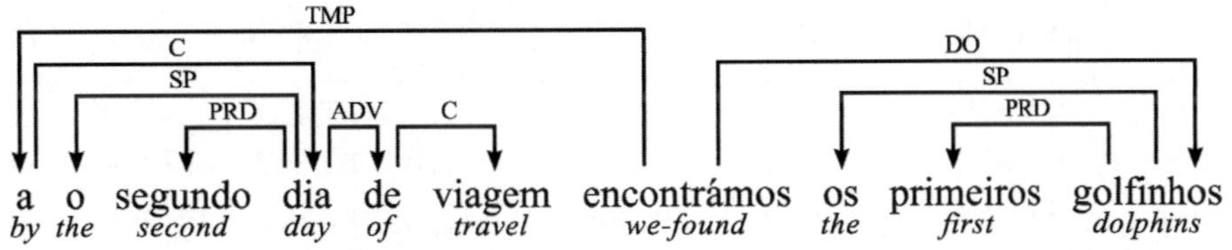

C(de, viagem)	SP(dia, o)	C(a, dia)
ADV(dia, de)	PRD(golfinhos, primeiros)	TMP(encontrámos, a)
PRD(dia, segundo)	SP(golfinhos, os)	DO(encontrámos, golfinhos)

Figure 1: Dependency representation

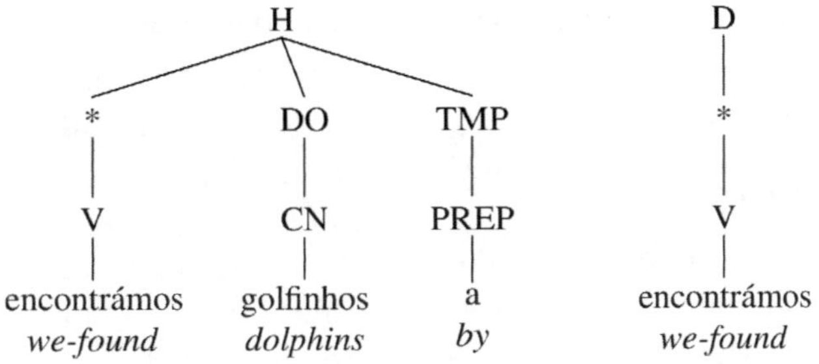

Figure 2: Features for SVM-light-TK

model. It is based on a second-order hidden Markov model extended with linear smoothing of parameters to address data-sparseness issues and suffix analysis for handling unknown words. TnT was used as a supertagger in (Dridan, 2009), where it achieved the best results for this task, and is thus a good representative for this approach to supertagging. We run it out-of-the-box using the default settings.

SVMTool is another statistical sequential tagger which, as the name indicates, is based on support-vector machines. It is extremely flexible in allowing to define which features should be used in the model (e.g. size of word window, number of POS bigrams, etc.) and the tagging strategy (left to right, bidirectional, number of passes, etc). In fact, due to this flexibility, it is described as being a tagger generator. It beat TnT in a POS tagging task (Giménez and Màrquez, 2004), so we use it in the current paper to evaluate whether that lead is kept in a supertagging task. We used the simplest settings, "M0 LR", which uses Model 0 in a left to right tagging direction.[6]

[6]See (Giménez and Màrquez, 2006) for an explanation of these settings.

The type distribution in the dataset is highly skewed. For instance, from the number of common noun types that occur in this corpus, the two most frequent ones are enough to account for 57% of all the common noun tokens. Such skewed category distributions are usually a problematic issue for machine-learning approaches since the number of instances of the more rare categories is too small to properly estimate the parameters of the model.

For many types there are not enough instances in the dataset to train a classifier. Hence, the evaluation that follows is done only for the most frequent types. For instance, top-10 means picking the 10 most frequent types in the corpus, training one-vs-one classifiers for those types, and evaluating only over tokens with one of those types. In addition, we show only the evaluation results of verb types, for which SCF information is more varied and relevant.

Table 1 show the accuracy results for each tool over the top-10, top-20 and top-30 most frequent verb types.

Comparing both sequential supertaggers, one finds that SVMTool is consistently better than TnT, which is in accordance with the results for POS tagging reported in (Giménez and Màrquez, 2004).

Our TK approach beats both supertaggers when

	TnT	SVMTool	TK
top-10	92.98%	94.22%	94.71%
top-20	91.53%	92.39%	90.21%
top-30	91.42%	92.38%	88.70%

Table 1: Accuracy over frequent verb types

dataset	sentences	tokens	unique	oov
base	5,422	51,483	8,815	10.0%
+ Público	10,727	139,330	18,899	7.6%
+ Wiki	15,108	205,585	24,063	6.6%
+ Folha	21,217	288,875	30,204	6.0%

Table 2: Cumulative size of datasets

looking at the top-10 verb types, but falls behind as soon as the number of types under consideration increases. This seems to point towards data-sparseness issues, an hypothesis we test by automatically extending the dataset, as discussed next.

5.1 Experiments with an Extended Dataset

The extended datasets were created by taking additional sentences from the Público newspaper, as well as sentences from the Portuguese Wikipedia and from the Folha de São Paulo newspaper, preprocessing them with a POS tagger, and running them through LXGram.

Such an approach is only made possible because LXGram, like many other modern HPSG grammars, includes a stochastic disambiguation module that automatically chooses the most likely analysis among all those returned in the parse forest, instead of requiring a manual choice by a human annotator (Branco and Costa, 2010). The authors do not provide a complete evaluation of this disambiguation module. Instead, they perform a manual evaluation of a sample of 50 sentences that indicates that this module picks the correct reading in 40% of the cases.

If this ratio is kept, 60% of the sentences in the extended datasets will have an analysis that is, in some way, the wrong analysis, though it is not clear how this translates into errors in the lexical types that end up being assigned to the tokens. For instance, when faced with the rather common case of PP-attachment ambiguity, the disambiguation module may choose the wrong attachment, which will count as being a wrong analysis though most lexical types assigned to the words in the sentence may be correct.

To evaluate this, we tested the disambiguation module over the base dataset, where we know what the correct parses are, and found that the grammar picks the correct parse in 44% of the cases. If we just look at whether the lexical types are correct, the grammar picks a sentence with fully correct types in 68% of the cases.

LXGram displayed a coverage of roughly 30%, and allowed us to build progressively larger datasets as more data was added. The cumulative sizes of the resulting datasets are shown in Table 2. The Table also shows the ratio of OOV words, which was determined by taking the average of the ratio for each of the 10 folds (i.e. words that occur in a fold but not in any of the other 9 folds).

We can now evaluate the tools over the four progressively larger datasets and plot their learning curves. In the following Figures, the errors bars represent a 95% confidence interval.

All learning curves in the following Figures tell a somewhat similar story.

The lead that SVMTool has over TnT when looking only at the base corpus is kept in the extended corpora. Both sequential supertaggers only start to benefit from the increased dataset at the final stage, when sentences from Folha de São Paulo are added. Before that stage the added data seems to be slightly detrimental to them, possibly due to them being sensitive to noise in the automatically generated data.

The learning curves give credence to the hypothesis put forward earlier that our TK approach was being adversely affected by data-sparseness issues when classifying a greater number of verb types, and that it has much to gain by an increase in the amount of training data.

For the top-10 verb types, for which there is enough data in the base dataset, TK starts ahead from the outset and significantly increases its margin over the two supertaggers.

For the top-20 and top-30 verb types, TK starts behind but its accuracy raises quickly as more data are added, ending slightly ahead of SVMTool when running over the largest dataset.

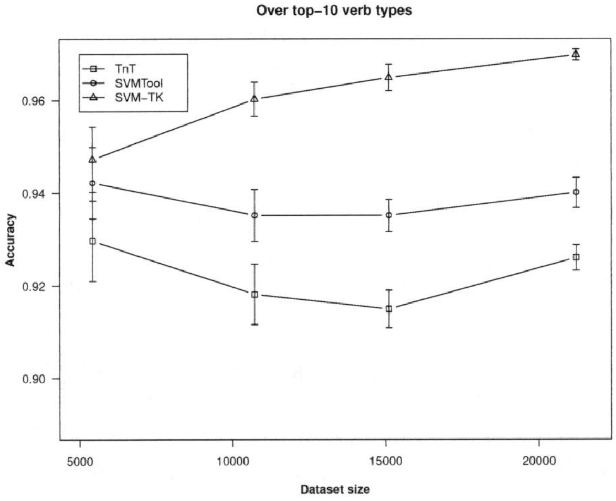

Figure 3: Learning curves (over top-10 verb types)

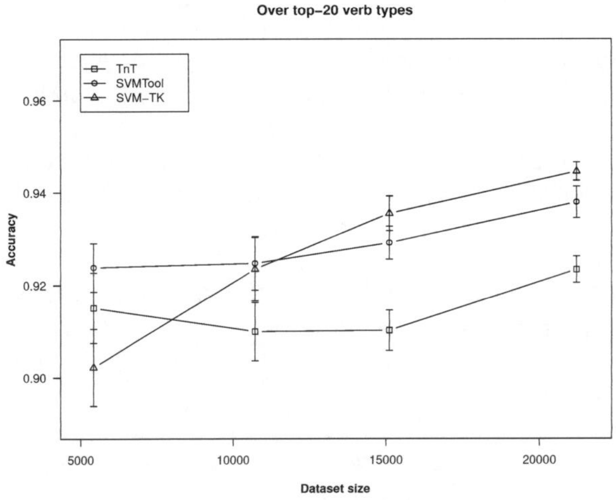

Figure 4: Learning curves (over top-20 verb types)

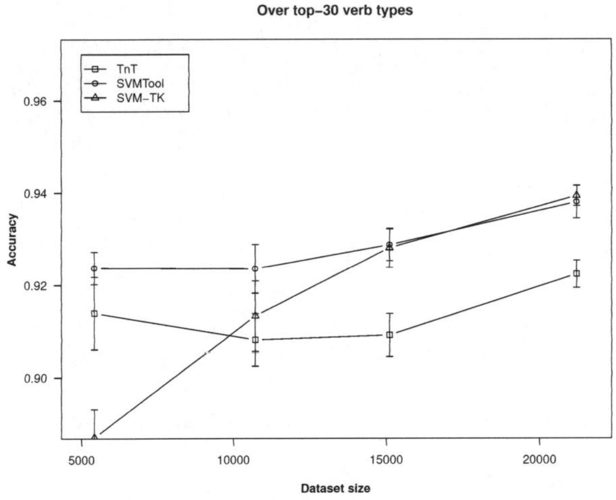

Figure 5: Learning curves (over top-30 verb types)

dataset	accuracy
base	87.24%
+ Público	82.67%
+ Wiki	82.30%
+ Folha	83.92%

Table 3: MaltParser labeled accuracy

5.2 Running over Predicted Dependencies

In the previous section, we were concerned with evaluating the classifier itself. Accordingly, the features used by the classifier were the gold dependencies in the corpus. However, on a running system, the features used by the classifier will be automatically generated by a dependency parser. To evaluate this setup, we used MaltParser (Nivre et al., 2007).

Like the other tools, the parser was run out-of-the-box. The 10-fold average labeled accuracy scores for each dataset shown in Table 3 can thus be seen as a lower bound on the achievable accuracy. Despite this, the performance over the base dataset is extremely good, on par with the best scores achieved for other languages (cf. (Nivre et al., 2007)). However, performance drops sharply when automatically annotated data is used, only beginning to pick up again when running over the largest dataset.

As expected, the noisy features that result from the automatic process have a detrimental effect on the accuracy of the classifier. For the same set of experiments reported previously, the accuracy of the SVM-TK classifier when running over predicted dependencies tends to trail 2.0–2.5% points behind that of the classifier that uses gold dependencies, as shown in Table 4.

6 Concluding Remarks

In this paper we reported on an novel approach to assigning deep lexical types. It uses an SVM classifier with a tree kernel that allows it to seamlessly work with features encoding discrete structures representing the grammatical dependencies between words.

Evaluation over the top-10 most frequent verb types showed that the grammatical dependencies of a word, which can be seen as information on its SCF, are very helpful in allowing the classifier to accurately assign lexical types. Our classifier clearly im-

dataset	top-10 gold	top-10 pred.	top-20 gold	top-20 pred.	top-30 gold	top-30 pred.
base	94.71%	93.14%	90.21%	88.66%	88.70%	87.01%
+ Público	96.02%	93.83%	92.34%	90.35%	91.32%	88.97%
+ Wiki	96.48%	93.95%	93.54%	91.29%	92.80%	90.21%
+ Folha	96.98%	94.55%	94.46%	92.26%	93.93%	91.50%

Table 4: SVM-TK classifier accuracy over gold and predicted features

proves over TnT, which had displayed the best supertagging performance in other studies.

When running the classifier for a greater number of verb types, data-sparseness issues led to a drop in performance, which motivated additional experiments where the dataset was extended with automatically annotated data. This allowed us to plot learning curves that show that our approach can maintain a lead in accuracy when given more training data.

Running the classifier over predicted features shows an expected drop in performance. However, we anticipate that using larger corpora will also be effective in raising these scores since additional training data not only improve the classifier, but also the underlying parser that provides the dependencies that are used as features.

References

Timothy Baldwin. 2005. Bootstrapping deep lexical resources: Resources for courses. In Timothy Baldwin, Anna Korhonen, and Aline Villavicencio, editors, *Proceedings of the ACL-SIGLEX Workshop on Deep Lexical Acquisition*, pages 67–76.

Srinivas Bangalore and Aravind Joshi. 1994. Disambiguation of super parts of speech (or supertags): Almost parsing. In *Proceedings of the 15th Conference on Computational Linguistics (COLING)*, pages 154–160.

Srinivas Bangalore and Aravind Joshi. 1999. Supertagging: An approach to almost parsing. *Computational Linguistics*, 25(2):237–265.

António Branco and Francisco Costa. 2008. A computational grammar for deep linguistic processing of Portuguese: LX-Gram, version A.4.1. Technical Report DI-FCUL-TR-08-17, University of Lisbon.

António Branco and Francisco Costa. 2010. A deep linguistic processing grammar for Portuguese. In *Proceedings of the 9th Encontro para o Processamento Computacional da Língua Portuguesa Escrita e Falada (PROPOR)*, LNAI, pages 86–89. Springer.

António Branco, Francisco Costa, and Filipe Nunes. 2008. The processing of verbal inflection ambiguity: Characterization of the problem space. In *Proceedings of the 21st Encontro Anual da Associação Portuguesa de Linguística (APL)*, pages 2577–2583.

Thorsten Brants. 2000. TnT — a statistical part-of-speech tagger. In *Proceedings of the 6th Applied Natural Language Processing Conference and the 1st North American Chapter of the Association for Computational Linguistics*, pages 224–231.

Michael Brent. 1991. Automatic acquisition of subcategorization frames from untagged text. In *Proceedings of the 29th Annual Meeting of the Association for Computational Linguistics*, pages 209–214.

Ted Briscoe and John Carroll. 1997. Automatic extraction of subcategorization from corpora. In *Proceedings of the 5th Applied Natural Language Processing Conference*, pages 356–363.

Stephen Clark and James Curran. 2007. Wide-coverage efficient statistical parsing with CCG and log-linear models. *Computational Linguistics*, 33:493–552.

Michael Collins and Nigel Duffy. 2002. New ranking algorithms for parsing and tagging: Kernels over discrete structures, and the voted perceptron. In *Proceedings of the 40th Annual Meeting of the Association for Computational Linguistics*, pages 263–270.

Nello Cristianini and John Shawe-Taylor. 2000. *An Introduction to Support Vector Machines and Other Kernel-Based Learning Methods*. Cambridge University Press.

Rebecca Dridan. 2009. *Using Lexical Statistics to Improve HPSG Parsing*. Ph.D. thesis, University of Saarland.

Mikel Galar, Alberto Fernandéz, Edurne Barrenechea, Humberto Bustince, and Francisco Herrera. 2011. An overview of ensemble methods for binary classifiers in multi-class problems: Experimental study in one-vs-one and one-vs-all schemes. *Pattern Recognition*, 44:1761–1776.

Jesús Giménez and Lluís Màrquez. 2004. SVMTool: A general POS tagger generator based on support vector machines. In *Proceedings of the 4th Language Resources and Evaluation Conference (LREC)*.

Jesús Giménez and Lluís Màrquez, 2006. *SVMTool: Technical Manual v1.3*. TALP Research Center, LSI Department, Universitat Politecnica de Catalunya.

Thorsten Joachims. 1999. Making large-scale SVM learning practical. In B. Schölkopf, C. Burges, and A. Smola, editors, *Advances in Kernel Methods — Support Vector Learning*, chapter 11, pages 169–184. MIT Press, Cambridge, MA.

Maria Helena Mira Mateus, Ana Maria Brito, Inês Duarte, Isabel Hub Faria, Sónia Frota, Gabriela Matos, Fátima Oliveira, Marina Vigário, and Alina Villalva. 2003. *Gramática da Língua Portuguesa*. Caminho, 5th edition.

Takuya Matsuzaki, Yusuke Miyao, and Jun'ichi Tsujii. 2007. Efficient HPSG parsing with supertagging and CFG-filtering. In *Proceedings of the 20th International Joint Conference on Artificial Intelligence (IJCAI)*, pages 1671–1676.

Ruslan Mitkov, editor. 2004. *The Oxford Handbook of Computational Linguistics*. Oxford University Press.

Alessando Moschitti. 2006. Making tree kernels practical for natural language learning. In *Proceedings of the 11th European Chapter of the Association for Computational Linguistics*.

Joakim Nivre, Johan Hall, Jens Nilsson, Atanas Chanev, Gülsen Eryigit, Sandra Kübler, Svetoslav Marinov, and Erwin Marsi. 2007. MaltParser: A language-independent system for data-driven dependency parsing. *Natural Language Engineering*, 13(2):95–135.

Robbert Prins and Gertjan van Noord. 2003. Reinforcing parser preferences through tagging. *Traitment Automatique des Langues*, 44:121–139.

Using an SVM Ensemble System for Improved Tamil Dependency Parsing

Nathan Green, Loganathan Ramasamy and Zdeněk Žabokrtský
Charles University in Prague
Institute of Formal and Applied Linguistics
Faculty of Mathematics and Physics
Prague, Czech Republic
{green,ramasamy,zabokrtsky}@ufal.mff.cuni.cz

Abstract

Dependency parsing has been shown to improve NLP systems in certain languages and in many cases helps achieve state of the art results in NLP applications, in particular applications for free word order languages. Morphologically rich languages are often short on training data or require much higher amounts of training data due to the increased size of their lexicon. This paper examines a new approach for addressing morphologically rich languages with little training data to start.

Using Tamil as our test language, we create 9 dependency parse models with a limited amount of training data. Using these models we train an SVM classifier using only the model agreements as features. We use this SVM classifier on an edge by edge decision to form an ensemble parse tree. Using only model agreements as features allows this method to remain language independent and applicable to a wide range of morphologically rich languages.

We show a statistically significant 5.44% improvement over the average dependency model and a statistically significant 0.52% improvement over the best individual system.

1 Introduction

Dependency parsing has made many advancements in recent years. A prime reason for the quick advancement has been the CoNLL shared task competitions, which gave the community a common training/testing framework along with many open source systems. These systems have, for certain languages, achieved high accuracy ranging from on average from approximately 60% to 80% (Buchholz and Marsi, 2006). The range of scores are more often language dependent rather than system dependent, as some languages contain more morphological complexities. While some of these languages are morphologically rich, we would like to additionally address dependency parsing methods that may help under-resourced languages as well, which often overlaps with morphologically rich languages. For this reason, we have chosen to do the experiments in this paper using the Tamil Treebank (Ramasamy and Žabokrtský, 2012).

Tamil belongs to Dravidian family of languages and is mainly spoken in southern India and also in parts of Sri Lanka, Malaysia and Singapore. Tamil is agglutinative and has a rich set of morphological suffixes. Tamil has nouns and verbs as two major word classes, and hundreds of word forms can be produced by the application of concatenative and derivational morphology. Tamil's rich morphology makes the language free word order except that it is strictly *head final*.

When working with small datasets it is often very difficult to determine which dependency model will best represent your data. One can try to pick the model through empirical means on a tuning set but as the data grows in the future this model may no longer be the best choice. The change in the best model may be due to new vocabulary or through a domain shift. If the wrong single model is chosen early on when training is cheap, when the model is applied in semi supervised or self training it could lead to significantly reduced annotation accuracy.

For this reason, we believe ensemble combinations are an appropriate direction for lesser resourced languages, often a large portion of morphologically rich languages. Ensemble methods are robust as data sizes grow, since the classifier can easily be retrained with additional data and the ensemble model chooses the best model on an edge by edge basis. This cost is substantially less than retraining multiple dependency models.

2 Related Work

Ensemble learning (Dietterich, 2000) has been used for a variety of machine learning tasks and recently has been applied to dependency parsing in various ways and with different levels of success. (Surdeanu and Manning, 2010; Haffari et al., 2011) showed a successful combination of parse trees through a linear combination of trees with various weighting formulations. Parser combination with dependency trees have been examined in terms of accuracy (Sagae and Lavie, 2006; Sagae and Tsujii, 2007; Zeman and Žabokrtský, 2005; Søgaard and Rishøj, 2010). (Sagae and Lavie, 2006; Green and Žabokrtský, 2012) differ in part since their method guarantees a tree while our system can, in some situations, produce a forest. POS tags were used in parser combination in (Hall et al., 2007) for combining a set of Malt Parser models with an SVM classifier with success, however we believe our work is novel in its use of an SVM classifier solely on model agreements. Other methods of parse combinations have shown to be successful such as using one parser to generate features for another parser. This was shown in (Nivre and McDonald, 2008; Martins et al., 2008), in which Malt Parser was used as a feature to MST Parser.

Few attempts were reported in the literature on the development of a treebank for Tamil. Our experiments are based on the openly available treebank (TamilTB) (Ramasamy and Žabokrtský, 2012). Development of TamilTB is still in progress and the initial results for TamilTB appeared in (Ramasamy and Žabokrtský, 2011). Previous parsing experiments in Tamil were done using a rule based approach which utilized morphological tagging and identification of clause boundaries to parse the sentences. The results were also reported for Malt Parser and MST parser.

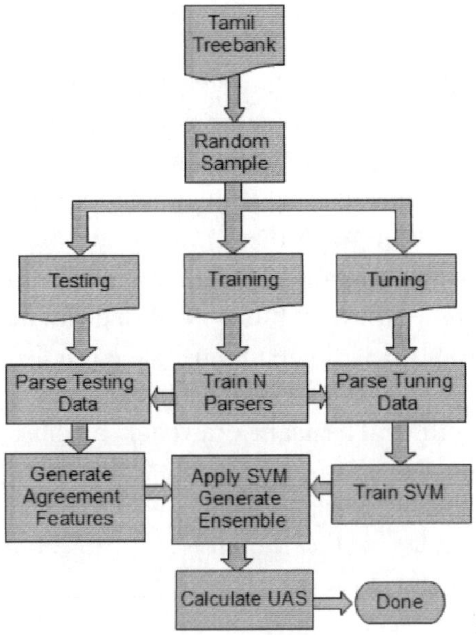

Figure 1: Process Flow for one run of our SVM Ensemble system. This Process in its entirety was run 100 times for each of the 8 data set splits.

When the morphological tags were available during both training and testing, the rule based approach performed better than Malt and MST parsers. For other Indian languages, treebank development is active mainly for Hindi and Telugu. Dependency parsing results for them are reported in (Husain et al., 2010).

3 Methodology

3.1 Process Flow

When dealing with small data sizes it is often not enough to show a simple accuracy increase. This increase can be very reliant on the training/tuning/testing data splits as well as the sampling of those sets. For this reason our experiments are conducted over 7 training/tuning/testing data split configurations. For each configuration we randomly sample without replacement the training/tuning/testing data and rerun the experiment 100 times. These 700 runs, each on different samples, allow us to better show the overall effect on the accuracy metric as well as the statistically significant changes as described in Section 3.5. Figure 1 shows this process flow for one run of this experiment.

3.2 Parsers

A dependency tree is a special case of a dependency graph that spawns from an artificial root, is connected, follows a single-head constraint and is acyclic. Because of this we can look at a large history of work in graph theory to address finding the best spanning tree for each dependency graph. The most common form of this type of dependency parsing is Graph-Based parsing also called arc-factored parsing and deals with the parameterization of the edge weights. The main drawback of these methods is that for projective trees, the worst case scenario for most methods is a complexity of $O(n^3)$ (Eisner, 1996). However, for non-projective parsing Chu-Liu-Edmond's algorithm has a complexity of $O(n^2)$ (McDonald et al., 2005). The most common tool for doing this is MST parser (McDonald et al., 2005). For this parser we generate two models, one projective and one non-projective to use in our ensemble system.

Transition-based parsing creates a dependency structure that is parameterized over the transitions. This is closely related to shift-reduce constituency parsing algorithms. The benefit of transition-based parsing is the use greedy algorithms which have a linear time complexity. However, due to the greedy algorithms, longer arc parses can cause error propagation across each transition (Kübler et al., 2009). We make use of Malt Parser (Nivre et al., 2007), which in the CoNLL shared tasks was often tied with the best performing systems. For this parser we generate 7 different models using different training parameters, seen in Table 1, and use them as input into our ensemble system along with the two Graph-based models described above. Each parser has access to gold POS information as supplied by the TamilTB described in 3.4.

Dependency parsing systems are often optimized for English or other major languages. This optimization, along with morphological complexities, lead other languages toward lower accuracy scores in many cases. The goal here is to show that while the corpus is not the same in size or scope of most CoNLL data, a successful dependency parser can still be trained from the annotated data through model combination for morphologically rich languages.

Training Parameter	Model Description
nivreeager	Nivre arc-eager
nivrestandard	Nivre arc-standard
stackproj	Stack projective
stackeager	Stack eager
stacklazy	Stack lazy
planar	Planar eager
2planar	2-Planar eager

Table 1: Table of the Malt Parser Parameters used during training. Each entry represents one of the parsing algorithms used in our experiments. For more information see http://www.maltparser.org/options.html

3.3 Ensemble SVM System

We train our SVM classifier using only model agreement features. Using our tuning set, for each correctly predicted dependency edge, we create $\binom{N}{2}$ features where N is the number of parsing models. We do this for each model which predicted the correct edge in the tuning data. So for $N = 3$ the first feature would be a 1 if model 1 and model 2 agreed, feature 2 would be a 1 if model 1 and model 3 agreed, and so on. This feature set is novel and widely applicable to many languages since it does not use any additional linguistic tools.

For each edge in the ensemble graph, we use our classifier to predict which model should be correct, by first creating the model agreement feature set for the current edge of the unknown test data. The SVM predicts which model should be correct and this model then decides to which head the current node is attached. At the end of all the tokens in a sentence, the graph may not be connected and will likely have cycles. Using a Perl implementation of minimum spanning tree, in which each edge has a uniform weight, we obtain a minimum spanning forest, where each subgraph is then connected and cycles are eliminated in order to achieve a well formed dependency structure. Figure 2 gives a graphical representation of how the SVM decision and MST algorithm create a final Ensemble parse tree which is similar to the construction used in (Hall et al., 2007; Green and Žabokrtský, 2012). Future iterations of this process could use a multi-label SVM or weighted edges based on the parser's accuracy on tuning data.

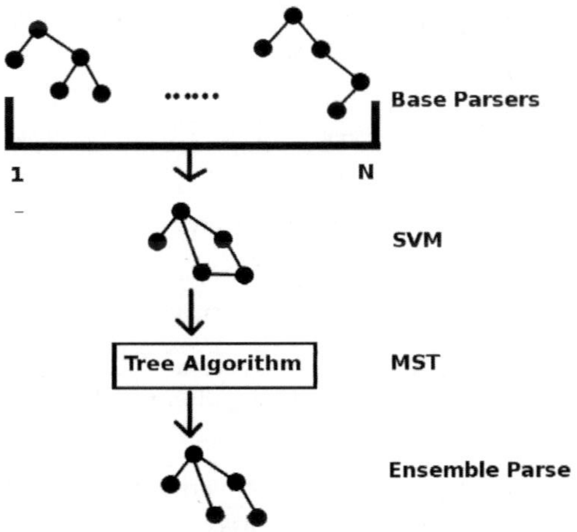

Figure 2: General flow to create an Ensemble parse tree

3.4 Data Sets

Table 2 shows the statistics of the TamilTB Treebank. The last 2 rows indicate how many word types have unique tags and how many have two tags. Also, Table 2 illustrates that most of the word types can be uniquely identified with single morphological tag and only around 120 word types take more than one morphological tag.

Description	Value
#Sentences	600
#Words	9581
#Word types	3583
#Tagset size	234
#Types with unique tags	3461
#Types with 2 tags	112

Table 2: TamilTB: data statistics

Since this is a relatively small treebank and in order to confirm that our experiments are not heavily reliant on one particular sample of data we try a variety of data splits. To test the effects of the training, tuning, and testing data we try 7 different data splits. The tuning data in the Section 4 use the format training-tuning-testing. So 70-20-10 means we used 70% of the TamilTB for training, 20% for tuning the SVM classifier, and 10% for evaluation.

3.5 Evaluation

Made a standard in the CoNLL shared tasks competition, two standard metrics for comparing dependency parsing systems are typically used. *L*abeled *a*ttachment *s*core (LAS) and *u*nlabeled *a*ttachment *s*core (UAS). UAS studies the structure of a dependency tree and assesses whether the output has the correct head and dependency arcs. In addition to the structure score in UAS, LAS also measures the accuracy of the dependency labels on each arc (Buchholz and Marsi, 2006). Since we are mainly concerned with the structure of the ensemble parse, we report only UAS scores in this paper.

To test statistical significance we use Wilcoxon paired signed-rank test. For each data split we have 100 iterations each with different sampling. Each model is compared against the same samples so a paired test is appropriate in this case. We report statistical significance values for $p < 0.01$ and $p < 0.05$.

4 Results and Discussion

Data Split	Average SVM UAS	% Increase over Avg	% Increase over Best
70-20-10	76.50%	5.13%	0.52%
60-20-20	76.36%	5.68%	0.72%
60-30-10	75.42%	5.44%	0.52%
60-10-30	75.66%	4.83%	0.10%
85-5-10	75.33%	3.10%	-1.21%
90-5-5	75.42%	3.19%	-1.10%
80-10-10	76.44%	4.84%	0.48%

Table 3: Average increases and decreases in UAS score for different Training-Tuning-Test samples. The average was calculated over all 9 models while the best was selected for each data split

For each of the data splits, Table 3 shows the percent increase in our SVM system over both the average of the 9 individual models and over the best individual model. As the Table 3 shows, our approach seems to decrease in value along with the decrease in tuning data. In both cases when we only used 5% tuning data we did not get any improvement in our average UAS scores. Examining Table 4, shows that the decrease in the 90-5-5 split is not statistically significant however the decrease in 85-5-10 is a statistically significant drop. However, the increases in all data splits are statistically significant except for the 60-20-20 data split. It appears that

Model	70-20-10	60-20-20	60-30-10	60-10-30	85-5-10	90-5-5	80-10-10
2planar	*	*	*	*	*	*	**
mstnonproj	*	*	*	*	*	*	**
mstproj	*	*	*	*	*	*	**
nivreeager	*	*	*	*	**	x	*
nivrestandard	*	*	**	x	*	*	*
planar	*	*	*	*	*	*	**
stackeager	*	*	*	x	*	**	*
stacklazy	*	*	*	x	*	**	*
stackproj	**	*	*	x	**	**	**

Table 4: Statistical Significance Table for different Training-Tuning-Test samples. Each experiment was sampled 100 times and Wilcoxon Statistical Significance was calculated for our SVM model's increase/decrease over each individual model. $* = p < 0.01$, $** p =< 0.05$, $x = p \geq 0.05$

the size of the tuning and training data matter more than the size of the test data given the low variance in Table 5. Since the TamilTB is relatively small when compared to other CoNLL treebanks, we expect that this ratio may shift more when additional data is supplied since the amount of out of vocabulary, OOV, words will decrease as well. As OOV words decrease, we expect the use of additional test data to have less of an effect.

Data Splits	SVM Variance
70-20-10	0.0011
60-20-20	0.0005
60-30-10	0.0010
60-10-30	0.0003
85-5-10	0.0010
90-5-5	0.0028
80-10-10	0.0010

Table 5: Variance of the UAS Scores of our Ensemble SVM System over 100 data splits

The traditional approach of using as much data as possible for training does not seem to be as effective as partitioning more data for tuning an SVM. For instance the highest training percentage we use is 90% applied to training with 5% for tuning and testing each. In this case the best individual model had a UAS of 76.25% and the SVM had a UAS of 75.42%. One might think using 90% of the data would achieve a higher overall UAS than using less training data. On the contrary, we achieve a better UAS score on average using only 60%, 70%, 80%, and 85% of the data towards training. This additional data spent for tuning appears to be worth the cost.

5 Conclusion

We have shown a new SVM based ensemble parser that uses only dependency model agreement features. The ability to use only model agreements allows us to keep this approach language independent and applicable to a wide range of morphologically rich languages. We show a statistically significant 5.44% improvement over the average dependency model and a statistically significant 0.52% improvement over the best individual system.

In the future we would like to examine how our data splits' results change as more data is added. This might be a prime use for self training. Since the tuning data size for the SVM seems most important, the UAS may be improved by only adding self training data to our tuning sets. This would have the additional benefit of eliminating the need to retrain the individual parsers, thus saving computation time. The tuning size may have a reduced effect for larger treebanks but in our experiments it is critical to the smaller treebank. Additionally, a full comparison of various ensemble parsing error distributions will be needed.

6 Acknowledgments

This research has received funding from the European Commission's 7th Framework Program (FP7) under grant agreement n° 238405 (CLARA)

References

Sabine Buchholz and Erwin Marsi. 2006. CoNLL-X shared task on multilingual dependency parsing. In *Proceedings of the Tenth Conference on Computational Natural Language Learning*, CoNLL-X '06, pages 149–164, Stroudsburg, PA, USA. Association for Computational Linguistics.

Thomas G. Dietterich. 2000. Ensemble methods in machine learning. In *Proceedings of the First International Workshop on Multiple Classifier Systems*, MCS '00, pages 1–15, London, UK. Springer-Verlag.

Jason Eisner. 1996. Three new probabilistic models for dependency parsing: An exploration. In *Proceedings of the 16th International Conference on Computational Linguistics (COLING-96)*, pages 340–345, Copenhagen, August.

Nathan Green and Zdeněk Žabokrtský. 2012. Hybrid Combination of Constituency and Dependency Trees into an Ensemble Dependency Parser. In *Proceedings of the Workshop on Innovative Hybrid Approaches to the Processing of Textual Data*, pages 19–26, Avignon, France, April. Association for Computational Linguistics.

Gholamreza Haffari, Marzieh Razavi, and Anoop Sarkar. 2011. An ensemble model that combines syntactic and semantic clustering for discriminative dependency parsing. In *Proceedings of the 49th Annual Meeting of the Association for Computational Linguistics: Human Language Technologies*, pages 710–714, Portland, Oregon, USA, June. Association for Computational Linguistics.

Johan Hall, Jens Nilsson, Joakim Nivre, Gülsen Eryigit, Beáta Megyesi, Mattias Nilsson, and Markus Saers. 2007. Single Malt or Blended? A Study in Multilingual Parser Optimization. In *Proceedings of the CoNLL Shared Task Session of EMNLP-CoNLL 2007*, pages 933–939.

Samar Husain, Prashanth Mannem, Bharat Ram Ambati, and Phani Gadde. 2010. The icon-2010 tools contest on indian language dependency parsing. In *Proceedings of ICON-2010 Tools Contest on Indian Language Dependency Parsing*, pages 1–8.

Sandra Kübler, Ryan McDonald, and Joakim Nivre. 2009. *Dependency parsing*. Synthesis lectures on human language technologies. Morgan & Claypool, US.

André F. T. Martins, Dipanjan Das, Noah A. Smith, and Eric P. Xing. 2008. Stacking dependency parsers. In *Proceedings of the Conference on Empirical Methods in Natural Language Processing*, EMNLP '08, pages 157–166, Stroudsburg, PA, USA. Association for Computational Linguistics.

Ryan McDonald, Fernando Pereira, Kiril Ribarov, and Jan Hajic. 2005. Non-projective dependency parsing using spanning tree algorithms. In *Proceedings of Human Language Technology Conference and Conference on Empirical Methods in Natural Language Processing*, pages 523–530, Vancouver, British Columbia, Canada, October. Association for Computational Linguistics.

Joakim Nivre and Ryan McDonald. 2008. Integrating graph-based and transition-based dependency parsers. In *Proceedings of ACL-08: HLT*, pages 950–958, Columbus, Ohio, June. Association for Computational Linguistics.

Joakim Nivre, Johan Hall, Jens Nilsson, Atanas Chanev, Gulsen Eryigit, Sandra Kübler, Svetoslav Marinov, and Erwin Marsi. 2007. MaltParser: A language-independent system for data-driven dependency parsing. *Natural Language Engineering*, 13(2):95–135.

Loganathan Ramasamy and Zdeněk Žabokrtský. 2011. Tamil dependency parsing: results using rule based and corpus based approaches. In *Proceedings of the 12th international conference on Computational linguistics and intelligent text processing - Volume Part I*, CICLing'11, pages 82–95, Berlin, Heidelberg.

Loganathan Ramasamy and Zdeněk Žabokrtský. 2012. Prague dependency style treebank for Tamil. In *Proceedings of LREC 2012*, İstanbul, Turkey.

Kenji Sagae and Alon Lavie. 2006. Parser combination by reparsing. In *Proceedings of the Human Language Technology Conference of the NAACL, Companion Volume: Short Papers*, pages 129–132, New York City, USA, June. Association for Computational Linguistics.

Kenji Sagae and Jun'ichi Tsujii. 2007. Dependency parsing and domain adaptation with LR models and parser ensembles. In *Proceedings of the CoNLL Shared Task Session of EMNLP-CoNLL 2007*, pages 1044–1050, Prague, Czech Republic, June. Association for Computational Linguistics.

Anders Søgaard and Christian Rishøj. 2010. Semi-supervised dependency parsing using generalized tri-training. In *Proceedings of the 23rd International Conference on Computational Linguistics (Coling 2010)*, pages 1065–1073, Beijing, China, August.

Mihai Surdeanu and Christopher D. Manning. 2010. Ensemble models for dependency parsing: cheap and good? In *HLT: The 2010 Annual Conference of the North American Chapter of the Association for Computational Linguistics*, HLT '10, pages 649–652, Stroudsburg, PA, USA. Association for Computational Linguistics.

Daniel Zeman and Zdeněk Žabokrtský. 2005. Improving parsing accuracy by combining diverse dependency parsers. In *In: Proceedings of the 9th International Workshop on Parsing Technologies*.

Korean Treebank Transformation for Parser Training

DongHyun Choi
Dept. of Computer Science
KAIST
Korea
cdh4696@world.kaist.ac.kr

Jungyeul Park
Les Editions
an Amzer Vak
France
park@amzer-vak.fr

Key-Sun Choi
Dept. of Computer Science
KAIST
Korea
kschoi@cs.kaist.ac.kr

Abstract

Korean is a morphologically rich language in which grammatical functions are marked by inflections and affixes, and they can indicate grammatical relations such as subject, object, predicate, etc. A Korean sentence could be thought as a sequence of eojeols. An eojeol is a word or its variant word form agglutinated with grammatical affixes, and eojeols are separated by white space as in English written texts. Korean treebanks (Choi et al., 1994; Han et al., 2002; Korean Language Institute, 2012) use eojeol as their fundamental unit of analysis, thus representing an eojeol as a prepreterminal phrase inside the constituent tree. This eojeol-based annotating schema introduces various complexity to train the parser, for example an entity represented by a sequence of nouns will be annotated as two or more different noun phrases, depending on the number of spaces used. In this paper, we propose methods to transform eojeol-based Korean treebanks into entity-based Korean treebanks. The methods are applied to Sejong treebank, which is the largest constituent treebank in Korean, and the transformed treebank is used to train and test various probabilistic CFG parsers. The experimental result shows that the proposed transformation methods reduce ambiguity in the training corpus, increasing the overall F1 score up to about 9 %.

1 Introduction

The result of syntactic parsing is useful for many NLP applications, such as named entity recognition (Finkel and Manning, 2009), semantic role labeling (Gildea and Jurafsky, 2002), or sentimental analysis (Nasukawa and Yi, 2003). Currently most of the state-of-the-art constituent parsers take statistical parsing approach (Klein and Manning, 2003; Bikel, 2004; Petrov and Klein, 2007), which use manually annotated syntactic trees to train the probabilistic models of each consituents.

Even though there exist manually annotated Korean treebank corpora such as Sejong Treebank (Korean Language Institute, 2012), very few research projects about the Korean parser, especially using phrase structure grammars have been conducted. In this paper, we aim to transform the treebank so that it could be better used as training data for the already-existing English constituent parsers.

Most of Korean treebank corpora use eojeols as their fundamental unit of analysis. An eojeol is a word or its variant word form agglutinated with grammatical affixes, and eojeols are separated by white space as in English written texts (Choi et al., 2011). Figure 1 is one of the example constituent tree from the Sejong Treebank. As can be observed, an eojeol is always determined as a prepreterminal phrase [1]. But this kind of bracketing guideline could cause ambiguities to the existing algorithms for parsing English, because: (1) English does not have the concept of "eojeol", and (2) an eojeol can contain two or more morphemes with different grammatical roles. For example, Korean case par-

[1]A node is a prepreterminal if all the children of this node are preterminals (Part-Of-Speech tags such as NNP and JKG). Preterminal is defined to be a node with one child which is itself a leaf (Damljanovic et al., 2010).

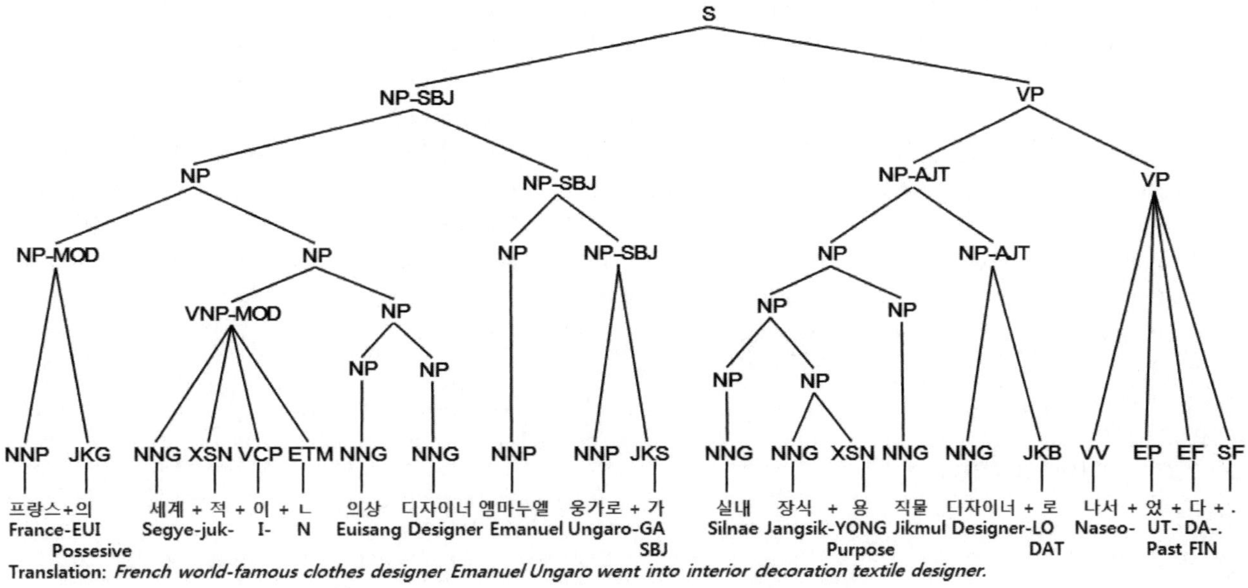

Figure 1: An example constituent tree and morphological analysis result from the Sejong treebank

ticles ('josa') are normally written inside the same eojeol with their argument nouns, but the whole eojeol is always considered as a prepreterminal noun phrase in the Korean treebank, as can be seen in the eojeol *Ungaro-GA*. Considering that the case particles in Korean play important role in determining the syntactic structure of a sentence, this could cause loss of information during the training phase. Moreover, *Emanuel Ungaro* is considered as two different noun phrases, because they simply belong to the two different eojeols (that is, a space exists between eojeols *Emanuel* and *Ungaro-GA*).

In this paper, we propose methods to refine the Sejong treebank which is currently the largest Korean treebank corpus. The methods are aimed at decreasing the ambiguities during the training phase of parsers, by separating phrases which are integrated into the same prepreterminal phrase due to the reason that they happen to be in the same eojeol, and integrating phrases into the same prepreterminal phrase which are separated because they happen to be in different eojeols. The refined datasets are trained and tested against three state-of-the-art parsers, and the evaluation results for each dataset are reported.

In section 2, the work about Korean parsers are briefly introduced. Sejong treebank is described with more detailed explanation in section 3, while the methods to transform the treebank are introduced in section 4. In section 5 the evaluation results of the transformed treebank using the three existing state-of-the-art parsers are introduced with an error report, and we discuss conclusions in section 6.

2 Related Work

There were some trials to build Korean constituent parsers, but due to the lack of appropriate corpus those trials were not able to acheive a good result. (Smith and Smith, 2004) tried to build a Korean parser by bilingual approach with English, and achieved labeled precision/recall around 40 % for Korean. More recently, (Park, 2006) tried to extract tree adjoining grammars from the Sejong treebank, and (Oh et al., 2011) build a system to predict a phrase tag for each eojeol.

Due to the partial free word order and case pariicles which can decide the grammatical roles of noun phrases, there exist some works to build statistical dependency parsers for Korean. (Chung, 2004) presented a dependency parsing model using surface contextual model. (Choi and Palmer, 2011) converted the Sejong treebank into the dependency treebank, and applied the SVM algorithm to learn the dependency model.

NNG	General noun	IC	Interjection	JKQ	Quotational CP	XSV	Verb DS
NNP	Proper noun	MM	Adnoun	JX	Auxiliary PR	XSA	Adjective DS
NNB	Bound noun	MAG	General adverb	JC	Conjunctive PR	XR	Base morpheme
NP	Pronoun	MAJ	Conjunctive adverb	EP	Prefinal EM	SN	Number
NR	Numeral	JKS	Subjective CP	EF	Final EM	SL	Foreign word
VV	Verb	JKC	Complemental CP	EC	Conjunctive EM	SH	Chinese word
VA	Adjective	JKG	Adnomial CP	ETN	Nominalizing EM	NF	Noun-like word
VX	Auxiliary predicate	JKO	Objective CP	ETM	Adnominalizing EM	NV	Verb-like word
VCP	Copula	JKB	Adverbial CP	XPN	Noun prefix	NA	Unknown word
VCN	Negation adjective	JKV	Vocative CP	XSN	Noun DS	SF,SP,SS,SE,SO,SW	

Table 1: POS tags used in Sejong treebank (CP: case particle, EM: ending marker, DS: derivational suffix, PR: particle, SF SP SS SE SO: different types of punctuations, SW: currency symbols and mathematical symbols. Table borrowed from (Choi and Palmer, 2011))

Apart from the Sejong Treebank, there are few other Korean treebanks available. The KAIST treebank (Choi et al., 1994) contains constituent trees about approximately 30K sentences from newspapers, novels and textbooks. Also, the Penn Korean Treebank (Han et al., 2002) contains 15K constituent trees constructed from the sentences of newswire and military domains. The proposed methods are evaluated using the Sejong treebank because it is the most recent and the largest Korean treebank among those which is currently available.

3 Sejong Treebank

The Sejong treebank is the largest constituent treebank in Korean. It contains approximately 45K manually-annotated constituent trees, and their sources cover various domains including newspapers, novels and cartoon texts. Figure 1 shows an example of the Sejong constituent tree.

The tree consists of phrasal nodes and their functional tags as described in table 2. Each eojeol could contain one or more morphemes with different POS tags (Table 1 shows the POS tagset). In most cases, eojeols are determined by white spaces. As stated in its bracketing guidelines, the Sejong treebank uses eojeols as its fundamental unit of analysis [2]. This means that an eojeol is always treated as one prepreterminal phrase. This could cause confusions to the training system, because an eojeol could contain many morphemes which have very different grammatical roles, as can be seen in the example of *Ungaro-GA* - word *Ungaro* is a noun, where the nominative case particle *GA* suggests that this eojeol is used as a subject.

Table 2 shows phrase tags and functional tags used to construct the Sejong treebank. Some phrases are annotated with functional tags to clarify their grammatical role inside the sentence. There are three special phrase tags beside those in table 2: X indicates phrases containing only case particles or ending markers, L and R indicate left and right parenthesis.

Phrase-level tags		Functional tags	
S	Sentence	SBJ	Subject
Q	Quotative clause	OBJ	Object
NP	Noun phrase	CMP	Complement
VP	Verb phrase	MOD	Modifier
VNP	Copula phrase	AJT	Adjunct
AP	Adverb phrase	CNJ	Conjunctive
DP	Adnoun phrase	INT	Vocative
IP	Interjection phrase	PRN	parenthetical

Table 2: Phrase tags used in Sejong treebank.

4 Transforming Methods: from Eojeol-based to Entity-based

In this section, we describe the methods to transform the annotation schema of the Korean treebank from eojeol-based to entity-based using the examples of the Sejong treebank.

4.1 Method 1: POS Level Preprocessing

Before starting the actual transforming process, the system first detects emails, phone numbers and dates

[2]The bracketing guidelines could be requested from the Sejong project, but available only in Korean

based on their unique POS patterns. If the system detects a sequence of morphemes matching with one of predefined POS patterns inside an eojeol, then it groups those morphemes into one entity and tags it as a noun. This procedure aims to reduce the ambiguity of the corpus by reducing many miscellaneous mrophemes which in fact forms one phone number, email address or date information into one entity. Figure 2 shows an example of an eojeol whose five morphemes toghether represent one date, and its transformation result.

Figure 2: Example of an eojeol containing date: five morphemes are merged into one morpheme representing date.

Also, the morphemes representing chinese characters (POS: `SH`) and other foreign characters (POS: `SL`) are considered as nouns, since they are normally used to rewrite Korean nouns that have their foreign origin such as Sino-Korean nouns.

4.2 Method 2: Detecting NPs inside an Eojeol

Although an eojeol is considered to be one prepreterminal phrase as a whole, many eojeols contain separated noun components inside them. For example, a noun phrase *Ungaro-GA* in Figure 3 consists of a separated noun component *Ungaro* in it, plus josa *GA*. The system separates noun components from other endings and case particles, creates a new phrase containing those words and tags it as an NP. By doing so, the boundaries of the NP are more clarified - before transforming prepreterminal NPs could contain case particles and endings, but after the transformation it is not possible. Also the internal syntactic structures of phrases are revealed, providing more information to the parser.

4.3 Method 3: Finding Arguments of Josa

In this step, the system tries to find out the actual argument of each josa. For example, in figure 4 the actual argument of the nominative josa *GA* is the whole person name *Emanuel Ungaro*, not only *Ungaro*. The system tries to find out the actual argument of each josa by using a rather simple heuristic:

1. Traverse the constituent parse tree in bottom-up, right-to-left manner.
2. If a phrase node is NP, its parent is also NP, and it directly dominates josa(s), then:
   (a) Create a new NP.
   (b) Attach the node to that NP, except the josa(s).
   (c) Attach all the other children of the parent node to the newly-created NP.
   (d) Remove all the children of the parent, and attach the new NP and remaining josa part to the parent node.
3. After the procedure ends, find and remove redundant NPs, if exist.

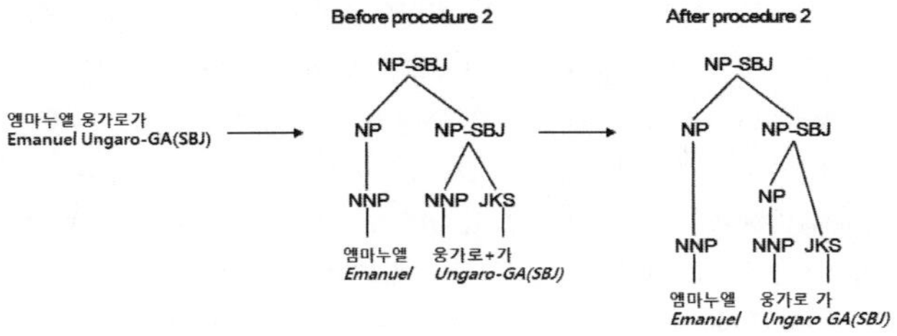

Figure 3: Detecting NP inside an eojeol: Case of a verb phrase

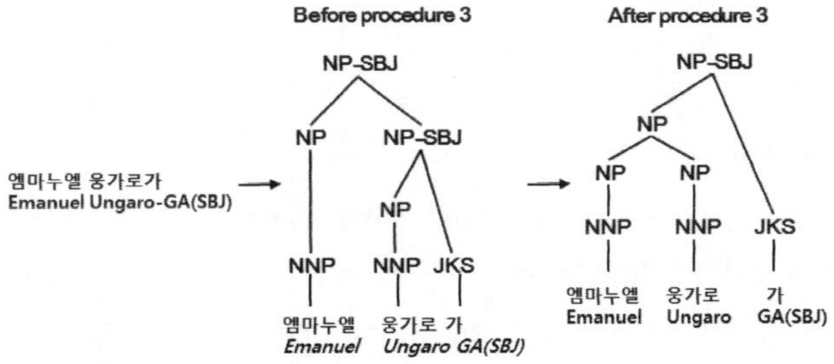

Figure 4: Example of applying the transformation heuristic

Method 3 is dependent on method 2, since method 2 first determines boundary of NPs which do not include any case particles.

4.4 Method 4: Integrating a Sequence of Nouns into One NP

Some of entities represented as sequences of nouns are considered as two or more separated noun phrases since their components belong to the different eojeols. This could be problematic because an entity could sometimes be written without any whitespace between its component nouns. Figure 5 shows one of the case: person name *Emanuel Ungaro* is considered as two separated NPs since there exists a whitespace between a noun *Emanual* and a noun *Ungaro*. In this step, we aim to solve this problem.

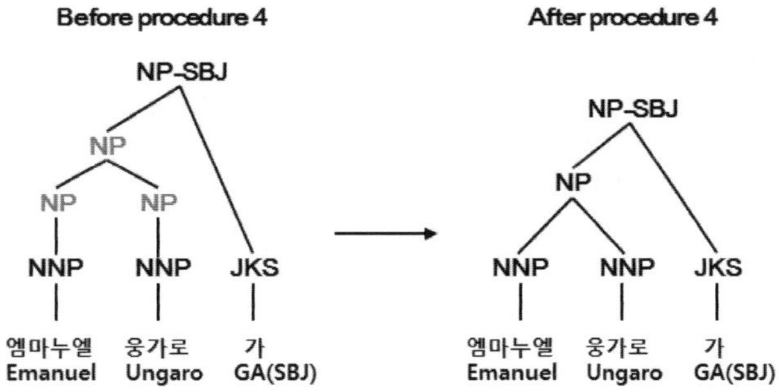

Figure 5: Integrating sequence of nouns representing one entity into one prepreterminal noun phrase

The system finds out an NP which has two NP children which dominates only the noun preterminal children. If the system finds such an NP, then it removes NP children and attaches their children directly to the found NP. Figure 5 shows an application example of the method.

This method is dependent on method 3, since this method assumes that an NP with its parent also NP does not have any case particles - which cannot be hold if method 3 is not applied.

4.5 Method 5: Dealing with Noun Conjunctions

The system tries to enumerate the noun conjunctions, rather than expressing those conjunctions in binary format. Current Sejong treebank expresses noun conjunctions in binary format - that is, to express the constituent tree for noun conjunctions, the nonterminal node has one NP child on its left which contains information about the first item of the conjunction, and the rest of conjunctions are expressed on the right child. Figure 6[3] shows an example of the Sejong constituent tree expressing the noun conjunctions, and its transformed version.

Korean Sentence	마이크와 스피커가 장착되어 있다.
Pronounciation	*Mike-WA(CNJ) Speaker-GA(SBJ) JangChak-DOI-UH IT-DA.*
English translation	Microphone and speaker are installed.

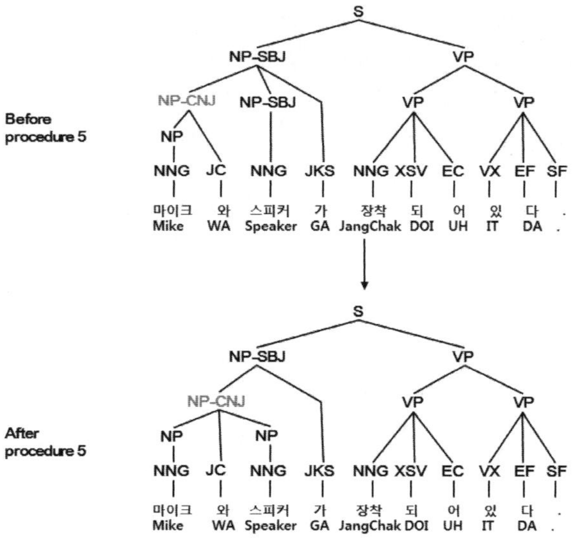

Figure 6: Enumerating Noun Conjunctions

By converting noun conjunctions into rather the 'enumerated' forms, two benefits could be gained: first, the resultant constituent tree will resemble more to the Penn-treebank constituent trees. Since most of the existing English parsers are trained on the Penn Treebank, we can expect that the enumerated form of conjunctions will more 'fit' to those parsers. Second, the conjunctions are expressed in much more explicit format, so the human users can more easily understand the conjunctive structures inside the constituent trees.

4.6 Method 6: Re-tagging Phrase Tags

In this step, the system re-tags some of phrase tags to clarify their types and to decrease training ambiguities. For example, a noun phrase with and without case particles should be distinguished. The system re-tags those noun phrases with case particles to JSP[4] to distinguish them from the pure noun phrases which consist of only nouns. Also, VP-MOD and VNP-MOD are re-tagged to DP, since they have very similar lexical formats with existing DPs. NP-MOD is converted into JSP-MOD - most of them consist of a NP with josa JKG, forming possesive cases. S-MOD remains as S-MOD if its head is JSP-MOD:

[3]*Mike-WA_*(CNJ) *Speaker-GA_*(NOM) *Jangchak-DOI-UH IT-DA.* ('Microphone and speaker are installed.')

[4]It stands for a 'Josa Phrase'.

otherwise, it is also re-tagged to a DP. Figure 7[5] shows a re-tagging example.

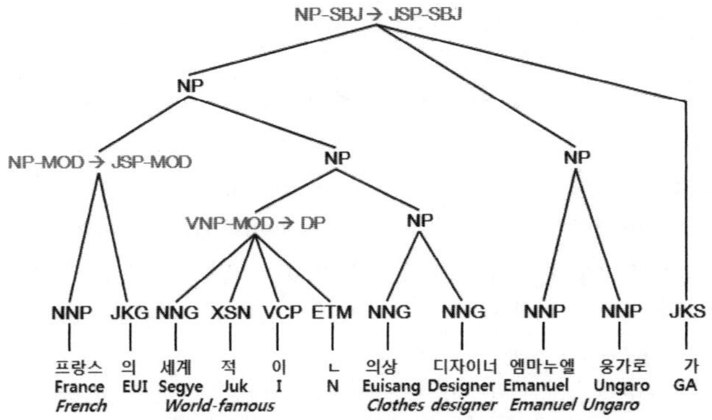

Figure 7: Example of retagging phrase tags: VP-MOD to DP, NP-MOD to JSP-MOD, and NP-SBJ to JSP-SBJ.

5 Evaluations

In this section, several experiment results using the standard F1 metric $(2PR/(P+R))$ are introduced to show the effect of each transforming method, and the most frequently shown error cases are explained.

5.1 Experiments using the Sejong Treebank

The proposed transformation methods are applied to the Sejong treebank, and the converted treebanks are used to train and test three different well-known statistical parsers, namely Stanford parser (Klein and Manning, 2003), Bikel-Collins parser (Bikel, 2012) and Berkeley parser (Petrov et al., 2006). To figure out the effect of each method, all six methods are sequentially applied one by one, and each version of the treebank is used to train and test each parser. The baseline treebank is the original Sejong treebank without any transformations. For the Korean head word extraction which will be used during parsing, the head percolation rule of (Choi and Palmer, 2011) is adapted. According to that paper, particles and endings were the most useful morphemes to determine dependencies between eojeols. Based on the observation, their rules are changed so that they give the best priorities on those morphemes. We use the preprocessing method described in (Park, 2006) for training trees. It replaces symboles with Penn-Treebank-like tags and corrects wrong morpheme boundary marks within the eojeol. Methods are applied cumulatively; for example, symbol 'M 1-6' means the version of a treebank to which method 1, 2, 3, 4, 5 and 6 are applied cumulatively.[6]

System	Corpus	P	R	F1
Stan.	**Baseline**	67.88%	61.77%	64.69%
	M 1	68.34%	61.93%	64.98%
	M 1-2	71.78%	67.50%	69.58%
	M 1-3	71.28%	67.91%	69.56%
	M 1-4	71.06%	67.08%	69.01%
	M 1-5	71.35%	67.27%	69.26%
	M 1-6	75.85%	72.07%	73.92%
Bikel.	**Baseline**	74.81%	70.39%	72.53%
	M 1	74.87%	70.45%	72.59%
	M 1-2	77.05%	73.84%	75.41%
	M 1-3	75.87%	72.88%	74.34%
	M 1-4	75.33%	72.10%	73.68%
	M 1-5	75.29%	72.18%	73.70%
	M 1-6	73.70%	71.05%	72.35%
Berk.	**Baseline**	75.25%	72.72%	73.96%
	M 1	74.54%	71.97%	73.23%
	M 1-2	77.27%	75.05%	76.14%
	M 1-3	75.60%	73.19%	74.38%
	M 1-4	75.69%	73.32%	74.49%
	M 1-5	76.53%	74.30%	75.40%
	M 1-6	78.60%	76.03%	77.29%

Table 3: Evaluation results of parsers, with various transformed versions of the Sejong treebank.

Table 3 shows the experimental results on each version of the treebanks using each parser. Since the corpus covers various domains (i.e. the style of sentences is not homogeneous.), we perform 10-fold cross-validation for our experiments. **Stan.** represents Stanford parser, **Bikel.** represents Bikel-Collins parser, and **Berk.** means Berkeley parser. For the Berkeley parser, we set the number of iteration as two for latent annotations. In this set of experiments, only phrase tags are the target of training and testing, not including functional tags.

As can be observed from the evaluation result, the performance is improved due to methods 2 and 6 are quite big compared to the effect of other four

[5] See Figure 1 for its transcription and translation.

[6] As pointed out by reviewers, we are planning the reversibility of transformations to be evaluated on the same trees for meaning comparison.

System	Corpus	P	R	F1
Stan.	**Baseline**	71.48%	69.40%	70.43%
	M 1	71.89%	69.75%	70.81%
	M 1-2	75.90%	73.44%	74.65%
	M 1-3	72.32%	69.76%	71.02%
	M 1-4	72.37%	69.97%	71.16%
	M 1-5	72.80%	70.28%	71.52%
	M 1-6	72.32%	69.81%	71.05%
Bikel.	**Baseline**	69.65%	66.80%	68.19%
	M 1	69.73%	66.97%	68.32%
	M 1-2	74.33%	71.90%	73.09%
	M 1-3	63.94%	64.57%	64.25%
	M 1-4	63.95%	65.04%	64.49%
	M 1-5	64.09%	65.05%	64.57%
	M 1-6	62.94%	64.16%	63.54%
Berk.	**Baseline**	76.82%	75.28%	76.04%
	M 1	76.73%	75.06%	75.89%
	M 1-2	79.59%	77.91%	78.74%
	M 1-3	75.24%	72.16%	73.67%
	M 1-4	75.02%	73.01%	74.00%
	M 1-5	75.58%	73.61%	74.58%
	M 1-6	74.37%	71.93%	73.13%

Table 4: Evaluation results of parsers, with phrase tags and functional tags together as learning target.

methods. Especially, the performance increase due to the method 6 strongly suggests that Sejong phrase tagsets are not enough to distinguish the types of phrases effectively. Except those two methods, only the method 5 increases the overall performance slightly, and methods 1, 3 and 4 do not have any significant effect on the performance or even somesometimes decrease the overall performance.

Although the usage of functional tags is different from that of phrase tags, the Sejong treebank has a very rich functional tag set. Considering the results of the previous experiments, it is highly likely that some of phrasal information is encoded into the functional tags. To prove that, another set of experiments is carried out. In this time, parsers are trained not only on phrase tags but also on functional tags. Table 4 shows the evaluation results.

As can be observed, by keeping functional tags to train and test parsers, the baseline performance increases 3 to 6 % for the Stanford and Berkeley parsers. Only the performance of the Bikel parser is decreased - it is highly possible that the parser fails to find out the appropriate head word for each possible tag, because the number of possible tags is increased greatly by using the functional tags along with the phrase tags.

In both set of experiments, the method 3 decreases the overall performance. This strongly suggests that finding the actual argument of josa directly is quite a challenging work. The performance drop is considered mainly because the branching problem at the higher level of the constituent tree is counted twice due to the josa.

5.2 Experiments using the Penn Korean Treebank

To show the effect of the transformation methods more clearly, the Penn Korean Treebank (Han et al., 2002) is used as another treebank for experimentation: (Chung et al., 2010) describes about major difficulties of parsing Penn Korean Treebank. The same three parsers are trained and tested using the treebank. Due to the different annotation guidelines and different tagsets, transformation methods 1, 5 and 6 cannot be applied on the treebank. Thus, only method 2, 3 and 4 are used to transform the treebank. Table 5 shows the evaluation results.

System	Corpus	P	R	F1
Stan.	**Baseline**	82.84%	80.28%	81.54%
	M 2	85.29%	83.25%	84.26%
	M 2-3	84.52%	82.71%	83.61%
	M 2-4	84.52%	82.92%	83.72%
Bikel.	**Baseline**	81.49%	78.20%	79.81%
	M 2	75.82%	74.47%	75.13%
	M 2-3	73.50%	69.66%	71.53%
	M 2-4	73.45%	69.66%	71.51%
Berk.	**Baseline**	85.11%	81.90%	83.47%
	M 2	83.40%	81.04%	82.20%
	M 2-3	82.36%	80.52%	81.43%
	M 2-4	82.97%	81.28%	82.12%

Table 5: Evaluation on Penn Korean Treebank.

The overall performance of training the Penn Korean treebank is higher than that of the Sejong treebank. There could be two possible explanations. First one is, since the Penn Korean treebank tries to follow English Penn treebank guidelines as much as possible, thus annotation guidelines of the Korean Penn treebank could be much "familiar" to the parsers than that of the Sejong treebank. The second explanation is, since the domain of the Penn Korean treebank is much more restricted than that of the Sejong treebank, the system could be trained for the specific domain. The best performance was gained with the Stanford parser, with the treebank transformed by method 2. Actually, (Chung et al., 2010) also investigated parsing accuracy on the Penn Korean treebank; the direct comparison could be very difficult because parsing criteria is different.

5.3 Error Analysis

In this section, some of the parsing error cases are reported. Berkeley parser trained with the Sejong treebank is used for error analysis. Both phrase tags and functional tags are used to train and test the system.

5.3.1 Locating Approximate Positions of Errors

As the first step to analyze the errors, we tried to figure out at which points of the constituent tree errors frequently occur – do the errors mainly occur at the bottom of the trees? Or at the top of the trees? If we can figure out approximate locations of errors, then the types of errors could be predicted.

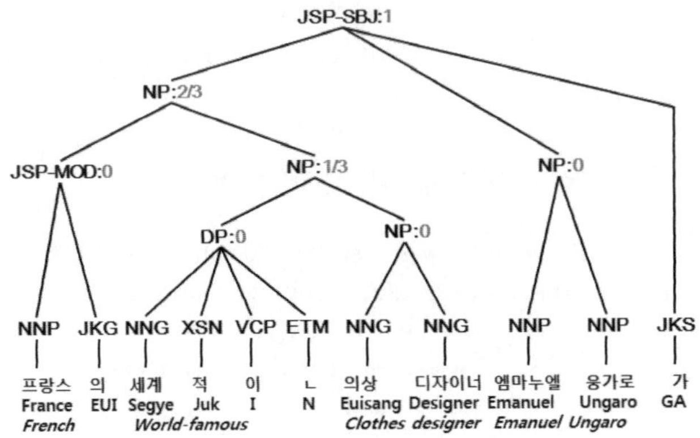

Figure 8: Example of assigning levels to each phrasal node.

To define the level of each nonterminal node of the constituent tree, the following rules are used:

- The level of prepreterminal node is 0.
- The levels of other phrasal nodes are defined as: the maximal level of their children + 1.
- Once the levels of all the phrasal nodes are calculated, normalize the levels so that they have the values between 0 and 1.

Figure 8 shows an example of constituent tree with levels assigned to its phrasal nodes. All the prepreterminal nodes have level value 0, and the topmost node has level 1.

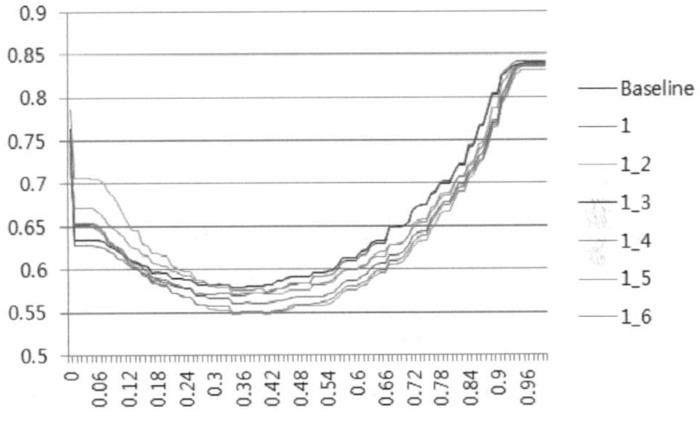

Figure 9: Performance of the system on each level of the parse tree

Once the levels are assigned to each constituent tree, only those constituents with levels larger than or equal to the predefined threshold μ are used to evaluate the system. μ are increased from 0 to 1 with value 0.01. Higher μ value means that the system is evaluated only for those constituents positioned at the top level of the constituent tree.

Figure 9 shows the evaluation results. X-axis represents the value of μ, and Y-axis represents the F1-score. As can be observed, most of the errors occur at the mid-level of the constituent trees. Also, the effects of some methods are explicitly shown on the graph. For example, method 2 greatly increases the performance at low level of the constituent tree, suggesting improved consistency in detemining prepreterminal NP nodes. Also, it is shown that the proposed methods does not affect the performance of mid-level and top-level constituent decisions - this suggests that the future works should be more focused on providing more information about those mid-level decision to the treebank annotation.

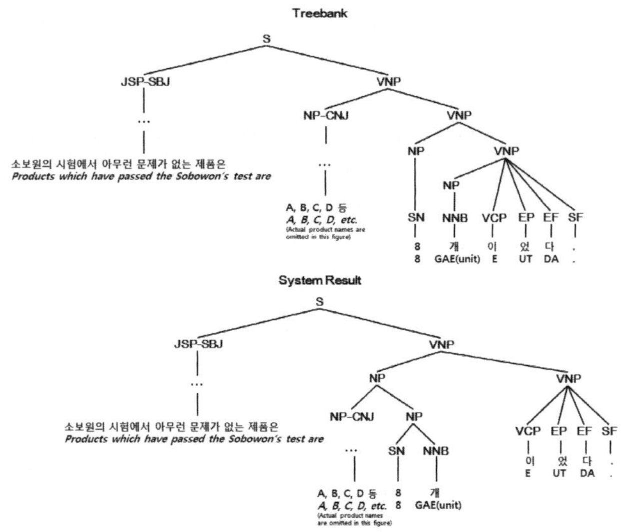

Figure 10: Example of NP boundary detection error. Part of parse tree as well as name of the enumerated products are omitted to more clearly show the example itself.

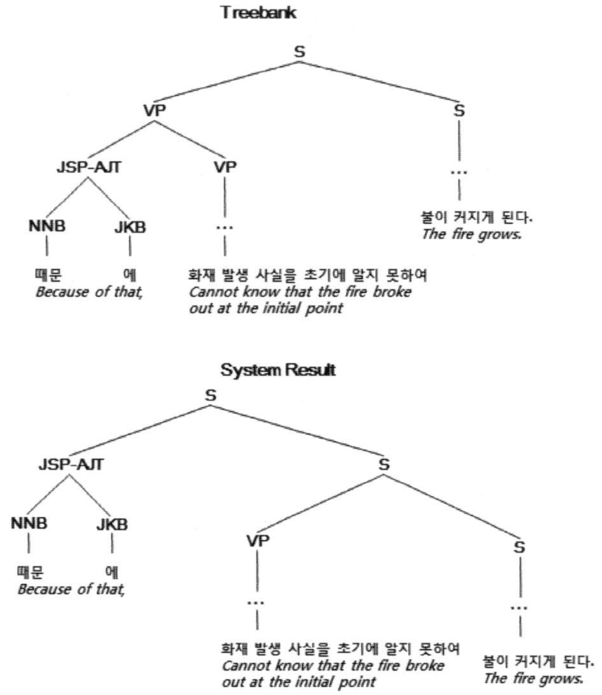

Figure 11: Example of a phrase (**JSP-AJT**) which failed to find its right modifee.

5.3.2 Frequent Error Cases

In this section, four major parsing error cases are described.

Detecting Boundaries of NP. Although the method 4 tries to find and gather the sequence of nouns which actually belong to one NP, it misses some of the cases. Figure 10 shows such example. Some parts of the tree are omitted using the notation '...' to show the example more simply. Although it is counted as the parser error, the result of the parser is more likely to be an answer - the number of those products is 8, not their action. The Sejong treebank tree is annotated in that way because the number '8' and bound noun *Gae* ('unit'), representing as units, are separated by a space. To detect such kind of separated NPs and transform them into one NP will be our next task.

Finding an Appropriate Modifee. Some phrases modifying other phrases were failed to find their appropriate modifees. Figure 11 shows an example of such kind of error case.

Detecting an Appropriate Subject of the Sentence. This case frequently occurs when a sentence is quotated inside the other sentence. In this case, the subject of quotated sentence is often considered as the subject of the whole sentence, because the quotated sentences in Korean are usually first stated and then the subject of the whole sentence shows up. Figure 12 shows an example of the erroneously detected subject.

The Wrongly-tagged Topmost Node. Some of Sejong treebank trees have phrases which are not tagged as **S** as their topmost nodes. This could cause confusion during the training. Figure 13 shows such example.

6 Conclusion and Future Work

Although there exist some manually-annotated large-enough constituent treebanks such as Sejong treebank, it was hard to apply the algorithms for English parsers to Korean treebanks, because they were annotated in eojeol-based scheme, which concept does not exist in English. In this paper, we showed the possibility of acquiring good training and testing results with the existing parsers trained using the existing Korean treebanks, if it undergoes some simple transforming procedures. The error analysis result shows that, indeed the proposed method improves the performance of parser at the lower level of constituent tree.

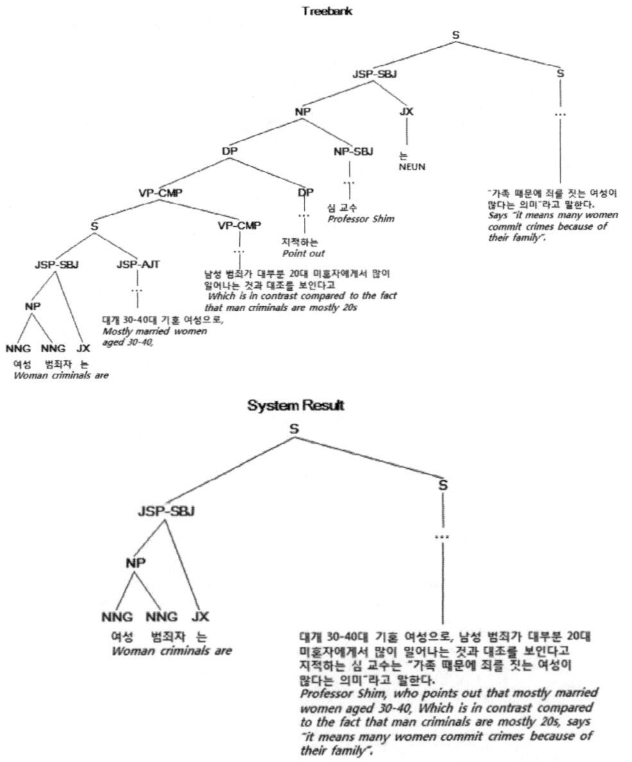

Figure 12: Example of a wrongly-detected subject.

Although there exists a performance gain due to the transforming methods, there are still many gaps for improvement. The evaluation results and error analysis results suggests the need to define the phrase tagset of Sejong treebank in more detail. Also, the transforming methods themselves are not perfect yet - we believe still they could be improved more to increase consistency of the resultant treebanks.

We will continuously develop our transforming methods to improve the parsing result. Furthermore, we are planning to investigate methods to determine the appropriate "detailedness" of phrase tag set, so that there are no missing information due to too small number of tags as well as no confusion due to too many tags.

Acknowledgement

This research was supported by Basic Science Research Program through the National Research Foundation of Korea (NRF) funded by the Ministry of Education, Science and Technology (No. 2011-0026718)

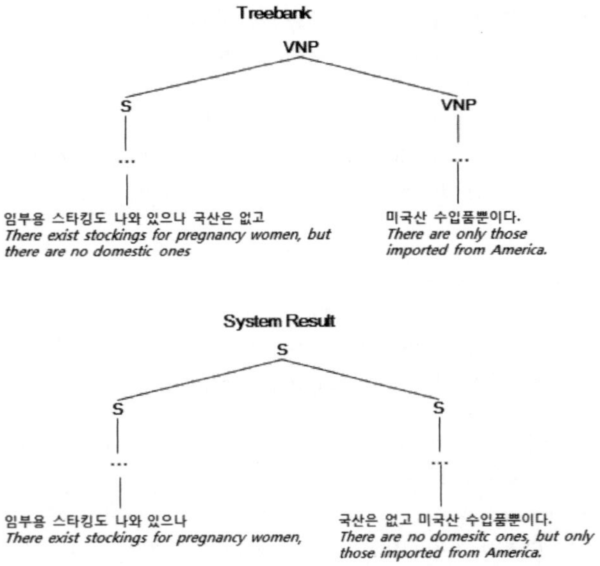

Figure 13: Example of the wrongly-tagged topmost node. Some trees in the treebank have Non-**S** topmost phrase nodes.

References

Dan Bikel. 2004. *On the Parameter Space of Generative Lexicalized Statistical Parsing Models*. Ph.D. thesis, University of Pennsylvania.

Dan Bikel. 2012. Bikel parser. `http://www.cis.upenn.edu/~dbikel/software.html`.

Jinho D. Choi and Martha Palmer. 2011. Statistical dependency parsing in Korean: From corpus generation to automatic parsing. In *The Second Workshop on Statistical Parsing of Morphologically Rich Languages*, pages 1–11.

Key-Sun Choi, Young S. Han, Young G. Han, and Oh W. Kwon. 1994. KAIST tree bank project for Korean: Present and future development. In *Proceedings of the International Workshop on Sharable Natural Language Resources*, pages 7–14.

Key-Sun Choi, Isahara Hitoshi, and Maosong Sun. 2011. Language resource management – word segmentation of written texts – part 2: Word segmentation for Chinese, Japanese and Korean. In *ISO 24614-2*. ISO.

Tagyoung Chung, Matt Post, and Daniel Gildea. 2010. Factors affecting the accuracy of korean parsing. In *Proceedings of the NAACL HLT 2010 First Workshop on Statistical Parsing of Morphologically-Rich Languages*, pages 49–57, Los Angeles, CA, USA, June. Association for Computational Linguistics.

Hoojung Chung. 2004. *Statistical Korean Dependency Parsing Model based on the Surface Contextual Information*. Ph.D. thesis, Korea University.

Danica Damljanovic, Milan Agatonovic, and Hamish Cunningham. 2010. Identification of the question focus: Combining syntactic analysis and ontology-based lookup through the user interaction. In *Proceedings of 7th Language Resources and Evaluation Conference (LREC)*, pages 361–368.

Jenny Rose Finkel and Christopher D. Manning. 2009. Joint parsing and named entity recognition. In *NAACL '09 Proceedings of Human Language Technologies: The 2009 Annual Conference of the North American Chapter of the Association for Computational Linguistics*, pages 326–334.

Daniel Gildea and Daniel Jurafsky. 2002. Automatic labeling of semantic roles. *Computational Linguistics*, 28(3):245–288.

Chung-Hye Han, Na-Rae Han, Eon-Suk Ko, Heejong Yi, and Martha Palmer. 2002. Penn Korean treebank: Development and evaluation. In *Proceedings of the 16th Pacific Asia Conference on Language, Information and Computation*.

Dan Klein and Christopher D. Manning. 2003. Accurate unlexicalized parsing. In *Proceedings of the 41st Meeting of the Association for Computational Linguistics*, pages 423–430.

Korean Language Institute. 2012. Sejong treebank. `http://www.sejong.or.kr`.

Tetsuya Nasukawa and Jeonghee Yi. 2003. Sentiment analysis: capturing favorability using natural language processing. In *Proceedings of the 2nd international conference on Knowledge capture*, pages 70–77.

Jin Young Oh, Yo-Sub Han, Jungyeul Park, and Jeong-Won Cha. 2011. Predicting phrase-level tags using entropy inspired discriminative models. In *2011 International Conference on Information Science and Applications (ICISA)*, pages 1–5.

Jungyeul Park. 2006. Extraction of tree adjoining grammars from a treebank for Korean. In *Proceedings of the 21st International Conference on computational Linguistics and 44th Annual Meeting of the Association for Computational Linguistics: Student Research Workshop*, pages 73–78.

Slav Petrov and Dan Klein. 2007. Improved inference for unlexicalized parsing. In *Human Language Technologies 2007: The Conference of the North American Chapter of the Association for Computational Linguistics; Proceedings of the Main Conference*, pages 404–411, Rochester, New York, April. Association for Computational Linguistics.

Slav Petrov, Leon Barrett, Romain Thibaux, and Dan Klein. 2006. Learning accurate, compact, and interpretable tree annotation. In *Proceedings of the COLING-ACL 2006*, pages 433–440.

David A. Smith and Noah A. Smith. 2004. Bilingual parsing with factored estimation: Using English to parse Korean. In *Proceedings of the EMNLP*, pages 49–56.

Generative Constituent Parsing and Discriminative Dependency Reranking: Experiments on English and French

Joseph Le Roux[◇] **Benoît Favre**[†] **Alexis Nasr**[†] **Seyed Abolghasem Mirroshandel**[†,⋆]
[◇]LIPN, Université Paris Nord – CNRS UMR 7030, Villetaneuse, France
[†]LIF, Université Aix-Marseille – CNRS UMR 7279, Marseille, France
[⋆]Computer Engineering Department, Sharif university of Technology, Tehran, Iran
leroux@univ-paris13.fr, benoit.favre@lif.univ-mrs.fr,
alexis.nasr@lif.univ-mrs.fr, ghasem.mirroshandel@lif.univ-mrs.fr

Abstract

We present an architecture for parsing in two steps. A phrase-structure parser builds for each sentence an n-best list of analyses which are converted to dependency trees. These dependency structures are then rescored by a discriminative reranker. Our method is language agnostic and enables the incorporation of additional information which are useful for the choice of the best parse candidate. We test our approach on the the Penn Treebank and the French Treebank. Evaluation shows a significative improvement on different parse metrics.

1 Introduction

Two competing approaches exist for parsing natural language. The first one, called generative, is based on the theory of formal languages and rewriting systems. Parsing is defined here as a process that transforms a string into a tree or a tree forest. It is often grounded on phrase-based grammars – although there are generative dependency parsers – in particular context-free grammars or one of their numerous variants, that can be parsed in polynomial time. However, the independence hypothesis that underlies this kind of formal system does not allow for precise analyses of some linguistic phenomena, such as long distance and lexical dependencies.

In the second approach, known as discriminative, the grammar is viewed as a system of constraints over the correct syntactic structures, the words of the sentence themselves being seen as constraints over the position they occupy in the sentence. Parsing boils down to finding a solution that is compatible with the different constraints. The major problem of this approach lies in its complexity. The constraints can, theoretically, range over any aspect of the final structures, which prevents from using efficient dynamic programming techniques when searching for a global solution. In the worst case, final structures must be enumerated in order to be evaluated. Therefore, only a subset of constraints is used in implementations for complexity reasons. This approach can itself be divided into formalisms relying on logic to describe constraints, as the model-theoretic syntax (Pullum and Scholz, 2001), or numerical formalisms that associate weights to lexico-syntactic substructures. The latter has been the object of some recent work thanks to progresses achieved in the field of Machine Learning. A parse tree is represented as a vector of features and its accuracy is measured as the distance between this vector and the reference.

One way to take advantage of both approaches is to combine them sequentially, as initially proposed by Collins (2000). A generative parser produces a set of candidates structures that constitute the input of a second, discriminative module, whose search space is limited to this set of candidates. Such an approach, parsing followed by reranking, is used in the Brown parser (Charniak and Johnson, 2005). The approach can be extended in order to feed the reranker with the output of different parsers, as shown by (Johnson and Ural, 2010; Zhang et al., 2009).

In this paper we are interested in applying reranking to dependency structures. The main reason is that many linguistic constraints are straightforward to implement on dependency structures, as, for example, subcategorization frames or selectional constraints that are closely linked to the notion of dependents of a predicate. On the other hand, dependencies extracted from constituent parses are known to be more accurate than dependencies obtained from dependency parsers. Therefore the solution we choose is an indirect one: we use a phrase-based parser to generate n-best lists and convert them to lists of dependency structures that are reranked. This approach can be seen as trade-off between phrase-based reranking experiments (Collins, 2000) and the approach of Carreras et al. (2008) where a discriminative model is used to score lexical features representing unlabelled dependencies in the Tree Adjoining Grammar formalism.

Our architecture, illustrated in Figure 1, is based on two steps. During the first step, a syntagmatic parser processes the input sentence and produces n-best parses as well as their probabilities. They are annotated with a functional tagger which tags syntagms with standard syntactic functions *subject, object, indirect object*... and converted to dependency structures by application of percolation rules. In the second step, we extract a set of features from the dependency parses and the associated probabilities. These features are used to reorder the n-best list and select a potentially more accurate parse. Syntagmatic parses are produced by the implementation of a PCFG-LA parser of (Attia et al., 2010), similar to (Petrov et al., 2006), a functional tagger and dependency converter for the target language. The reranking model is a linear model trained with an implementation of the MIRA algorithm (Crammer et al., 2006)[1].

Charniak and Johnson (2005) and Collins (2000) rerank phrase-structure parses and they also include head-dependent information, in other words unlabelled dependencies. In our approach we take into account grammatical functions or labelled dependencies.

It should be noted that the features we use are very generic and do not depend on the linguistic knowledge of the authors. We applied our method to English, the de facto standard for testing parsing technologies, and French which exhibits many aspects of a morphologically rich language. But our approach could be applied to other languages, provided that the resources – treebanks and conversion tools – exist.

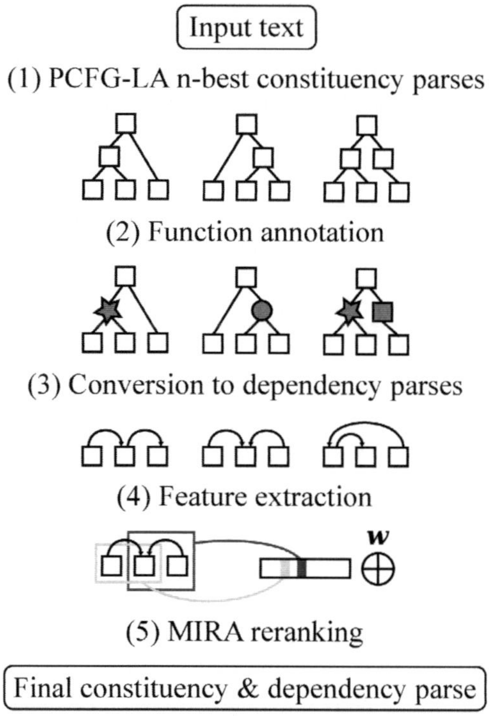

Figure 1: The parsing architecture: production of the n-best syntagmatic trees (1) tagged with functional labels (2), conversion to a dependency structure (3) and feature extraction (4), scoring with a linear model (5). The parse with the best score is considered as final.

The structure of the paper is the following: in Section 2 we describe the details of our generative parser and in Section 3 our reranking model together with the features templates. Section 4 reports the results of the experiments conducted on the Penn Treebank (Marcus et al., 1994) as well as on the Paris 7 Treebank (Abeillé et al., 2003) and Section 5 concludes the paper.

2 Generative Model

The first part of our system, the syntactic analysis itself, generates surface dependency structures in a sequential fashion (Candito et al., 2010b; Candito et al., 2010a). A phrase structure parser based on Latent Variable PCFGs (PCFG-LAs) produces tree structures that are enriched with functions and then converted to labelled dependency structures, which will be processed by the parse reranker.

[1]This implementation is available at `https://github.com/jihelhere/adMIRAble`.

2.1 PCFG-LAs

Probabilistic Context Free Grammars with Latent Annotations, introduced in (Matsuzaki et al., 2005) can be seen as automatically specialised PCFGs learnt from treebanks. Each symbol of the grammar is enriched with annotation symbols behaving as subclasses of this symbol. More formally, the probability of an unannotated tree is the sum of the probabilities of its annotated counterparts. For a PCFG-LA G, R is the set of annotated rules, $D(t)$ is the set of (annotated) derivations of an unannotated tree t, and $R(d)$ is the set of rules used in a derivation d. Then the probability assigned by G to t is:

$$P_G(t) = \sum_{d \in D(t)} P_G(d) = \sum_{d \in D(t)} \prod_{r \in R(d)} P_G(r) \quad (1)$$

Because of this alternation of sums and products that cannot be optimally factorised, there is no exact polynomial dynamic programming algorithm for parsing. Matsuzaki et al. (2005) and Petrov and Klein (2007) discuss approximations of the decoding step based on a Bayesian variational approach. This enables cubic time decoding that can be further enhanced with coarse-to-fine methods (Charniak and Johnson, 2005).

This type of grammars has already been tested on a variety of languages, in particular English and French, giving state-of-the-art results. Let us stress that this phrase-structure formalism is not lexicalised as opposed to grammars previously used in reranking experiments (Collins, 2000; Charniak and Johnson, 2005). The notion of lexical head is therefore absent at parsing time and will become available only at the reranking step.

2.2 Dependency Structures

A syntactic theory can either be expressed with phrase structures or dependencies, as advocated for in (Rambow, 2010). However, some information may be simpler to describe in one of the representations. This equivalence between the modes of representations only stands if the informational contents are the same. Unfortunately, this is not the case here because the phrase structures that we use do not contain functional annotations and lexical heads, whereas labelled dependencies do.

This implies that, in order to be converted into labelled dependency structures, phrase structure parses must first be annotated with functions. Previous experiments for English and French as well (Candito et al., 2010b) showed that a sequential approach is better than an integrated one for context-free grammars, because the strong independence hypothesis of this formalism implies a restricted domain of locality which cannot express the context needed to properly assign functions. Most functional taggers, such as the ones used in the following experiments, rely on classifiers whose feature sets can describe the whole context of a node in order to make a decision.

3 Discriminative model

Our discriminative model is a linear model trained with the Margin-Infused Relaxed Algorithm (MIRA) (Crammer et al., 2006). This model computes the score of a parse tree as the inner product of a feature vector and a weight vector representing model parameters. The training procedure of MIRA is very close to that of a perceptron (Rosenblatt, 1958), benefiting from its speed and relatively low requirements while achieving better accuracy.

Recall that parsing under this model consists in (1) generating a n-best list of constituency parses using the generative model, (2) annotating each of them with function tags, (3) converting them to dependency parses, (4) extracting features, (5) scoring each feature vector against the model, (6) selecting the highest scoring parse as output.

For training, we collect the output of feature extraction (4) for a large set of training sentences and associate each parse tree with a loss function that denotes the number of erroneous dependencies compared to the reference parse tree. Then, model weights are adjusted using MIRA training so that the parse with the lowest loss gets the highest score. Examples are processed in sequence, and for each of them, we compute the score of each parse according to the current model and find an updated weight vector that assigns the first rank to the best parse (called *oracle*). Details of the algorithm are given in the following sections.

3.1 Definitions

Let us consider a vector space of dimension m where each component corresponds to a feature: a parse tree p is represented as a sparse vector $\phi(p)$. The model is a weight vector w in the same space where each weight corresponds to the importance of the features for characterizing good (or bad) parse trees. The score $s(p)$ of a parse tree p is the scalar product of its feature vector $\phi(p)$ and the weight vector w.

$$s(p) = \sum_{i=1}^{m} w_i \phi_i(p) \quad (2)$$

Let L be the n-best list of parses produced by the generative parser for a given sentence. The highest scoring parse $\hat{p}$ is selected as output of the reranker:

$$\hat{p} = \underset{p \in L}{\operatorname{argmax}}\, s(p) \quad (3)$$

MIRA learning consists in using training sentences and their reference parses to determine the weight vector w. It starts with $w = 0$ and modifies it incrementally so that parses closest to the reference get higher scores. Let $l(p)$, loss of parse p, be the number of erroneous dependencies (governor, dependent, label) compared to the reference parse. We define o, the oracle parse, as the parse with the lowest loss in L.

Training examples are processed in sequence as an instance of online learning. For each sentence, we compute the score of each parse in the n-best list. If the highest scoring parse differs from the oracle ($\hat{p} \neq o$), the weight vector can be improved. In this case, we seek a modification of w ensuring that o gets a better score than $\hat{p}$ with a difference at least proportional to the difference between their loss. This way, very bad parses get pushed deeper than average parses. Finding such weight vector can be formulated as the following constrained optimization problem:

$$\text{minimize: } ||w||^2 \quad (4)$$

$$\text{subject to: } s(o) - s(\hat{p}) \geq l(o) - l(\hat{p}) \quad (5)$$

Since there is an infinity of weight vectors that satisfy constraint 5, we settle on the one with the smallest magnitude. Classical constrained quadratic optimization methods can be applied to solve this problem: first, Lagrange multipliers are used to introduce the constraint in the objective function, then the Hildreth algorithm yields the following analytic solution to the non-constrained problem:

$$w^\star = w + \alpha\,(\phi(o) - \phi(\hat{p})) \quad (6)$$

$$\alpha = \max\left[0, \frac{l(o) - l(\hat{p}) - [s(o) - s(\hat{p})]}{||\phi(o) - \phi(\hat{p})||^2}\right] \quad (7)$$

Here, $w^\star$ is the new weight vector, α is an update magnitude and $[\phi(o) - \phi(\hat{p})]$ is the difference between the feature vector of the oracle and that of the highest scoring parse. This update, similar to the perceptron update, draws the weight vector towards o while pushing it away from $\hat{p}$. Usual tricks that apply to the perceptron also apply here: (a) performing multiple passes on the training data, and (b) averaging the weight vector over each update[2]. Algorithm 1 details the instructions for MIRA training.

Algorithm 1 MIRA training

```
for i = 1 to t do
  for all sentences in training set do
    Generate n-best list L from generative parser
    for all p ∈ L do
      Extract feature vector φ(p)
      Compute score s(p) (eq. 2)
    end for
    Get oracle o = argmin_p l(p)
    Get best parse p̂ = argmax_p s(p)
    if p̂ ≠ o then
      Compute α (eq. 7)
      Update weight vector (eq. 6)
    end if
  end for
end for
Return average weight vector over updates.
```

3.2 Features

The quality of the reranker depends on the learning algorithm as much as on the feature set. These features can span over any subset of a parse tree, up to the whole tree. Therefore, there are a very large set of possible features to choose from. Relevant features must be general enough to appear in as many

[2]This can be implemented efficiently using two weight vectors as for the averaged perceptron.

parses as possible, but specific enough to characterize good and bad configurations in the parse tree.

We extended the feature set from (McDonald, 2006) which showed to be effective for a range of languages. Our feature templates can be categorized in 5 classes according to their domain of locality. In the following, we describe and exemplify these templates on the following sentence from the Penn treebank, in which we target the PMOD dependency between "at" and "watch."

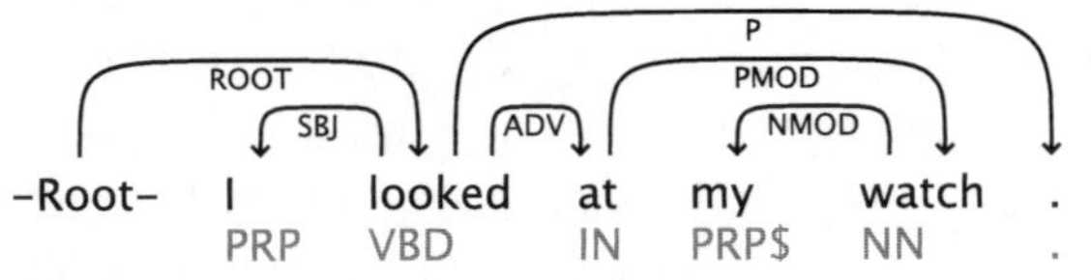

Probability Three features are derived from the PCFG-LA parser, namely the posterior probability of the parse (eq. 1), its normalized probability relative to the 1-best, and its rank in the n-best list.

Unigram Unigram features are the most simple as they only involve one word. Given a dependency between position i and position j of type l, governed by x_i, denoted $x_i \xrightarrow{l} x_j$, two features are created: one for the governor x_i and one for the dependent x_j. They are described as 6-tuples (word, lemma, pos-tag, is-governor, direction, type of dependency). Variants with wildcards at each subset of tuple slots are also generated in order to handle sparsity.

In our example, the dependency between "looked" and "at" generates two features:

`[at, at, IN, G, R, PMOD]` and `[looked, look, NN, D, L, PMOD]`

And also wildcard features such as:

`[-, at, IN, G, R, PMOD], [at, -, IN, G, R, PMOD] ... [at, -, -, -, -, PMOD]`

This wildcard feature generation is applied to all types of features. We will omit it in the remainder of the description.

Bigram Unlike the previous template, bigram features model the conjunction of the governor and the dependent of a dependency relation, like bilexical dependencies in (Collins, 1997). Given dependency $x_i \xrightarrow{l} x_j$, the feature created is (word x_i, lemma x_i, pos-tag x_i, word x_j, lemma x_j, pos-tag x_j, distance[3] from i to j, direction, type).

The previous example generates the following feature:

`[at, at, IN, watch, watch, NN, 2, R, PMOD]`

Where 2 is the distance between "at" and "watch".

Linear context This feature models the linear context between the governor and the dependent of a relation by looking at the words between them. Given dependency $x_i \xrightarrow{l} x_j$, for each word from $i+1$ to $j-1$, a feature is created with the pos-tags of x_i and x_j, and the pos tag of the word between them (no feature is create if $j = i+1$). An additional feature is created with pos-tags at positions $i-1$, i, $i+1$, $j-1$, j, $j+1$. Our example yields the following features:

[**IN**, PRP$, **NN**], and [VBD, **IN**, PRP$, PRP$, **NN**, .].

Syntactic context: siblings This template and the next one look at two dependencies in two configurations. Given two dependencies $x_i \xrightarrow{l} x_j$ and $x_i \xrightarrow{m} x_k$, we create the feature (word, lemma, pos-tag for x_i, x_j and x_k, distance from i to j, distance from i to k, direction and type of each of the two dependencies). In our example:

`[looked, look, VBD, I, I, PRP, at, at, IN, 1, 1, L, SBJ, R, ADV]`

Syntactic context: chains Given two dependencies $x_i \xrightarrow{l} x_j \xrightarrow{m} x_k$, we create the feature (word, lemma, pos-tag of x_i, x_j and x_k, distance from i to j, distance from i to k, direction and type of each of the two dependencies). In our example:

`[looked, look, VBD, at, at, IN, watch, watch, NN, 1, 2, R, ADV,`

[3]In every template, distance features are quantified in 7 classes: 1, 2, 3, 4, 5, 5 to 10, more.

R, PMOD]

It is worth noting that our feature templates only rely on information available in the training set, and do not use any external linguistic knowledge.

4 Experiments

In this section, we evaluate our architecture on two corpora, namely the Penn Treebank (Marcus et al., 1994) and the French Treebank (Abeillé et al., 2003). We first present the corpora and the tools used for annotating and converting structures, then the performances of the phrase structure parser alone and with the discriminative reranker.

4.1 Treebanks and Tools

For English, we use the Wall Street Journal sections of the Penn Treebank. We learn the PCFG-LA from sections 02-21[4]. We then use FUNTAG (Chrupała et al., 2007) to add functions back to the PCFG-LA analyses. For the conversion to dependency structures we use the LTH tool (Johansson and Nugues, 2007). In order to get the gold dependencies, we run LTH directly on the gold parse trees. We use section 22 for development and section 23 for the final evaluation.

For French, we use the Paris 7 Treebank (or French Treebank, FTB). As in several previous experiments we decided to divide the 12,350 phrase structure trees in three sets: train (80%), development (10%) and test (10%). The syntactic tag set for French is not fixed and we decided to use the one described in (Candito and Crabbé, 2009) to be able to compare this system with recent parsing results on French. As for English, we learn the PCFG-LA without functional annotations which are added afterwards. We use the dependency structures developed in (Candito et al., 2010b) and the conversion toolkit BONSAÏ. Furthermore, to test our approach against state of the art parsing results for French we use word clusters in the phrase-based parser as in (Candito and Crabbé, 2009).

For both languages we constructed 10-fold training data from train sets in order to avoid overfitting the training data. The trees from training sets were divided into 10 subsets and the parses for each subset were generated by a parser trained on the other 9 subsets. Development and test parses are given by a parser using the whole training set. Development sets were used to choose the best reranking model.

For lemmatisation, we use the MATE lemmatiser for English and a home-made lemmatiser for French based on the le*fff* lexicon (Sagot, 2010).

4.2 Generative Model

The performances of our parser are summarised in Figure 2, (a) and (b), where F-score denotes the Parseval F-score[5], and LAS and UAS are respectively the Labelled and Unlabelled Attachment Score of the converted dependency structures[6]. We give oracle scores (the score that our system would get if it selected the best parse from the n-best lists) when the parser generates n-best lists of depth 10, 20, 50 and 100 in order to get an idea of the effectiveness of the reranking process.

One of the issues we face with this approach is the use of an imperfect functional annotator. For French we evaluate the loss of accuracy on the resulting dependency structure from the gold development set where functions have been omitted. The UAS is 100% but the LAS is 96.04%. For English the LAS from section 22 where functions are omitted is 95.35%.

From the results presented in this section we can make two observations. First, the results of our parser are at the state of the art on English (90.7% F-score) and on French (85.7% F-score). So the reranker will be confronted with the difficult task of improving on these scores. Second, the progression margin is sensible with a potential LAS error reduction of 41% for English and 40.2% for French.

4.3 Adding the Reranker

4.3.1 Learning Feature Weights

The discriminative model, i.e. template instances and their weights, is learnt on the training set parses obtained via 10-fold cross-validation. The generative parser generates 100-best lists that are used as learning example for the MIRA algorithm. Feature extraction produces an enormous number of features: about 571 millions for English and 179 mil-

[4]Functions are omitted.

[5]We use a modified version of `evalb` that gives the oracle score when the parser outputs a list of candidates for each sentence.

[6]All scores are measured without punctuation.

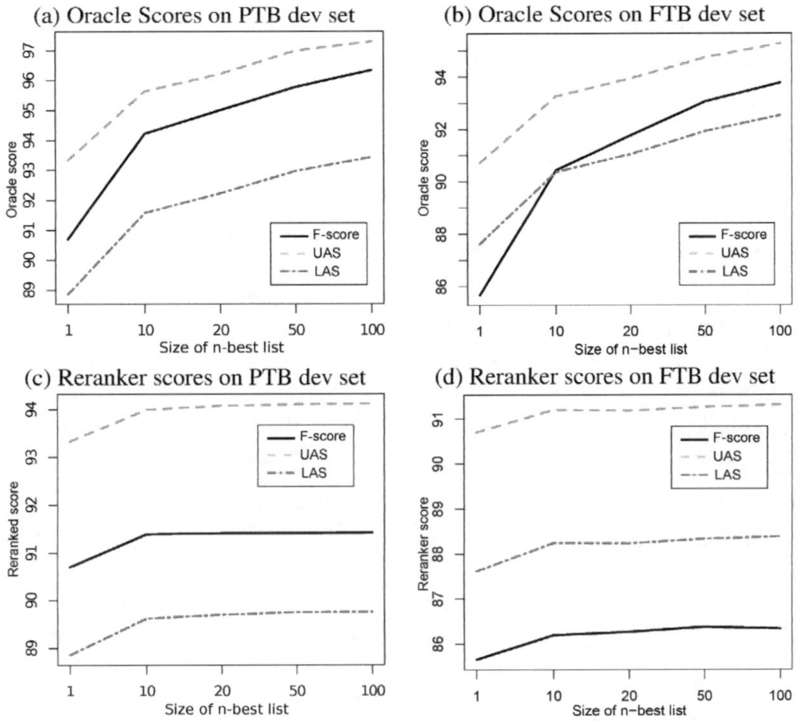

Figure 2: Oracle and reranker scores on PTB and FTB data on the dev. set, according to the depth of the n-best.

lions for French. Let us remark that this large set of features is not an issue because our discriminative learning algorithm is online, that is to say it considers only one example at a time, and it only gives non-null weights to useful features.

4.3.2 Evaluation

In order to test our system we first tried to evaluate the impact of the length of the n-best list over the reranking predictions[7]. The results are shown in Figure 2, parts (c) and (d).

For French, we can see that even though the LAS and UAS are consistently improving with the number of candidates, the F-score is maximal with 50 candidates. However the difference between 50 candidates and 100 candidates is not statistically significant. For English, the situation is simpler and scores improve continuously on the three metrics.

Finally we run our system on the test sets for both treebanks. Results are shown[8] in Table 1 for English, and Table 2 for French. For English the improvement is 0.9% LAS, 0.7% Parseval F-score and 0.8% UAS.

	Baseline	Reranker
F	90.4	91.1
F $<$ 40	91.0	91.7
LAS	88.9	89.8
UAS	93.1	93.9

Table 1: System results on PTB Test set

For French we have improvements of 0.3/0.7/0.9. If we add a template feature indicating the agreement between part-of-speech provided by the PCFG-LA parser and a part-of-speech tagger (Denis and Sagot, 2009), we obtain better improvements: 0.5/0.8/1.1.

	Baseline	Reranker	Rerank + MElt
F	86.6	87.3	87.4
F $<$ 40	88.7	89.0	89.2
LAS	87.9	89.0	89.2
UAS	91.0	91.9	92.1

Table 2: System results on FTB Test set

[7]The model is always trained with 100 candidates.

[8]F $<$ 40 is the parseval F-score for sentences with less than 40 words.

4.3.3 Comparison with Related Work

We compare our results with related parsing results on English and French.

For English, the main results are shown in Table 3. From the presented data, we can see that indirect reranking on LAS may not seem as good as direct reranking on phrase-structures compared to F-scores obtained in (Charniak and Johnson, 2005) and (Huang, 2008) with one parser or (Zhang et al., 2009) with several parsers. However, our system does not rely on any language specific feature and can be applied to other languages/treebanks. It is difficult to compare our system for LAS because most systems evaluate on gold data (part-of-speech, lemmas and morphological information) like Bohnet (2010).

Our system also compares favourably with the system of Carreras et al. (2008) that relies on a more complex generative model, namely Tree Adjoining Grammars, and the system of Suzuki et al. (2009) that makes use of external data (unannotated text).

	F	LAS	UAS
Huang, 2008	91.7	–	–
Bohnet, 2010	–	90.3	–
Zhang et al, 2008	91.4	–	93.2
Huang and Sagae, 2010	–	–	92.1
Charniak et al, 2005	91.5	90.0	94.0
Carreras et al. 2008	–	–	93.5
Suzuki et al. 2009	–	–	93.8
This work	91.1	89.8	93.9

Table 3: Comparison on PTB Test set

For French, see Table 4, we compare our system with the MATE parser (Bohnet, 2010), an improvement over the MST parser (McDonald et al., 2005) with hash kernels, using the MELT part-of-speech tagger (Denis and Sagot, 2009) and our own lemmatiser.

We also compare the French system with results drawn from the benchmark performed by Candito et al. (2010a). The first system (BKY-FR) is close to ours without the reranking module, using the Berkeley parser adapted to French. The second (MST-FR) is based on MSTParser (McDonald et al., 2005). These two system use word clusters as well.

The next section takes a close look at the models of the reranker and its impact on performance.

	$F < 40$	LAS	UAS
This work	**89.2**	**89.2**	**92.1**
MATE + MELT	–	89.2	91.8
BKY-FR	88.2	86.8	91.0
MST-FR	–	88.2	90.9

Table 4: Comparison on FTB Test set

4.3.4 Model Analysis

It is interesting to note that in the test sets, the one-best of the syntagmatic parser is selected 52.0% of the time by the reranker for English and 34.3% of the time for French. This can be explained by the difference in the quantity of training data in the two treebanks (four times more parses are available for English) resulting in an improvement of the quality of the probabilistic grammar.

We also looked at the reranking models, specifically at the weight given to each of the features. It shows that 19.8% of the 571 million features have a non-zero weight for English as well as 25.7% of the 179 million features for French. This can be explained by the fact that for a given sentence, features that are common to all the candidates in the n-best list are not discriminative to select one of these candidates (they add the same constant weight to the score of all candidates), and therefore ignored by the model. It also shows the importance of feature engineering: designing relevant features is *an art* (Charniak and Johnson, 2005).

We took a closer look at the 1,000 features of highest weight and the 1,000 features of lowest weight (negative) for both languages that represent the most important features for discriminating between correct and incorrect parses. For English, 62.0% of the positive features are backoff features which involve at least one wildcard while they are 85.9% for French. Interestingly, similar results hold for negative features. The difference between the two languages is hard to interpret and might be due in part to lexical properties and to the fact that these features may play a balancing role against towards non-backoff features that promote overfitting.

Expectedly, posterior probability features have the highest weight and the n-best rank feature has the highest negative weight. As evidenced by Table 5,

	en (+)	en (-)	fr (+)	fr (-)
Linear	30.4	36.1	44.8	44.0
Unigram	20.7	16.3	9.7	8.2
Bigram	27.4	29.1	20.8	24.4
Chain	15.4	15.3	13.7	19.4
Siblings	5.8	3.0	10.8	3.6

Table 5: Repartition of weight (in percentage) in the 1,000 highest (+) and lowest (-) weighted features for English and French.

among the other feature templates, linear context occupies most of the weight mass of the 1,000 highest weighted features. It is interesting to note that the unigram and bigram templates are less present for French than for English while the converse seems to be true for the linear template. Sibling features are consistently less relevant.

In terms of LAS performance, on the PTB test set the reranked output is better than the baseline on 22.4% of the sentences while the opposite is true for 10.4% of the sentences. In 67.0% of the sentences, they have the same LAS (but not necessarily the same errors). This emphasises the difficulty of reranking an already good system and also explains why oracle performance is not reached. Both the baseline and reranker output are completely correct on 21.3% of the sentences, while PCFG-LA correctly parses 23% of the sentences and the MIRA brings that number to 26%.

Figures 3 and 4 show hand-picked sentences for which the reranker selected the correct parse. The French sentence is a typical difficult example for PCFGs because it involves a complex rewriting rule which might not be well covered in the training data (SENT $\rightarrow$ NP VP PP PONCT PP PONCT PP PONCT). The English example is tied to a wrong attachment of the prepositional phrase to the verb instead of the date, which lexicalized features of the reranker handle easily.

5 Conclusion

We showed that using a discriminative reranker, on top of a phrase structure parser, based on converted dependency structures could lead to significant improvements over dependency and phrase structure parse results. We experimented on two treebanks for two languages, English and French and we measured the improvement of parse quality on three different metrics: Parseval F-score, LAS and UAS, with the biggest error reduction on the latter. However the gain is not as high as expected by looking at oracle scores, and we can suggest several possible improvements on this method.

First, the sequential approach is vulnerable to cascading errors. Whereas the generative parser produces several candidates, this is not the case of the functional annotators: these errors are not amendable. It should be possible to have a functional tagger with ambiguous output upon which the reranker could discriminate. It remains an open question as how to integrate ambiguous output from the parser and from the functional tagger. The combination of n-best lists would not scale up and working on the ambiguous structure itself, the packed forest as in (Huang, 2008), might be necessary. Another possibility for future work is to let the phrase-based parser itself perform function annotation, but some preliminary tests on French showed disappointing results.

Second, designing good features, sufficiently general but precise enough, is, as already coined by Charniak and Johnson (2005), *an art*. More formally, we can see several alternatives. Dependency structures could be exploited more thoroughly using, for example, tree kernels. The restricted number of candidates enables the use of more global features. Also, we haven't used any language-specific syntactic features. This could be another way to improve this system, relying on external linguistic knowledge (lexical preferences, subcategorisation frames, copula verbs, coordination symmetry ...). Integrating features from the phrase-structure trees is also an option that needs to be explored.

Third this architecture enables the integration of several systems. We experimented on French using a part-of-speech tagger but we could also use another parser and either use the methodology of (Johnson and Ural, 2010) or (Zhang et al., 2009) which fusion n-best lists form different parsers, or use stacking methods where an additional parser is used as a guide for the main parser (Nivre and McDonald, 2008).

Finally it should be noted that this system does not rely on any language specific feature, and thus can be applied to languages other that French or English

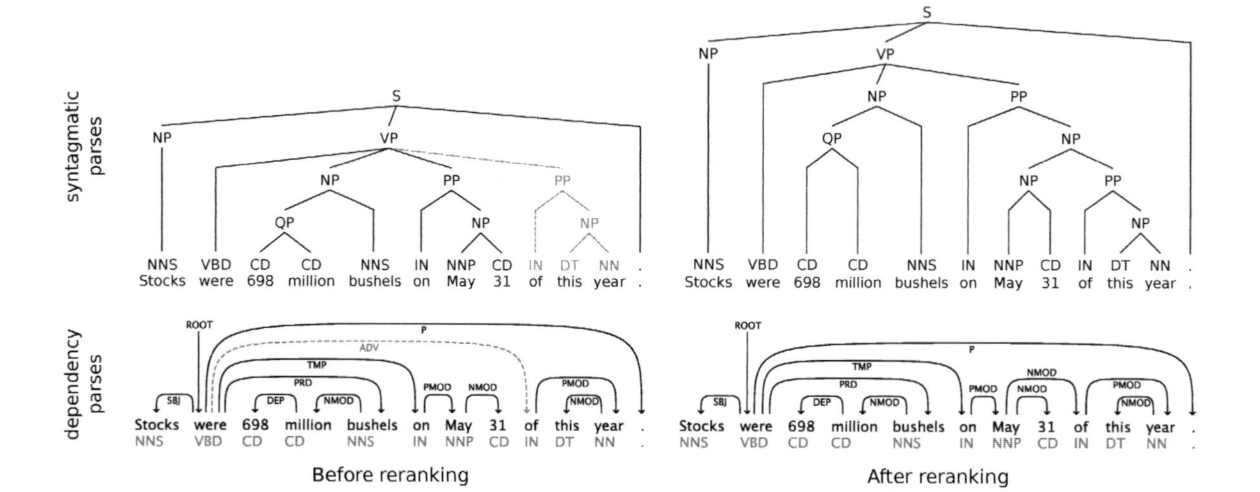

Figure 3: English sentence from the WSJ test set for which the reranker selected the correct tree while the first candidate of the n-best list suffered from an incorrect attachment.

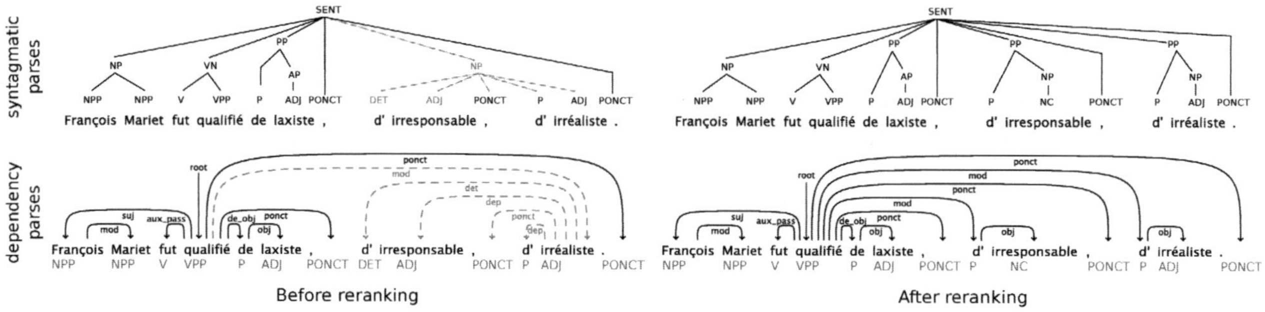

Figure 4: Sentence from the FTB for which the best parse according to baseline was incorrect, probably due to the tendency of the PCFG-LA model to prefer rules with more support. The reranker selected the correct parse.

without re-engineering new reranking features. This makes this architecture suitable for morphologically rich languages.

Acknowledgments

This work has been funded by the French Agence Nationale pour la Recherche, through the project SEQUOIA (ANR-08-EMER-013).

References

Anne Abeillé, Lionel Clément, and Toussenel François, 2003. *Treebanks*, chapter Building a treebank for French. Kluwer, Dordrecht.

M. Attia, J. Foster, D. Hogan, J. Le Roux, L. Tounsi, and J. van Genabith. 2010. Handling Unknown Words in Statistical Latent-Variable Parsing Models for Arabic, English and French. In *Proceedings of SPMRL*.

Bernd Bohnet. 2010. Top Accuracy and Fast Dependency Parsing is not a Contradiction. In *Proceedings of COLING*.

M.-H. Candito and B. Crabbé. 2009. Improving Generative Statistical Parsing with Semi-Supervised Word Clustering. In *Proceedings of IWPT 2009*.

M.-H. Candito, J. Nivre, P. Denis, and E. Henestroza Anguiano. 2010a. Benchmarking of Statistical Dependency Parsers for French. In *Proceedings of COLING'2010*.

Marie Candito, Benoît Crabbé, and Pascal Denis. 2010b. Statistical French Dependency Parsing : Treebank Conversion and First Results. In *Proceedings of LREC2010*.

Xavier Carreras, Michael Collins, and Terry Koo. 2008. TAG, Dynamic Programming and the Perceptron for Efficient, Feature-rich Parsing. In *CONLL*.

Eugene Charniak and Mark Johnson. 2005. Coarse-to-Fine n-Best Parsing and MaxEnt Discriminative Reranking. In *Proceedings of ACL*.

Grzegorz Chrupała, Nicolas Stroppa, Josef van Genabith, and Georgiana Dinu. 2007. Better training for function labeling. In *Proceedings of RANLP*, Borovets, Bulgaria.

Michael Collins. 1997. Three Generative, Lexicalised Models for Statistical Parsing. In *Proceedings of the 35th Annual Meeting of the ACL*.

Michael Collins. 2000. Discriminative Reranking for Natural Language Parsing. In *Proceedings of ICML*.

Koby Crammer, Ofer Dekel, Joseph Keshet, Shai ShalevShwartz, and Yoram Singer. 2006. Online Passive-Aggressive Algorithm. *Journal of Machine Learning Research*.

Pascal Denis and Benoît Sagot. 2009. Coupling an annotated corpus and a morphosyntactic lexicon for state-of-the-art pos tagging with less human effort. In *Proceedings PACLIC 23*, Hong Kong, China.

Liang Huang. 2008. Forest Reranking: Discriminative Parsing with Non-Local Features. In *Proceedings of ACL*.

Richard Johansson and Pierre Nugues. 2007. Extended constituent-to-dependency conversion for English. In *Proceedings of NODALIDA 2007*, pages 105–112, Tartu, Estonia, May 25-26.

Mark Johnson and Ahmet Engin Ural. 2010. Reranking the Berkeley and Brown Parsers. In *Human Language Technologies: The 2010 Annual Conference of the North American Chapter of the Association for Computational Linguistics*, pages 665–668, Los Angeles, California, June. Association for Computational Linguistics.

Mitchell Marcus, Grace Kim, Mary Ann Marcinkiewicz, Robert MacIntyre, Ann Bies, Mark Ferguson, Karen Katz, and Britta Schasberger. 1994. The penn treebank: Annotating predicate argument structure. In *Proceedings of the ARPA Speech and Natural Language Workshop*.

Takuya Matsuzaki, Yusuke Miyao, and Jun ichi Tsujii. 2005. Probabilistic CFG with Latent Annotations. In *Proceedings of ACL*.

Ryan McDonald, Koby Crammer, and Fernando Pereira. 2005. Online Large-Margin Training of Dependency Parsers. In *Association for Computational Linguistics (ACL)*.

Ryan McDonald. 2006. *Discriminative Training and Spanning Tree Algorithms for Dependency Parsing*. Ph.D. thesis, University of Pennsylvania.

J. Nivre and R. McDonald. 2008. Integrating graph-based and transition-based dependency parsers. In *Proceedings of ACL*, pages 950–958.

Slav Petrov and Dan Klein. 2007. Improved Inference for Unlexicalized Parsing. In *HLT-NAACL*, pages 404–411.

Slav Petrov, Leon Barrett, Romain Thibaux, and Dan Klein. 2006. Learning Accurate, Compact, and Interpretable Tree Annotation. In *ACL*.

Geoffrey K. Pullum and Barbara C. Scholz. 2001. On the distinction between model-theoretic and generative-enumerative syntactic frameworks. In *Logical Aspects of Computational Linguistics*.

Owen Rambow. 2010. The Simple Truth about Dependency and Phrase Structure Representations: An Opinion Piece. In *NAACL HLT*.

Frank Rosenblatt. 1958. The Perceptron: A Probabilistic Model for Information Storage and Organization in the Brain. *Psychological Review*.

Benoît Sagot. 2010. The lefff, a freely available and large-coverage lexicon for french. In *Proceedings of LREC 2010, La Valette, Malta*.

J. Suzuki, H. Isozaki, X. Carreras, and M. Collins. 2009. An empirical study of semi-supervised structured conditional models for dependency parsing. In *Proceedings of the 2009 Conference on Empirical Methods in Natural Language Processing: Volume 2-Volume 2*, pages 551–560. Association for Computational Linguistics.

Hui Zhang, Min Zhang, Chew Lim Tan, and Haizhou Li. 2009. K-best combination of syntactic parsers. In *Proceedings of EMNLP*.

Author Index